DATE DUE

Demco, Inc. 38-293

CREIGHTON UNIVERSITY

VISIONARY CLOSURE IN THE MODERN NOVEL

Visionary Closure in the Modern Novel

William R. Thickstun

St. Martin's Press   New York

#16466841

4-13-04

All rights reserved. For information, write:
Scholarly & Reference Division,
St. Martin's Press, Inc., 175 Fifth Avenue, New York, NY 10010

First published in the United States of America in 1988

Printed in Hong Kong

ISBN 0–312–01339–6

Library of Congress Cataloguing-in-Publication Data
Thickstun, William R.
Visionary closure in the modern novel.
Bibliography: p.
Includes index.
1. English fiction—20th century—History and criticism.
2. Visions in literature. 3. Closure (Rhetoric)
4. Modernism (Literature) 5. Faulkner, William,
1987–1962. Sound and the fury. I. Title.
PR888.V56T45 1988   823′.912′09   87–20816
ISBN 0–312–01339–6

For Margaret

Contents

Acknowledgements

The author and publishers would like to thank the following for permission to reproduce copyright material.

From *Howards End* by E. M. Forster, copyright 1921 by E. M. Forster; reprinted by permission of Random House, Inc. and Edward Arnold (Publishers) Ltd.

From *The Rainbow* by D. H. Lawrence, copyright 1915 by David Herbert Lawrence, copyright 1943 by Frieda Lawrence; reprinted by permission of Viking Penguin, Inc., Laurence Pollinger Ltd. and the Estate of Mrs. Frieda Lawrence Ravagli.

From *Ulysses* by James Joyce, copyright 1914, 1918 by Margaret Caroline Anderson, copyright renewed 1942, 1946 by Nora Joseph Joyce, copyright 1934 by the Modern Library, Inc., copyright renewed 1961 by Lucia and George Joyce; reprinted by permission of Random House Inc., The Bodley Head, and The Society of Authors on behalf of the literary Executors of the Estate of James Joyce.

From *To the Lighthouse* by Virginia Woolf, copyright 1927 by Harcourt Brace Jovanovich, Inc., copyright renewed 1955 by Leonard Woolf; reprinted by permission of Harcourt Brace Jovanovich, Inc., the author's estate and The Hogarth Press.

From *The Sound and the Fury* by William Faulkner, copyright 1929 by William Faulkner, copyright renewed 1956 by William Faulkner, copyright 1946 by Random House, Inc., reprinted by permission of Random House, Inc. and Curtis Brown Ltd.

From *Two Cheers for Democracy* by E. M. Forster, copyright 1951 by E. M. Forster, renewed 1979 by Donald Parry; reprinted by permission of Harcourt Brace Jovanovich, Inc. and Edward Arnold (Publishers) Ltd.

From *The Diary of Virginia Woolf*, ed. Anne Olivier Bell, reprinted by permission of Harcourt Brace Jovanovich, Inc., the author's estate and The Hogarth Press.

From *A Portrait of the Artist as a Young Man* by James Joyce, copyright 1916 by B. W. Huebsch, copyright renewed 1944 by Nora Joyce, definitive text copyright (c) 1964 by The Estate of James Joyce, reprinted by permission of Viking Penguin, Inc., Jonathan Cape Ltd., the Executors of the James Joyce Estate, and The Society of Authors as the literary Executors of the Estate of James Joyce.

From 'The Idea of Order at Key West' from *The Palm at the End of the Mind* by Wallace Stevens, copyright 1967, 1969, 1971 by Holly Stevens; reprinted by permission of Random House, Inc. and Faber & Faber Ltd.

In the course of my work on this project I have received help and advice from numerous people. Daniel R. Schwarz has provided unwearying support from the beginning; he helped to shape my understanding of the English novel, and his incisive commentary on successive drafts of the study has been invaluable. I am grateful to M. H. Abrams for sharing his vast and detailed knowledge of Romantic literature and intellectual history, and to James McConkey for responding with sensitivity and perceptiveness to my work from the perspective of a working creative writer. Phillip L. Marcus has also read most of the book at various stages; I have profited from his extensive knowledge of the historical contexts of modernism. Walter Slatoff read my chapter on Faulkner with a generous if skeptical eye, helping me to anticipate many potential challenges. I owe less easily definable gratitude to the other teachers, colleagues and friends who have read chapters of the book, contributed useful suggestions, or influenced my growth as reader, writer, and critic: John Elder, Robert Hill, Stephen Parrish, Scott Elledge, Evan Radcliffe, Richard DuRocher, Nancy Shaw, Karen Cherewatuk, Megan Macomber, Paul Russell, Kim Noling, Stephen Sicari, Richard Johnson, and William Quillian. I am deeply grateful to my editor at Macmillan, Frances Arnold, for her advice, support and patience in helping me prepare the book for publication.

My largest debt, both personal and professional, is acknowledged in the dedication.

1
Visionary Closure and the Embodied Muse

I

Between 1910 and 1929, five writers ended major novels with moments of vision. The novels are E. M. Forster's *Howards End* (1910), D. H. Lawrence's *The Rainbow* (1915), James Joyce's *Ulysses* (1922), Virginia Woolf's *To the Lighthouse* (1927), and William Faulkner's *The Sound and the Fury* (1929). In the final section of each of these novels, a woman has a visionary experience that transcends full expression in language and that seems to make possible a concluding affirmation or image of order. Many critics have found these endings feeble, artificially positive, or inconsistent with the works in which they appear; such dismissals stand up well enough in studies of individual novels and authors, but cannot adequately explain what led five writers to employ such endings in major novels written within a span of twenty years. I believe that these writers created in these novels an altogether new fictional form, drawing upon religious and Romantic traditions to attempt endings that would combine unconstricted vitality of character with the aesthetic demands of closure.

In *Aspects of the Novel*, E. M. Forster identifies marriage and death as the two most common ways of ending a novel. The 'average novelist' relies on these events, he argues, because they are 'almost his only connection between his characters and his plot'.[1] If this observation now seems less self-evident than it would have in 1927, it is because Forster and the other English modernists did more than any previous group of writers to challenge the inevitability of these two patterns. Forster's generalization applies to earlier novels with considerable aptness, though many novelists attempted to vary the two patterns in unexpected ways. I would like to approach the modernist experiment with visionary endings by briefly surveying the earlier forms of closure that the modernists rejected.

In the two early works that helped to create the English novel, Samuel Richardson offers his successors models for what would become the two dominant modes of novelistic closure. The plot of *Pamela* (1740) is

1

essentially completed in the marriage of its heroine, though it is characteristic of Richardson's concerns and values that the text continues for many pages after this event until Pamela is acknowledged by her husband's family and written into his will. In *Clarissa* (1748), Richardson structures the ending around his heroine's death; again, however, the narrative continues beyond the main climax, until moral justice is achieved in the death of Lovelace. Most readers have agreed that Richardson's high moral seriousness is more effectively embodied in the tragic form and closure of *Clarissa*. At the same time, Richardson's contemporary Henry Fielding, in *Joseph Andrews* (1742) and *Tom Jones* (1749), established marriage as the dominant form of closure in comic novels. In Fielding the denouement also involves a rise in the fortunes of the hero and a discovery of his true birth; these elements occasionally recur in the endings of later novels, often in company with a culminating marriage. The greatest novelist of culminating marriage, however, eschewed such high comic improbabilities in order to create the kind of morally serious comedy that Richardson had failed to achieve in *Pamela*. All of Jane Austen's novels end in the marriage of their heroines; the first two – *Sense and Sensibility* (1811) and *Pride and Prejudice* (1813) – provide double plots that revolve around two sisters and end in two marriages. These and Austen's later novels – *Northanger Abbey* (1818), *Mansfield Park* (1814), *Emma* (1816), and *Persuasion* (1818) – delight in proposing an almost infinite variety of ways to the most unsurprising of ends.[2]

Even when later nineteenth-century novelists experimented extensively with fictional form, they rarely abandoned entirely the alternatives of marriage and death as culminating events. Despite their innovations in narrative perspective and structure, the Brontës employed essentially conventional endings: Charlotte Brontë's *Jane Eyre* (1847) ends with the marriage of Jane and Rochester; Emily Brontë's *Wuthering Heights* (1847) with the death of Heathcliff. A variant on the marital ending emerges in novels which conclude with the second marriages of their protagonists: in Thackeray's *Vanity Fair* (1848) Amelia Sedley remarries to William Dobbin; in Dickens's *David Copperfield* (1850) David remarries to Agnes Wickfield; in Eliot's *Middlemarch* (1872) Dorothea Brooke remarries to Will Ladislaw. But this variant pattern created its own special problems. The writers intend these second marriages to be better than the characters' first ones, yet readers have found all three second marriages in one way or other dissatisfying, perhaps because they inevitably proceed from dislocations of the original narrative direction and thus seem sentimentally imposed rather than natural resolutions of the plots. The form of *Vanity Fair*, for example, is essentially that of two inverted parabolas: initially, while Amelia's fortunes are falling, Becky Sharpe's are rising; finally, when Becky's fall, Amelia's gradually rise again. The design demands that they should re-encounter each other at the end of the book, and that the culminating events should somehow involve them both; but Becky's sudden interest in helping Dobbin to win Amelia is not fully explicable in terms of either her motivating self-interest or her redeeming *joie de vivre*.

Dickens innovated most persistently of all the nineteenth-century English novelists in constructing endings. *Dombey and Son* (1848) is an early and successful attempt to push the culminating marriage back in the structure of a novel; Florence Dombey and Walter Gay are united five chapters before the close, and Walter, who is absent at sea for most of the novel, never really becomes a major character. Dickens ends with Dombey's relenting toward his daughter, emphasizing the novel's central focus on their relationship. In *Bleak House* (1853) he experiments further: the novel repeatedly arrives at a satisfying and dramatic close – discovery, death, or marriage – then dissolves it into anti-climax and goes on; the effect of each new climax is to reorient the reader's perception of the novel's thematic centre. The detective-tale discovery of Tulkinghorn's murderer is superseded by the flight and death of Lady Dedlock; this seems an appropriate culmination to a work concerned with human fallibility, misunderstanding and injustice. But Dickens then turns to the issue of Esther's marriage, apparently to create a happier resolution in her union with John Jarndyce; this possibility, however, dissolves into her more fitting but less climactic marriage to the minor character Allan Woodcourt. While this shift is occuring, a newly-discovered will promises to resolve the great equity suit of Jarndyce and Jarndyce with which the book began; but this potential ending collapses with the suit itself, before the will can even be presented, because the whole substance of the estate has finally been consumed in costs. At this point Richard Carstone dies, most likely of consumption, his feeble strength of character destroyed by his fevered reliance on the suit; yet Dickens turns again in the final chapter to Esther's happy married life. Perhaps the success of these repeated reversals is related to Dickens's experiment with a double narrative structure; the climactic events occur in chapters narrated by Esther Summerson, but Dickens seems able to dissipate and supersede their closural effect by cutting away to the omniscient narrator after each crisis.[3]

The effect of closure on the thematic centre of a novel emerges again from a comparison of the alternative endings to *Great Expectations* (1861). Dickens originally planned neither a marriage nor a death for its close;

Pip was to end up a disillusioned bachelor, gaining only his clerkship in Herbert's firm. Since setting up Herbert in business was 'the one good thing he did in his prosperity', it was to be 'the only thing that endures and bears good fruit'.[4] The rewritten ending, which appears to promise a culminating marriage between Pip and Estella, seriously alters the moral shape and direction of the work. In his last completed novel, *Our Mutual Friend* (1865), Dickens again experimented with a sequence of final events. The marriage of John Rokesmith and Bella Wilfer is pushed back thirteen chapters from the end, that of Eugene Wrayburn and Lizzie Hexam six chapters; the early discovery that John Rokesmith is really John Harmon is superseded by the late discovery that Mr. Boffin was never really a miser; and the action of this otherwise comic and satiric novel essentially comes to rest in the grim deaths of Riderhood and Bradley Headstone. As in *Bleak House*, Dickens is deliberately trying to shake into new patterns the conventional endings in marriage, discovery and death; if he is less successful here, it is perhaps because the unified narrative is less forgiving of the alternations in tone that this variety of culminating events requires.

George Eliot was more interested in realistic character than Dickens, less interested in plot and formal questions; as a consequence, her endings are generally more conventional. *Adam Bede* (1859) ends in the marriage of Adam and Dinah; *The Mill on the Floss* (1860) in the deaths of Tom and Maggie; *Silas Marner* (1861) in the discoveries of Dunstan's crime and of Eppie's true parentage, though Eliot varies the conventional pattern in Eppie's refusal of her rise in fortune, a refusal finally ratified by her marriage. The double plot of *Middlemarch* leads to a more complex ending. Dorothea's culminating interview with Rosamund, like Becky Sharpe's intercession between Dobbin and Amelia at the end of *Vanity Fair*, finally brings the two plots fully together – more effectively so than in Thackeray's novel, since the motivation to intercede in helping the Lydgates arises naturally out of Dorothea's character. The overflowing of Dorothea's generosity in this scene believably engenders Rosamund's unique act of disinterested kindness in clearing up Dorothea's misunderstanding of Will Ladislaw, so that the novel can end with the sun rising on Dorothea's second marriage even as it sets on Lydgate's professional ambitions.

Nineteenth-century American and continental authors generally rely on the same patterns of closure as their English contemporaries, despite wide differences in style and subject. Hawthorne end *The Scarlet Letter* (1850) with Dimmesdale's dramatic death on the scaffold, and *The House of the Seven Gables* (1851) with a reconciliation of two families in the marriage of Phoebe and Holgrave. Melville's *Moby Dick* (1851) ends its epic quest into the nature of good and evil with the death not of an individual, but of almost its entire fictional population. Its final moment is unlike any other: a skyhawk, pinned by Tashtego's hammer to the mast, is tangled in Ahab's flag and dragged down with the ship, which 'like Satan, would not sink to hell till she had dragged a living part of heaven along with her'.[5] This cataclysmic and symbolic close contrasts sharply with Gustave Flaubert's quite different use of death to end his major novel of the same decade, *Madame Bovary* (1857). Emma's grim suicide is rendered in excruciatingly realistic detail, and the novel continues beyond it for three further chapters to end with the death of Charles Bovary and the mundane triumph of the pharmacist Homais.

The ending of Tolstoy's *Anna Karenina* (1876) partially foreshadows the visionary closure of the English modernists. Part VII of the novel concludes the action of the main plot, according to conventional models, with Anna's death. But the focus on Levin's revelatory experience in Part VIII gradually modulates this conclusion into an altogether different key. Levin has been near despair and suicide in his inability to discover the meaning of life; the solution that now comes to him is that one must live for one's soul, for truth, for God, rather than for one's own needs. He has always known this; searching for an answer has only compounded his confusion, since 'reason could not give me an answer – reason is incommensurable with the question'. This experience gives him a new spiritual tranquility; the novel's final sentence affirms his new faith that 'my life . . . is every moment of it no longer meaningless as it was before, but has an unquestionable meaning of goodness with which I have the power to invest it'.[6] The death of Anna still broods behind this affirmative close, but the sudden experience of a truth beyond the power of reason will reappear in the English visionary ending.

At the close of the nineteenth century and the beginning of the twentieth, Thomas Hardy and Joseph Conrad turned decisively away from the predominantly comic tradition of the English novel; their major novels all culminate in the deaths of their protagonists. Eustacia Vye is the real centre of interest in Hardy's *Return of the Native* (1878); the movement beyond her death to the final marriage of Thomasin and Venn both appears to be and was in fact an inconsistent afterthought.[7] Hardy's attempt to embody a tragic vision in fiction appears more clearly in the deaths that end *Tess of the d'Urbervilles* (1891) and *Jude the Obscure* (1895). The nature of Conrad's vision is more ambiguous: the deaths that conclude *Lord Jim* (1900), *Heart of Darkness* (1902), and *Nostromo* (1904) seem less deliberately tragic, the heros more seriously flawed.

Henry James is the first writer to perceive and discuss the problem that was to motivate the modernist experiments with closure. Early in his career, James rejected the conventional Victorian 'happy ending', which relies 'on a distribution at the last of prizes, pensions, husbands, wives, babies, millions, appended paragraphs, and cheerful remarks'.[8] But endings continued to trouble him; the problem of closure is the first major issue he takes up in his influential Prefaces to the 1909 New York edition of his works:

> the prime effect [of a fictional system of relations] is to lead on and on; while the fascination of following resides, by the same token, in the presumability *somewhere* of a convenient, of a visibly-appointed stopping place.

The problem is an essential conflict between the openness of life and the necessarily closed form of art:

> Really, universally, relations stop nowhere, and the exquisite problem of the artist is eternally but to draw, by a geometry of his own, the circle within which they shall happily *appear* to do so.

The painter of life must strive 'both to treat his chosen subject and to confine his necessary picture. It is only by doing such things that art becomes exquisite'.[9] But James does not suggest clearly how an exquisite reconciliation of life's continuity with art's confinement can be achieved; in his own fictions, the geometrical effects of plot and aesthetic patterning generally become compelling and inescapable at the close.

In *The Ambassadors* (1903), for example, which James called 'quite the best, "all round," of my productions',[10] the ending avoids all the conventional modes of closure only to impose its own equally rigid logic. Strether first loses his chance to marry Mrs. Newsome by championing Chad Newsome's relationship with Madame de Vionett, then loses his idealized vision of that relationship in the discovery that it is merely an ordinary liaison. In the novel's final scene he refuses Maria Gostrey's veiled marriage proposal, asserting that he must give her up 'to be right . . . That, you see, is my only logic. Not, out of the whole affair, to have got anything for myself'. This moment parallels the original ending of *Great Expectations*; it is what might be called anti-marital closure, a renunciation neither tragic nor comic, as Maria concedes: she 'sighed it at last all comically, all tragically, away'.[11] For Strether this renunciation is logical if unromantic; there is no problem about disappointing the lady's feelings, however, since she has existed from start to finish merely to serve reader's convenience as a sounding board for Strether's thinking. 'She is an enrolled, a direct, aid to lucidity; she is in fine, to tear off her mask, the most unmitigated and abandoned of *ficelles*', James admits in the preface.[12] One cannot easily imagine any life that might 'lead on and on' for these characters; the shape of the novel is so perfectly rounded at this point that they seem completely fixed and determined by its closing circle.

Before James began thinking so deeply about the theoretical problems of fiction, however, he created a far less schematic ending that looks forward in many ways to the innovations of his modernist heirs. The conclusion of *The Portrait of a Lady* (1881) revolves around the death of Ralph Touchett, and is in this sense conventional. But James makes Ralph's death the occasion for a series of discoveries on Isabel's part. From the sister of her husband, Gilbert Osmond, she learns that Osmond and Madame Merle have been lovers, that Osmond's daughter Pansy is their child, and that Osmond and Madame Merle have used Isabel for the sake of her money. From Madame Merle she learns that it was Ralph Touchett who made Isabel rich by convincing his father to leave her a fortune. From Ralph himself, dying, she learns that she has been loved; and from her perennial suitor, Caspar Goodwood, she learns in the novel's culminating scene just enough of heedless passion to reject it decisively, reaching her final decision to embrace the responsibility and pain of returning to Pansy and Osmond in Rome. Despite the presence of a great Victorian deathbed scene, the main weight of this conclusion rests on Isabel's decision; the ending is centred on her character rather than on the actual concluding events. She remains relatively uncircumscribed by the novel's form, still capable of developing and surprising the reader; one can only guess what she will do and how she will act in Rome.

II

James's response to the problem of closure was an increasing preoccupation with the management of artifice, with making relations appear to stop, with drawing the aesthetic circle exquisitely. The goal of the modernists after James is to draw the necessary aesthetic circle in such a way that human relations shall happily appear *not* to stop within it, leaving the reader free to imagine that the characters go on living – as if they were real people – after the novel's close. They begin where James began with closure and develop in precisely the opposite direction. In

Aspects of the Novel, Forster gives the following account of the formal problem involved in ending a novel:

> In the losing battle that the plot fights with the characters, it often takes a cowardly revenge. Nearly all novels are feeble at the end. This is because the plot requires to be wound up . . .
> [the novelist] has to round things off, and usually the characters go dead while he is at work, and our final impression of them is through deadness. . . . Incidents and people that occurred at first for their own sake now have to contribute to the *dénouement*.[13]

At the end of a conventional novel, Forster argues, the increasingly obvious artifice of plot destroys all illusion that the characters are real people, reducing them to mere fragments of a fictional design. Forster's account implicitly challenges the Aristotelian doctrine that writers 'do not employ action in order to achieve character portrayal, but they include character because of its relation to action'.[14] The modernists wish to invert Aristotle's hierarchy and give character priority over plot; as a result, they reject the use of conventional endings that too obviously seem to violate integrity and plausibility of character in the interest of predetermined aesthetic ends.

Virginia Woolf distills the modernist priority of character explicitly into the central premise of 'Mr. Bennett and Mrs. Brown' (1924):

> I believe that all novels . . . deal with character, and that it is to express character . . . that the form of the novels, so clumsy, verbose, and undramatic, so rich, elastic, and alive, has been evolved.

Men and women write novels 'because they are lured on to create some character'; the most important issue of novelistic craft is 'how to create characters that are real'.[15] When the modernists criticize the works of others – as Woolf condemns Galsworthy, Bennett and Wells in this essay – their criticism is almost always based on what they conceive to be failures to render character convincingly. Forster turns this standard against James himself in *Aspects of the Novel*.[16] Even Lawrence, in his famous letter about wanting to get away from the 'old stable ego of the character', justifies his complaint in terms of a desire for even deeper explorations beneath character into man's subconscious being.[17] Since the modern period, the priority of character in fiction has become common doctrine; the critic W. J. Harvey speaks for a broad consensus in asserting that 'most great novels exist to reveal and explore character'.[18]

The pre-eminent modernist concern with character emerges in Forster's focus on personal relations, in Lawrence's struggle to explore man's mythic subconsciousness, in the experiments of Joyce, Woolf and Faulkner with stream of consciousness and internal monologue. Early readers and critics of modernism were often confused by these experiments into believing that the primary goal of modernism was the presentation of form for its own sake; now that several decades have passed, it is easier to see how the formal experiments establish new conventions for rendering unexpected and previously neglected aspects of human experience. In the works of these writers the mimetic focus of the novel is turned inward to explore psychological and emotional experience; external detail and action appear only when they exert some influence upon the continual unfolding of an internal drama.[19] The modernist emphasis on character is related to what J. Hillis Miller has called 'the disappearance of God'; in a world from which God has withdrawn, or in which he is non-existent, men and women can only turn toward each other and into themselves in attempting to make order and meaning out of their experience: 'the drama has all been moved within the minds of the characters'.[20] Conventional endings in marriage and death become psychologically implausible because it is impossible to believe in any external power – implicitly, of God or his surrogates – to distribute prizes and impose punishments. Yet the modernists still wish to close the aesthetic circle, to provide some final connection between their characters and their plots.

This perception of a conflict between the demands of psychological verisimilitude and the demands of aesthetic form led the modernists to attempt extensive experiments with closure in the novel. In recent decades critics have divided sharply over how best to describe these experiments. The first theoretical position, that modern fiction breaks with traditional fiction in turning to various kinds of 'open form', has been proposed by Robert M. Adams in *Strains of Discord: Studies in Literary Openness* (1958), Beverly Gross in 'Narrative Time and the Open-Ended Novel' (1966), and Alan Friedman in *The Turn of the Novel* (1966).[21] Of these, Friedman's study offers the fullest discussion of modern fiction. He argues that whereas earlier writers 'worked to achieve endings which closed their novels', the modernists tried to achieve the 'hitherto unfamiliar phenomenon of allowing the expansion of experience to end without a final constriction, emotional or moral – to be still unchecked on the last page'. But Friedman's focus on 'experience' in the novel ties his discussion closely to the characters themselves and to their effect on the reader; he remains troubled by the problem that a writer must still attempt to reconcile openness of experience with the formal necessity for closure:

> How can he suggest at the end of his novel that these are the final pages of this particular rendering of experience – for practical necessity dictates that he must end – while at the same time he suggests that there is never a close to experience . . . how can he end without closing?

Friedman's answer to this question is that the novel's central characters must continually attempt

> to order finally, finally make sense of, finally limit, and hence transcend – their disturbing, expanding experience which *in fact* cannot be transcended, can never be transcended.

For Friedman, this answer seems no more impossible and irrational than the old myth that 'disturbing, expanding experience' can be ordered, limited and transcended.[22] But to pose and answer the question in these terms seems to me to evade the most interesting issue raised by modernist endings: given that the novelist wishes to leave the experience of his characters as open as possible, what forms and strategies are available for meeting the 'practical necessity' of closure, and how does he employ them?

Friedman discusses in detail only one of the five novels that I wish to focus on; of that novel's final vision he observes that

> the last paragraph of *The Rainbow* has annoyed almost everyone . . . [in] its abrupt, undue, and irrelevant social optimism. . . . Ursula's glowing vision remains, as social optimism, unpersuasive.

Friedman sees her vision as merely an awkward symbol for an inner process, one which helps to 'convey a movement in the soul'. With similar discontent, he suggests in passing that Lily Briscoe's vision at the end of *To the Lighthouse* may be 'a mere gimmick pulled from a grab-bag of tricks'.[23] In his chapter on Forster, *Howards End* is conspicuously absent; and he has almost nothing to say about *Ulysses*, that baffling and influential giant with which any theory of form in modern literature must ultimately come to terms. I think that Friedman's exclusive focus on 'open form' compels him to avoid or disparage those endings in modern fiction which attempt most fully to reconcile openness of experience for the characters with strong and compelling forms of narrative closure.

The second theoretical position on closure in the novel sees no radical break between traditional and modern endings, and views all novels as in some sense 'closed' aesthetic structures. Wayne Booth advanced this position in *The Rhetoric of Fiction* (1961):

> certainly those open structures which we admire always turn out, on close inspection, to be 'open' only in very limited respects; in so far as we think of them as great works, they somehow weave their various threads into a final harmony.[24]

Major studies in this line are Frank Kermode's *The Sense of an Ending* (1967), Barbara Herrnstein Smith's *Poetic Closure* (1968), David H. Richter's *Fable's End* (1974), and Marianna Torgovnick's *Closure in the Novel* (1981). Of these books, the more recent are the less useful to the present discussion. Torgovnick discusses none of the five novels I wish to study, and her general categories for novelistic closure – epilogue and scene – are not germane to the issues I wish to pursue.[25] Richter's book is primarily concerned with didactic fictions – such as *Gulliver's Travels* and *Lord of the Flies* – though he adheres to the general position that 'completeness and closure' in modern endings 'simply rest upon somewhat different principles from those governing more conventional represented actions'; further, he recognizes that the focus on character is central to the problem of closure in modern fiction.[26] Structuralist literary theory would also appear to be allied with this 'closed form' position; in *Structuralist Poetics* (1975), Jonathan Culler invokes Barthes and Gérard Genette to support his view that 'plot is subject to teleological determination'. But Culler also points out that the 'general ethos of structuralism runs counter to the notions of individuality and a rich psychological coherence'.[27] Such an ethos inevitably discounts the concern with character that motivated the modernists to experiment with endings; in a study of closure shaped by this ethos, *Narrative and its Discontents* (1981), D. A. Miller explicitly states that he is not interested in the 'frequently evoked conflict between the closed form of art . . . and the openness of life' but rather in the conflict within novels between 'the principles of production and the claims of closure to a resolved meaning'.[28] Since this frame of reference is unrelated to my own, and since Miller's analyses are confined to nineteenth century novels, I will not pursue his discussion further.

Barbara Herrnstein Smith's *Poetic Closure*, although not primarily concerned with fiction, offers a useful discussion of the psychological aims and effects of literary endings. Her argument rests on the 'basic proposition that closure – the sense of finality, stability, and integrity – is an effect that depends primarily upon the reader's experience of the structure of the entire poem'. We delight in endings that are designed; in a structured sequence of events, the terminal event confirms expectations that have been established by the preceding structure. But until a series 'is announced as *concluded*, we cannot be sure of the pattern'; the writer maintains our interest by introducing elements that sustain the work's structural 'instability'. As we read, we engage 'in a steady process of readjustment and retrospective patterning'; at the last word 'we should be able to re-experience the entire work, not now as a succession of events, but as an integral design'.[29] In her final chapter, Smith discusses the 'anti-closural tendencies of modern poetry (and modern art in general)', suggesting that such works exhibit 'the sort of conclusion that . . . without sounding arbitrary, manages to avoid sounding conclusive'. But effective closure, she believes, 'will always *involve* the reader's expectations' even though it will not always fulfill them. An unexpected ending

> forces and *rewards* a readjustment of the reader's expectations; it justifies itself retrospectively . . . [it] provides a perspective point from which the reader can now appreciate a significant pattern, principle, or motive not grasped before.[30]

The effect of 'retrospective patterning' may be even stronger in experimental works than in traditional ones, because it compels the reader to expand his awareness of the possible forms that literary order can achieve.

The best and most influential discussion of fictional closure places such retrospective patterning in a long historical perspective. In *The Sense of an Ending*, Frank Kermode argues that narrative structures always arise from their relation to endings; like the Christian temporal structure from which they derive, such structures attempt to organize time, to make it resemble human life by the provision of origins and ends. Men caught in the middle of time 'make considerable imaginative investments in coherent patterns which, by the provision of an end, make possible a satisfying consonance with the origins and with the middle'. Kermode takes the ticking of a clock as a model for the simplest kind of plot:

> *tick* is our word for a physical beginning, *tock* our word for an end. . . . We can perceive a duration only when it is organized. . . . We use fictions to enable the end to confer organization and form on the temporal structure.

In plots more complex than the ticking of a clock, more elaborate organizational devices still

> have to defeat the tendency of the interval between *tick* and *tock* to empty itself; to maintain within that interval following *tick* a lively expectation of *tock*, and a sense that however remote *tock* may be, all that happens happens as if *tock* were certainly following.

Plotting 'presupposes and requires that an end will bestow upon the whole duration and meaning'; the interval between beginning and end

> must be purged of simple chronicity, of the emptiness of *tock–tick*, humanly uninteresting successiveness. It is required to be a significant season, *kairos* poised between beginning and end. . . . Within this organization that which was conceived of as simply successive becomes charged with past and future: what was *chronos* becomes *kairos* . . .
> . . . *chronos* is 'passing time' or 'waiting time' – that which, according to Revelation, 'shall be no more' – and *kairos* is the season, a point in time filled with significance, charged with a meaning derived from its relation to the end.

Kermode suggests that 'when *tick-tock* seems altogether too easily fictional', we 'produce plots containing a good deal of *tock-tick*; such a plot is that of *Ulysses*. He identifies this structural complexity or 'narrative irony' with the Aristotelian 'peripeteia', reversal, a 'falsification of one's expectation of the end'; like Smith, he contends that our delight in a strategy of falsification is 'related to our wish to reach the discovery or recognition by an unexpected and instructive route'.[31]

III

In their experiments with visionary closure, the modernists are exploring one of these new and unexpected routes to the inevitable close in a work of fiction. The visionary ending offers a radical departure from the conventional fictional climax in death or marriage; it enables the work to end on a note of aesthetic finality that leaves future events in the lives of the characters relatively undetermined. The most influential model for visionary formal structure is the Bible, which parallels temporal structure – past, present, future – in moving structurally from Genesis, through Incarnation, to Revelation: 'I am the Alpha and Omega, the beginning and the ending, saith the Lord, which is, and which was, and which is to come' (Rev. 1:8 KJV). The Revelation of John prophetically forsees the end of this world, when 'there should be time no longer' (Rev. 10:6), and envisions 'a new heaven and a new earth: for the first heaven and the first earth were passed away' (Rev. 21:1). This visionary close reinterprets and rewrites the entire preceding narrative; all of Biblical history is retrospectively incorporated into a teleological progression toward apocalypse. Yet the writer leaves indefinite the exact nature, timing and manner of the promised future fulfillment; details of the 'new heaven and new earth' to come remain cryptic and undetermined, open to the reader's own interpretive imagination. This ambiguity offers a powerful model for effective closure that need not explicitly determine the fate or circumscribe the vitality of individual actors.

Their struggle to revitalize the portrayal of characters leads the modern novelists 'to go back and back', as Woolf remarks; 'to experiment with one thing and another'.[32] Although visionary endings are new to the novel in the modernist period, they trace back to a major poetic tradition deriving ultimately from Revelation. Dante ends *The Divine Comedy* with his beatific vision of the 'Eternal Light' of God, 'the love that moves the sun and the other stars'; the revelation is so powerful that although by the time of writing his 'vision almost wholly fades', yet 'still there drops within my heart the sweetness that was born of it'.[33] At the close of *Paradise Lost*, the archangel Michael takes Adam up the highest hill in Eden to give him a vision of providential history: history, that is, as it is given order and shape by God's redemption of man's fall. As scenes of early evil unfold before him, Adam cries out against 'visions ill foreseen'; but when Michael goes on to describe the Incarnation, sacrifice, and second coming of Christ, Adam learns to recognize God's 'goodness infinite', and to 'Acknowledge my Redeemer ever blest'.[34] This visionary ending retrospectively transforms Milton's poem about the fall of man into an affirmative, proleptic celebration of God's grace.

The Romantic poets took over the model of visionary closure from religious poetry and adapted it to secular experience. Wordsworth's account of his visionary experience on Snowdon, composed in 1804 to open the concluding book of *The Prelude*, offers a paradigmatic example of the 'Romantic Moment' used as a formal device to end a narrative poem.[35] Because I will refer back to it frequently in the pages that follow, I would like to examine it in some detail here. Although *The Prelude* is autobiographical narrative rather than fiction, its culmination in the Snowdon passage is particularly rich in narrative reversals; the result is that, in Kermode's terms, 'the end comes as expected, but not in the manner expected'.[36] But Wordsworth is simultaneously concerned to weave into the episode earlier motifs and metaphors that reinforce its 'retrospective patterning' of the poem as a whole. The passage recapitulates the poem's major themes and images by locating them within a new visionary experience; the effect of this strategy is retrospectively to reshape the reader's experience of the entire poem.[37] Wordsworth's location of such power over narrative in natural rather than religious experience marks an important transition in the historical development of visionary closure; the episode's closural effect in the thematic structure of *The Prelude* anticipates closely the role of visionary endings in modern fiction.[38]

Wordsworth begins his concluding narration by setting the scene and establishing certain expectations. He is travelling 'with a youthful friend',[39] but immediately overlooks the friend's presence, which will have no bearing on the meaning of the experience to follow: 'And westward took my way' (1. 4), he writes, not 'our' way. Their purpose is 'to see the sun / Rise from the top of Snowdon' (ll. 4–5), an experience never described in the passage which follows; the unexpected vision eclipses the expected one. They rouse the shepherd who is 'the stranger's usual guide' (1. 8), unconscious that this expedition will be an unusual one, of 'unhabitual influence' (1. 80). The effect of such language is to insist upon the ordinariness against which the extraordinary reversal of expectations will appear more striking by contrast.

The moment of vision occurs with the poet, rather than the guide, alone and leading: 'And I, as chanced, the foremost of the band' (1. 35). Although the poet ascribes this situation to chance, it corresponds to circumstances throughout *The Prelude* which deprive him of human guidance before a moment of revelatory experience. In Simplon Pass the 'band / Of travellers' whom Wordsworth and his companion have made 'our guides' dine with them and then rise, 'Leaving us at the board. Erelong we followed' (VI.494–501). The moment of revelation occurs before the guides are overtaken. Similarly, in the first of the spots of time, a human guide disappears:

> We were a pair of horsemen – honest James
> Was with me, my encourager and guide.
>   We had not travelled long ere some mischance
> Disjoined me from my comrade.

> (XI.282–5)

This persistent falling away of human guidance seems to suggest, implicitly, that as the visionary moment draws near, Nature herself takes over the role of guide: 'One evening – surely I was led by her – / I went alone into a shepherd's boat' (I.372–3). The opening of the boat-stealing episode establishes a pattern of solitary experience under Nature's guidance which will persist throughout the poem.

Initially, the poet's experience on Snowdon promises to be a gradual revelation: 'When at my feet the ground appeared to brighten, / And with a step or two seemed brighter still' (ll. 36–7). But as happens repeatedly in this passage, an expectation is introduced only to be reversed; the gradual brightening is suddenly usurped: 'For instantly a light upon the turf / Fell like a flash' (ll. 39–40). The suddenness of the experience bypasses the slow working of reason: 'Nor had I time to ask the cause of this' (l. 38). Like Saul on the Damascus road, the poet loses his bearings in a flash of light, and recovers to find 'sight / Of a new world' (XII.370–1).

At this point, Wordsworth identifies his own relation to the new world: 'on the shore / I found myself of a huge sea of mist / Which meek and silent rested at my feet' (ll. 42–4). This relationship is both literal and metaphorical: the passage, and *The Prelude* as a whole, are about Wordsworth's finding of himself, as a poet and in relation to the external world. The sea of mist, like the poet's personal crisis, can now be seen from above as a world where perception was dulled, and where the apparent 'opposition set' (l. 30) between the mind and nature was a false relation. The poet has come through an experience of impaired perception to a place where he can again see clearly. The vision on Snowdon is one of these rare moments in which sense perception is transcended: the real sea 'seemed', but *only* seemed, 'To dwindle and give up its majesty, / Usurped upon as far as sight could reach' (ll. 49–51). Though he cannot see the real sea, Wordsworth can imagine its presence beyond his line of sight, and so construct a truer world than that which his eye alone could give him.

The final aspect of the scene perceived by mind and moon

> Was a blue chasm, a fracture in the vapour,
> A deep and gloomy breathing-place, through which
> Mounted the roar of waters, torrents, streams
> Innumerable, roaring with one voice.
>   . . . in that breach
> Through which the homeless voice of waters rose,
> That dark deep thoroughfare, had Nature lodged
> The soul, the imagination of the whole.

>   (ll. 56–65)

The 'dark deep thoroughfare' leads back down through the mist out of which the poet has come, back through the time when he was lost and insensible to Nature, back down through mist and darkness to his beginnings. The voice that rises is 'homeless' because its source is no longer seen; it now inhabits the mind into which it has been infused. It seems to incorporate all the waters of the poet's experience, from that first, 'fairest of all rivers', who 'loved / To blend his murmurs with my nurse's song', and 'sent a voice / That flowed along my dreams' (I.272-6). It was the voice that gave him 'A knowledge, a dim earnest, of the calm / Which Nature breathes among the hills and groves' (I.284-5). Here on Snowdon the 'voice of waters' rises through a 'breathing-place', altered but not silenced in its passage through the 'deep and gloomy' fracture. The breach is the rift of connection between the child and the poet; it represents the continuity of that imagining power which has been associated throughout the poem with the sound of water.

Later in Book XIII Wordsworth will make explicit this use of the stream of water to represent poetic imagination:

> we have traced the stream
> From darkness, and the very place of birth
> In its blind cavern, whence is faintly heard
> The sound of waters; followed it to light
> And open day, accompanied its course
> Among the ways of Nature, afterwards
> Lost sight of it bewildered and engulphed,
> Then given it greeting as it rose once more
> With strength.
>
> (ll. 172-80)

During the passage through the mist he 'lost sight of it bewildered and engulfed', but now has heard it 'as it rose once more / With strength'. The 'deep dark thoroughfare' leads back to an 'under-presence', a subconscious power of imagination arising from earliest memory by which the whole scene is 'exalted' (l. 71). This language is Biblical in origin: 'Every valley shall be exalted' (Isaiah 40:4); 'For whosoever exalteth himself shall be abased; and he that humbleth himself shall be exalted' (Luke 14:11). But for Wordsworth it is not God who exalts: it is the imaginative 'under-presence' in the poet's mind which, paradoxically, 'exalts' not only itself, but the entire experience. The power to perceive and 'half-create' is a human power; the scene derives its grandeur only from the power of imagination in the observer who is to become a poet.

Nature has 'lodged / The soul, the imagination of the whole' in the mind of man.

The meditation that follows the experience on Snowdon is characteristic of the structural process Wordsworth employs throughout *The Prelude*: moments of remembered experience and meditations upon the significance of each experience succeed each other in alternation. Here, the main purpose of the meditative passage is to insist that the visionary moment be read metaphorically: 'it appeared to me / The perfect image of a mighty mind, / Of one that feeds upon infinity' (ll. 68–70). This mind is implicitly greater than Wordsworth's own; the vision suggests a Platonic idea of the poetic mind, 'In sense conducting to ideal form' (1850, l. 76).[40] The mind imaged on Snowdon 'feeds upon infinity', whereas Wordsworth's human poetic mind feeds only upon a few scattered recollections of former experience:

> the hiding-places of my power
> Seem open, I approach, and then they close;
> I see by glimpses now, when age comes on
> May scarcely see at all.

$$(XI.335–8)$$

These 'hiding-places' correspond to the chasm in the mist on Snowdon; in the idealized vision, the chasm is perenially open. But for Wordsworth himself the mist may one day close over the chasm, cutting him off from all connection with the sources of his imaginative power.

As we now know, the climbing of Snowdon took place in 1791, many years before the poet came to feel its final significance and weave it into its present place in *The Prelude*.[41] The experience occurred before his crisis and final restoration of imagination; at the time, he could not have seen it as a proleptic, metaphoric vision of his later crisis and recovery. He only perceives its significance in the light of that recovery, in the ability to look back upon his own growth and see it whole.[42] It is an experience 'recollected in tranquility'. But in constructing the poem Wordsworth brings the experience and the understanding of it together in one place; like Augustine before him, he intentionally alters biographical detail in the interest of thematic clarity.[43] The vision on Snowdon interweaves a metaphor for the poetic mind with a demonstration of the poetic imagination at work.[44] *The Prelude* has described the growth of a poet's mind; this concluding vision reveals that growth at its final and fullest stage.

IV

The first three modernist novels to experiment with visionary closure – *Howards End*, *The Rainbow*, and *Ulysses* – stand at similar points in their authors' careers. Each follows an autobiographical novel – *The Longest Journey*, *Sons and Lovers*, *A Portrait of the Artist* – and represents an attempt to move from a focus on the author's own consciousness toward the sympathetic rendering of a larger range of human experience. The visionary novels are all, in this sense, sequels to *The Prelude*, novelistic versions of the poem Wordsworth never completed 'On Man, on Nature, and on Human Life' to which *The Prelude* was to have been only a prologue. In his Prospectus to this unfinished work Wordsworth declares, invoking the name of Milton's Muse, 'Urania, I shall need / Thy guidance, or a greater Muse', because his subject is not Milton's heaven, hell and chaos, but the far deeper mysteries of 'the Mind of Man – / My haunt, and the main region of my song'.[45] One of the central discoveries of Wordsworth's poetry is that this 'greater Muse' is Nature herself; she leads him to discover his poetic identity in *The Prelude*, while her intercession in the growth of that identity simultaneously becomes the central subject of the poem.

For the modernists, the wish to render a larger sphere of human activity beyond the self demands a similar source of inspiration from outside the writer's own immediate experience. Literary tradition, in which the great preponderance of writers have been men, offers the relationship of male poet and female Muse as a conventional answer to this need for intellectual cross-fertilization. A definitive history of the Muse convention in western literature remains to be written; the only extended discussion of the subject emerges out of the frequently brilliant but largely unsubstantiated speculations of Robert Graves in *The White Goddess* (1948). Graves believes that the Northern European and Mediterranean peoples originally worshipped a female moon deity, who was later replaced by male gods to justify the shift to a patriarchal social system; the mystery-cults of Eleusis, the witch-covens of western Europe, and the Catholic worship of Mary are survivals into the historical era of the original goddess-worship. Poetry, according to Graves, is another such survival; 'a true poem is necessarily an invocation of the White Goddess, or Muse, the Mother of All living'. The classical Muses were originally three in number – Meditation, Memory and Song – representing the three poetic aspects of the one Goddess, but in the eighth century BC this triad of Muses was enlarged to three triads, in order to weaken her power further by 'departmentalization'; ultimately the male Apollo emerged as leader of the Muses and unchallenged God of poetry, though he still made no claim to *inspire* poems.[46] Inspiration, it would seem, remains a function of sexual difference.

The Muse in her most familiar aspect is the Muse of invocation –

> Sing, Goddess, the wrath of Achilles . . .
> Tell me, Muse, of that man, so ready at need . . .[47]

Milton uses the Muse convention in this way:

> Of man's first disobedience, and the fruit
> Of that forbidden tree . . .
> Sing Heav'nly Muse . . .[48]

Jonathan Culler suggests that 'apostrophe is perhaps always an indirect invocation of the muse', arguing that such invocations aim at 'constituting the object as another subject with whom the poetic subject might hope to strike up a harmonious relationship'. The 'apostrophizing poet' then uses this relationship to constitute himself:

> One who successfully invokes nature is one to whom nature might, in its turn, speak. He makes himself poet, visionary. Thus, invocation is a figure of vocation.

Culler distinguishes 'two forces in poetry, the narrative and the apostrophic', and suggests that 'the lyric is characteristically the triumph of the apostrophic'.[49] But the apostrophic Muse is not the only Muse; literature also offers notable examples of what might be called the embodied Muse, the figure of inspiration who appears as a character within the literary work. Like invocation, such evocation of the Muse helps to confirm the poet's identity; Graves goes so far as to argue that 'the test of a poet's vision . . . is the accuracy of his portrayal of the White Goddess'.[50] If, as Culler contends, invocation of the Muse is central to lyric poetry, evocation of the Muse is often equally central to narrative. Because, as Graves remarks, 'the Muse is a deity, but she is also a woman',[51] she is readily available to be rendered as a character in the course of a narrative action.

From classical times, such Muse figures have appeared in both literary and non-literary narratives. Plato locates an embodied Muse at the heart of his philosophic system in *The Symposium*. Despite Plato's idealization of union between male minds, Socrates identifies Diotima, 'a woman of

Mantinea', as his principal 'instructress in the art of love'. Diotima teaches Socrates to understand philosophic eros, the intellectual love upon which logic and reason are founded; such love mediates in the mind's apprehension of the highest good and beauty, which are inaccessible to reason alone. According to Diotima, the 'perfect revelation' to which 'love-mysteries' lead arises out of man's gradual ascent, in the objects he contemplates, from physical to moral to intellectual beauty; the final goal is 'the contemplation of absolute beauty'.[52] This pattern of female intercession in the ascent toward a final revelation recurs frequently in Western literature; in the twentieth century, all of the five modernist visionary novels combine, to some extent, an embodied Muse and a visionary close. This classical tradition of the embodied Muse is explicitly joined with the Biblical model for culminating vision in the roles of Saint Monica in Augustine's *Confessions* and of Beatrice in Dante's *Divine Comedy*.

In his movement towards Christianity, Augustine finds the church demands 'that certain things should be believed even though they could not be proved'.[53] This situation, like that of Socrates, requires a Muse figure, a female intercessor to teach those truths that are beyond man's unaided reason; Augustine finds such a figure in his mother, herself a Christian who has long prayed for his conversion. Early in the *Confessions* Monica has a dream vision foretelling Augustine's ultimate acceptance of 'the rule of faith', which consoles her in her distress at his sinful life (III.2). When Augustine at last achieves his conversion, he acknowledges that the event confirms her power of vision (VIII.12); addressing God, he asserts that all along 'you were speaking to me through her' (II.3). Finally, as a believer, Augustine himself shares a visionary experience with his mother at Ostia, shortly before her death. As they lean out a window, wondering about the eternal life of the saints,

> the flame of love burned stronger in us and raised us higher toward the eternal God . . . to that place of everlasting plenty. . . . While we spoke of the eternal Wisdom, longing for it and straining for it with all the strength of our hearts, for one fleeting instant we reached out and touched it. (IX.10)

This culminating moment functions structurally in bringing Augustine's narrative proper to a close; the shared vision confirms that he has achieved the faith beyond reason which Monica has always possessed. When Monica lies dying shortly after, she asks that he remember her 'at the altar of the Lord' (IX.2); at the time of writing the *Confessions*,

Augustine extends this request in a prayer: 'Lord . . . inspire those of them who read this book to remember Monica, your servant, at your altar.' The narrative of his life concludes with a final prophetic affirmation that his mother's last request 'shall be granted in the prayers of the many who read my confessions more fully than in mine alone' (IX.13). The visionary experience both confirms his vocation and confers effectual power upon his language, in a pattern of movement from vision to affirmation which also underlies the structure of the modernist visionary novels.

Dante employs the classical invocation of the uncharacterized Muse frequently throughout the *Commedia* (*Inf*. II.7 and XXXII.10, *Purg*. I.8 and XXIX.37-42, *Par*. II.8 and XVIII.82). But he also provides the most influential of all embodied Muse figures in the character of Beatrice, the idealized object of his youthful love, whose early death impressed her image still more deeply upon his creative imagination. Like Diotima and Monica, Beatrice leads her male follower upward to a beatific vision beyond reason and accessible only to faith. In Dante's allegorical elaboration of this pattern, Virgil – who symbolizes the poet's own power of reason – can lead Dante through hell and purgatory, but not paradise; Virgil says he will need 'a spirit fitter for that than I' as guide (*Inf*. I.121-3). Virgil twice mentions that he was sent to succour Dante by Beatrice herself, who has thus effectively set the whole poem in motion (*Inf*. II.49-72, *Purg*. I.52-4). As they advance through purgatory, Virgil refers Dante's questions about prayer, grace, and love to Beatrice: 'as far as reason sees here I can tell thee; beyond that wait only for Beatrice, for it is a matter of faith' (*Purg*. VI.43-8, XV.76-8, XVIII.46-8). Ultimately, at the close of the *Purgatorio*, Beatrice – who represents faith – herself assumes the role of spiritual guide.

Writing on 'The Raison d'Etre of Criticism in the Arts', E. M. Forster uses this moment as a metaphor for the final insufficiency of criticism – conceived of as a mode of rational inquiry – in attempting to explain our experience of art. Criticism

> has to withdraw when reality approaches, like Virgil from Dante on the summit of Purgatory. With the coming of love, we have to rely on Beatrice, whom we have loved all along, and if we have never loved Beatrice we are lost. . . . [Criticism] must be left behind at the entry of Heaven. [54]

Forster conceives of the highest human experience in aesthetic rather than religious terms, but it remains inaccessible to reason; for the highest understanding it is necessary to draw upon one's experience of love. In his commentary on the *Commedia*, John Sinclair asserts that Beatrice is for Dante the 'embodied revelation of the truth of God'. But at the same time she is still a woman, simultaneously 'the living spirit of truth . . . [and] the Beatrice who once showed him her youthful eyes. . . . Beatrice is the truth of God for him, and she is still Beatrice'.[55] The embodied Muse is at once human and transcendent; for Dante, Beatrice is 'she that imparadises my mind' (*Par.* XXVIII.1). She is the love that makes his vocation possible, the faith that leads him to the culminating vision of God that ends the *Paradiso*.

Along with the pattern of visionary closure, the embodied Muse convention was adopted and secularized by the English Romantic poets. In Wordsworth the mediating role of woman in the mind's access to vision is ascribed to Nature herself, the object of the poet's early love which was subsequently lost – like Beatrice for Dante – but is finally recovered in a triumphant affirmation of his poetic calling. Nature for Wordsworth is always feminine; it is the creative interchange of perception and stimulus between male mind and female universe that creates the world as he knows it. The sexual implications of this relationship appear most clearly when, as the boy in *Nutting*, he forces his way to a 'dear nook', where 'the hazels rose / Tall and erect, with tempting clusters hung, / A virgin scene!' After eyeing it for a time, 'voluptuous, fearless of a rival', he

> Dragged to earth both branch and bough, with crash
> And merciless ravage: and the shady nook
> Of hazels, and the green and mossy bower,
> Deformed and sullied, patiently gave up
> Their quiet being.[56]

Either the explicit sexuality or the violence of this interchange with Nature evidently troubled the poet; the episode, he says, was 'intended as part of a poem on my own life, but struck out as not being wanted there'.[57] Elsewhere his sexual relation with Nature is more carefully muted. In the Prospectus to *The Recluse*, he adopts the figure of apocalyptic marriage from Revelation to describe the millenial relation between mind and Nature, envisioning a time when 'the discerning intellect of Man' will be 'wedded to this goodly universe / In love and holy passion'. Wordsworth, 'long before the blissful hour arrives, / Would chant . . . the spousal verse / Of this great consummation'.[58]

Both Shelley and Keats combine visionary experience and the

embodied Muse in major poetic works. Shelley's *Prometheus Unbound* opens at the end of its dramatic action, when Prometheus, his hatred turning to pity, recalls the curse he had invoked on his tormentor Jupiter. In doing so, Prometheus discovers that his own hatred was what originally empowered Jupiter as a tyrant, his curse what created a fallen world. Prometheus's change of heart frees Asia, his long-sundered lover and bride, to rejoin him, much as Wordsworth is reunited with Nature and Dante with Beatrice. Descending in her journey to the realm of Demogorgon, Asia learns that 'the deep truth is imageless', inaccessible to reason and knowable only through love. The love she ultimately brings to Prometheus rejuvenates the world, creating 'a new earth and sea / And a heaven'; in the visionary fourth and final act of the poem, Asia's sisters Panthea and Ione watch as the earth and moon join in a great nuptial dance of celebration.[59] Keats's experience in *The Fall of Hyperion*, like Wordsworth's on Snowdon, provides a visionary affirmation of his poetic identity. In a dream vision, Keats enters an ancient temple and struggles to ascend the altar; there he confronts the veiled priestess Moneta, who first challenges and then implicitly confirms his sense of poetic vocation. As Muse, she offers to let him look inward through her eyes upon the fall of the Titans, in scenes that are for her 'still swooning vivid through my globed brain'. She is an explicitly embodied mediator in the poet's access to vision; when she puts back her veils, Keats sees 'a wan face',

> Not pined by human sorrows, but bright-blanch'd
> By an immortal sickness which kills not;
> It works a constant change, which happy death
> Can put no end to; deathwards progressing
> To no death was that visage; it had pass'd
> The lily and the snow.[60]

After this vivid evocation, Keats begins to recast his earlier fragment *Hyperion* as seen through Moneta's eyes. The poem is unfinished partly because, in this scene between poet and Muse which confirms his calling, Keats has unexpectedly both discovered and resolved his central theme.

Asia and Moneta are both powerful supernatural figures drawn from pre-Christian mythology; Wordsworth's grand conception of Nature in *The Prelude* evokes the entire external world as an animate female intercessor in his development toward poetic vision. But on the rare occasions when Wordsworth does embody his Muse in a specific character, she is clearly human rather than supernatural, and only slightly distinguished from Nature at large. The young woman of the Lucy poems is evoked almost entirely in natural images: she is 'a violet by a mossy stone', 'fair as a star', a 'flower' sown on earth to grow 'in sun and shower'. Nature chooses her at age three to grow up as 'A Lady of my own'; as Lucy listens to rural streams, 'beauty born of murmuring sound / Shall pass into her face'. When Lucy dies, the woman who grew out of the landscape is quietly reincorporated into it, 'Rolled round in earth's diurnal course, / With rocks, and stones, and trees'.[61] The embodied Wordsworthian Muse is simply Nature assuming human form. She makes her most paradigmatic appearance in *The Solitary Reaper*, a poem which closely anticipates the relations between writer, character and Muse in modern literature.

The aspect of the reaper's situation that Wordsworth insists upon most strongly in the poem's opening stanza is her solitude; she is 'single', 'solitary', 'by herself', 'alone'. When he stops and listens, he finds that her song is 'melancholy'; amid the natural scene, he has unexpectedly come upon 'the still, sad music of humanity'. Wordsworth characterizes the vale as 'overflowing' and 'profound', suggesting that it has become like the depths of the sea, the song welling up and spilling out of it in waves; the effect of this imagery is to bring the observer–poet inside the song. In the second stanza, the poet attempts a negative explanation of this experience by proposing two inadequate analogies. Both examples invoke desolate, wearying, lonely, distant situations; the effect of a bird's song in these settings is to bring unexpected joy to the hearers. But here in *The Solitary Reaper* it is a time of harvest and fair weather; characteristically for Wordsworth, the desolate setting must be in the listener's mind, as at the opening of *Resolution and Independence*. The reaper's song is 'welcome' and 'thrilling' because it shatters his mental bleakness. Paradoxically, only a sad song could touch him so deeply, because it identifies his own sadness with the sadness woven into the song, establishing a human bond and contact between the poet and the singer.

Wordsworth opens the third stanza with a rhetorical question: 'Will no one tell me what she sings?'[62] He makes two guesses at the subject: it may be a traditional highland ballad (but the woman sings 'for' rather than 'about' the story – her sympathy is fully engaged); or it may be 'some more humble lay, / Familiar matter of today', a subject in fact rather like those of Wordsworth's *Lyrical Ballads*. In suggesting this possibility the poet identifies himself with the singer, as Keats acknowledges a similar moment by exclaiming 'already with thee!' in *Ode to a Nightingale*. This identification in shared human sadness dissolves Wordsworth's isolation; the solitariness of the initial stanza is conspicuously absent in the final one. A new word – 'I' – appears for the first time in the poem; the poet's identity has been defined in the moment of human contact. The maiden's song has 'no ending' in a special sense, because when one's auditor is a poet, he can pass the experience on to others. 'The music in my heart I bore, / Long after it was heard no more', Wordsworth concludes; 'bore' means 'carried along', but it also implies giving new birth to the song in his own heart and with his own voice.[63]

This Muse who mediates a Wordsworthian interchange between man and nature reappears in Wallace Stevens's *The Idea of Order at Key West* (1935), a modern lyric written shortly after the group of five visionary novels. Like *The Solitary Reaper*, the poem presents a woman singing and a narrator–observer. Again, the words of the song are not given; the sound of song is what matters. Again, the observer first attempts negative explanations of the experience: 'The sea was not a mask. No more was she./The song and water were not medleyed sound.' Then he makes some tentative guesses about it, framed by the phrases 'even if' and 'it may be'. The sea in Stevens corresponds to Nature in Wordsworth, symbolizing life process that is inarticulate and 'inhuman'; the woman sings 'beyond the genius of the sea' because the sea 'was never formed to mind or voice', whereas she sings 'word by word'. The singer shapes and humanizes nature, translating its incomprehensible language into humanly under-standable sound. But the process is also 'more than that', more even than this translation; she is also adding something. The poem asserts in its first half that 'she was the maker of the song she sang'. But the phrase is repeated with a significant change in the second half: 'she was the single artificer of the world in which she sang'. The process of interchange between character and nature is reciprocal; the ordering of natural phenomena into human sound creates the whole world of the poem in which the singer appears. The sea itself gives up its own identity, 'whatever self it had', and 'became the self / That was her song, for she was the maker'.

In the process of this transformation the observer–poet, like Wordsworth, is caught up within the song; the effect of this change in perspective is to enhance his perception of order. The man-made boats and lights in the harbour are harmonized with the sea; natural and human worlds are made part of a larger unity. The utterance creates humanly perceptible order that the Universe cannot make alone. The central question of the poem – 'Ramon Fernandez, tell me, if you know' why the song makes the perception of order possible – is purely rhetorical, like Wordsworth's appeal for information. Reason and philosophy *cannot* finally describe the mysterious human power to create meaningful order out of the natural world. All ordering, rational, philosophical structures (which 'Mastered the night and portioned out the sea / Fixing emblazoned zones and fiery poles, / Arranging, deepening, enchanting night') are ultimately built upon a mystery akin to Plato's philosophic eros, dependent upon feminine intercession, founded in chaos and old night.[64]

V

Visionary closure in the modern novel draws upon both of these literary traditions: the culminating revelation that reinterprets the entire preceding narrative, and the embodied Muse who intercedes, from a position within the text, in the relations between mind and external world. The two traditions come together in Augustine and Dante, are adapted to secular literature in Romantic poetry, and are reshaped again by the modernists to create a new form of closure in the novel. The modernist strategy is to embody the Muse figure in a realistically rendered character, a woman who experiences a culminating moment of vision that radically reinterprets her own experience and alters the shape of the novel. The point of this strategy is to create closure that is dramatic and satisfying, that is focused on the experience of a character, and that is sufficiently indeterminate to leave the future lives of the characters relatively open in the reader's mind. Because this desire for indeterminacy becomes a central goal in modern fiction, however, the writers are quick to vary paradigms as soon as they perceive them; as a consequence, the five novels considered in this study seem to be the only five of comparable scope and influence in English that end in this way.[65] Even Woolf in *To the Lighthouse* and Faulkner in *The Sound and the Fury* are already engaged in revising the original model.

In the chapters that follow, I shall try to show how each novel is retrospectively reshaped by its culminating moment of vision. In some of the novels the centrality of the ending is emphasized by the title: *Howards End* puns on the place toward which the novel moves; *The Rainbow* is named for its culminating symbol; *To the Lighthouse* is titled for the movement toward its final goal. All five novels contain women who possess special power to translate the rhythms of nature into humanly comprehensible order: Mrs. Wilcox and Margaret Schlegel in *Howards End*; Anna and Ursula Brangwen in *The Rainbow*; Molly Bloom in *Ulysses*; Mrs. Ramsay and Lily Briscoe in *To the Lighthouse*; Dilsey in *The Sound and the Fury*. Forster and Lawrence were the first writers to experiment with visionary closure: in *Howards End*, Margaret Schlegel's concluding vision confirms her connection to a power in nature that lies beyond her ideas of order in daily life; at the end of *The Rainbow*, Ursula Brangwen envisions 'new heaven and new earth' beyond the flood of modern consciousness. With Joyce, the possibilities of visionary closure are perhaps most fully realized: Molly Bloom's final soliloquy unweaves the earlier form of *Ulysses*, like Penelope's nightly unweaving of her web, reversing the book's previous movement in the direction of increasing narrative and stylistic complexity. Woolf develops Lily Briscoe's concluding vision in *To the Lighthouse* to reshape the traditions of vision and Muse from the perspective of a female artist. Finally, in *The Sound and the Fury*, Faulkner adopts the visionary tradition to rewrite it completely; Caddy Compson should have inherited the power of culminating vision, but because she has been banished from her family and from the novel, the black servant Dilsey returns the visionary moment to the world of religious revelation. In the failure of her religious vision to provide adequate closure for the novel, Faulkner breaks the model employed in the earlier novels to create a new version of tragic form.

I will be concerned throughout my discussions of these novels with the relationship of character to form, of traditional mimesis to symbolic structure. In concluding with visionary experiences, the modernists are attempting to create structural connections between the realistic traditions of the novel and the symbolic traditions of mysticism and myth; the concluding visions are examples of *figura*, moments when, in Erich Auerbach's words,

> an occurrence on earth signifies not only itself but at the same time another, which it predicts or confirms, without prejudice to the power of its concrete reality here and now.[66]

Auerbach himself, writing during the dark years of World War II, concluded his great study of mimesis in western literature with a moving visionary hope for 'a common life of mankind on earth' to come. Though a work of scholarship rather than of imaginative literature, *Mimesis* itself arises inescapably out of the modernist era, as Auerbach was aware; it is an attempt to derive basic motifs from representative passages rather than to impose upon literature some comprehensive external scheme, just as the modern novelists 'hesitate to impose upon life, which is their subject, an order which it does not possess in itself'.[67]

This methodological deference to the properties of the literary works themselves governed most English and American literary criticism until five or ten years ago, and still seems to me the most sensitive and profitable way to approach the complex texts of modernism. I have not wished to see the novels merely as illustrations of some larger theoretical argument, but rather as complex aesthetic structures with their own individual forms of integrity and autonomy. I have also not attempted to write a literary history of modernism; the tradition of visionary closure I have set out to describe is only one modern tradition among many. Alongside these works, for example, stand other modern novels that end in counter-visions of alienation, loss, or desertion in an impersonal universe – Conrad's *Heart of Darkness*, Lawrence's *Sons and Lovers*, Wolfe's *Look Homeward, Angel*.[68] It would also be possible to trace the influence of modernist visionary closure upon more recent fictions. Gabriel Garcia Marquez, for example, ends *One Hundred Years of Solitude* with a visionary moment in which the last surviving character finally deciphers an encoded manuscript written one hundred years before and predicting in detail the entire history that the novel has unfolded. At this instant the manuscript becomes identical with the text we are reading; as the reader races through the final page, he discovers that an apocalyptic whirlwind is simultaneously destroying the entire internal world of the novel.[69] The continuing appearance of such vital responses to the modernist writers confirms that what Richard Ellmann said twenty-five years ago about Joyce is true in a broader sense of them all: we are still learning to be their contemporaries, still trying to understand our interpreters.

2

Ideas of Order in
Howards End

I

Readers have persistently criticized the conclusion of *Howards End* since
the novel's appearance in autumn 1910; early reviewers, while almost
unanimous in praising the novel as a whole, anticipated with considerable
accuracy the judgement on the ending that most later critics have
rendered.[1] In his influential critical study of Forster, Lionel Trilling
voices the general feeling that 'the nearly allegorical reconciliation is
rather forced', and expresses displeasure with the final 'rather contrived
scene of busyness and contentment in the hayfield'.[2] Forster himself
eventually joined this general consensus; he wrote in 1959 that the
conclusion of *Howards End* is 'certainly unsatisfactory, but perhaps [was]
less so at the time'.[3] The qualification is significant, however, because it
suggests that an ending which no longer holds up in 1959 may have been
worth attempting in 1910. I do not wish to overturn completely the
traditional assessment of Forster's flawed achievement in the conclusion
to *Howards End*. But I would like to explore what he was attempting to
achieve, try to see why it went wrong, and suggest how the ending
anticipates later modernist endings that were more successful. Because
these issues involve questions about Forster's formal and aesthetic
intentions, I would like to begin by exploring his general views on fiction
and art.

Virginia Woolf, in an essay on 'The Novels of E. M. Forster', argues
that novelists belong to 'two great camps':

> Speaking roughly, we may divide them into the preachers and the
> teachers, headed by Tolstoy and Dickens, on the one hand, and the
> pure artists, headed by Jane Austen and Turgenev, on the other. Mr.
> Forster, it seems, has a strong impulse to belong to both camps at
> once.[4]

Such a distinction is clearly limited in its usefulness (there is considerable

30

artistry in Dickens, and teaching in Austen), but it does help to identify a persistent one-sidedness in critical treatments of *Howards End*. Critics since Woolf have tended to concentrate more fully on Forster's social message than on his conscious artistry. Trilling's study, published in 1944, established the lines along which most subsequent discussion has run:

> *Howards End* is a novel about England's fate. It is a story of the class war. . . . The plot of *Howards End* is about the rights of property, about a destroyed will-and-testament and rightful and wrongful heirs. It asks the question, 'Who shall inherit England?'[5]

This forceful reading of the novel's social and historical message should be contrasted with Woolf's more subtle perception that Forster's

> vision is of a peculiar kind and his message of an elusive nature. He has not great interest in institutions. He has none of that social curiosity which marks the work of Mr. Wells. His concern is with the private life; his message is addressed to the soul.[6]

In a sense, both Trilling's and Woolf's responses are half-truths; Forster is clearly concerned with social issues, though his concern takes different forms from that of Wells. But Woolf's reading seems to me inherently closer to Forster's own values and priorities than Trilling's. Forster is persistently more interested in the private life than in institutions; his own view of art emphasizes its aesthetic value to individuals, not its potential to convey social teaching.

Although Forster never developed a systematic aesthetic theory, statements throughout his essays place him among those who hold what M. H. Abrams identifies as 'objective' theories of art, in company with adherents to the 'Art for Art's Sake' movement of the nineties and the New Criticism of the present century. Such theories characterize the work of art as an object detached from its creator and the environment of its creation, as an artifact which creates a 'world of its own', with its own autonomous laws, to be contemplated by the spectator without reference to anything beyond itself.[7] Nine years before the publication of *Howards End*, A. C. Bradley had proposed such an aesthetic theory in his widely influential *Oxford Lectures on Poetry*; the nature of poetry, Bradley writes, is to be a world by itself, independent, complete, autonomous: and to possess it fully you must enter that world, conform to its laws, and ignore for the time the beliefs, aims, and particular conditions which belong to you in the other world of reality.

The experience of reading poetry, Bradley argues, is 'an end in itself', and 'its *poetic* value is this intrinsic worth alone'. It may have 'ulterior value' as well, such as conveying 'instruction', but ulterior value cannot determine its poetic worth.[8] In 'Anonymity: An Inquiry', Forster establishes a similar distinction between 'atmosphere', which has no 'use', and 'information', which is merely useful and nothing more. He argues that art resides in the

power to create . . . a world, which, while it lasts, seems more real and solid than this daily existence . . . a universe that only answers to its own laws, supports itself, internally coheres, and has a new standard of truth.

Other key elements of objective theory appear in other Forster essays: 'Creation is disinterested'; 'The work of art assumes the existence of the perfect spectator.'[9]
Forster is careful, however, to disassociate himself from the excesses of the Art for Art's Sake movement:

Now we can easily dismiss those peacock's feathers and other affections – they are but trifles – but I want also to dismiss a more dangerous heresy, namely the silly idea that only art matters, an idea which has somehow got mixed up with the idea of art for art's sake, and has helped to discredit it. Many things, besides art, matter. It is merely one of the things that matter.[10]

This passage helps to explain Woolf's perception that Forster wishes to be at once moral teacher and pure artist. Unlike painting, music, and poetry, fiction does not have its own artistic medium; prose both 'serves us in daily life' and 'creates works of art'.[11] Some measure of social implication thus becomes inseparable from the language of fiction itself; to Forster the novelist, as to Forster the essayist, art is merely one of the things that matter. This divided allegiance in Forster's fiction to the demands of art and social teaching has been ignored by most critics since Woolf, however, resulting in the irony that a writer whose central artistic tenets are those of the 'pure artist', or formalist, has been read primarily as a novelist concerned with moral teaching and social message. But although non-formal concerns – such as the condition of England in 1910 – are important in a novel such as *Howards End*, they are not concerns which Forster himself would see as central to a critical assessment of his art. In 'The Raison d'Etre of Criticism in the Arts', he defines the 'aesthetic' purpose of criticism as that purpose which 'considers the object in itself, as an entity, and tells us what it can about its life'. All other uses of criticism, which involve describing 'the relation of the object to the rest of the world', are 'subsidiary'.[12]

In keeping with this formalist model, Forster consistently identifies order rather than beauty as the primary quality of art. He contends that art 'is valuable because it has to do with order, and creates little worlds of its own, possessing internal harmony'. Such harmony becomes the supremely valuable quality of art in the twentieth century because order has disappeared, or become impossibly remote from man, in commonly accepted descriptions of the external world. Works of art now appear to be 'the only objects in the material universe to possess internal order'; art remains 'the one orderly product which our muddling race has produced'.[13] The existence of art, for Forster, thus becomes the chief reason for being optimistic about mankind; at a level beyond any individual work of art, formal and social concerns again become inextricably connected.

The emergence of artistic order, however, is a complex and purely aesthetic matter. Such order 'is something evolved from within, not something imposed from without', yet a work of art also has 'a life of its own imposed on it by its creator'. The artist, Forster argues,

> creates through his sensitiveness and his power to impose form. . . . Form is not tradition. It alters from generation to generation. Artists always seek a new technique. . . . But form of some kind is imperative. It is the surface crust of the internal harmony, it is the outward evidence of order.[14]

External form seems to be that 'life' which is imposed on the work by its creator; internal order, a coherence which the work itself generates from within. The emergence of this coherence is beyond the artist's conscious control and is greeted afterwards with wonder:

> the artist, looking back on it, will wonder how on earth he did it. And indeed he did not do it on earth. . . . The creative state of mind is akin to a dream. . . . even . . . the most realistic artist [looks back on a finished

work with] the sense of withdrawal from his own creation, the sense of surprise.[15]

Internal order emerges in response to the artist's 'power to impose form', but is 'something evolved from within, not something imposed from without'. Yet the surface form remains as the 'outward evidence of order'. In Forster's own terms, therefore, the success or failure of a novel to achieve internal order – which is for him the supremely important purpose of art – may be determined by the extent to which a reader can trace such order through outward evidence embodied in the novel's form. Equipped with this distinction, I would like to take a fresh look at *Howards End*.

II

The narrative surface of *Howards End* is not static; it is in a continual state of flux. Forster employs rapid stylistic changes at the outset, foreshadowing continual changes at another level which will occur later. 'One may as well begin with Helen's letters to her sister',[16] he writes in a carefully careless, impersonal and lonely line of narrative, before plunging into an epistolary plot development reminiscent of the eighteenth century. Chapter II reverts to narrative heavily weighted with dialogue, and ends on a note of comic melodrama: 'But Aunt Juley was gone – gone irrevocably, and no power on earth could stop her' (p. 13), which anticipates chapter III's anti-climactic comedy of cross-purposes and social embarrassment. This stylistic variation, like the frantic pace of plot and action, is checked by the first appearance of Mrs. Wilcox (p. 22). In chapter IV the Forsterian narrator even finds sufficient breathing space to indulge in an exposition of the story and a history of the characters, using a style totally new to the novel. For the narrator, as for the characters, Mrs. Wilcox has provided shelter from the torrent of action; she acts exactly as the house does in Chapter XXIII, when Margaret 'heard the rains run this way and that where the watershed of the roof divided them' (p. 201).

The novel begins again in Chapter V with its famous rendition of the Schlegels' varying responses to Beethoven's Fifth Symphony, creating in the process a new lyrical style which stands out in striking contrast to all that has come before. The chapter also initiates a new line of action, apparently unrelated (except through its characters) to the first, one which continues in Chapter VI with its focus on the Basts. Finally, in

Chapter VII, the earlier action of the novel is united with the present one by means of a conventionally literary coincidence, when the Wilcoxes take a flat opposite Wickham Place. These initial stylistic changes continue somewhat less rapidly throughout the book; one critic has even argued that the portrayal of Leonard's state of mind on his final trip out to *Howards End* is an early version of stream-of-consciousness technique.[17] Such stylistic variety seems to indicate that, at least in this century, form not only 'alters from generation to generation' but even from chapter to chapter in a single work; in this respect Forster seems to anticipate Joyce, though in *Ulysses* the stylistic variation is far more strongly marked. Yet form is supposed to represent, for Forster, 'the surface crust of the internal harmony', and 'the outward evidence of order'. The form of *Howards End* – its vitally important 'outward evidence of order' – must therefore lie at a level below the immediate surface of the narrative.

Forster seems to try, rather, to locate the unifying form of the novel in the minds and relationships of its central characters. In *Aspects of the Novel*, he assigns two lectures – twice as many as to anything else – to 'People'. In 'What I Believe', he asks himself 'Where do I start?' and answers:

> With personal relationships. Here is something comparatively solid in a world full of violence and cruelty. . . . Starting from them, I get a little order into the contemporary chaos.[18]

Forster's belief in personal relationships emerges from the Arnoldian tradition that in the modern world people must be 'true to one another' because older sources of order and certainty have vanished.[19] Attempting to centre a novel's form on its characters would be to identify human relations more closely with that internal artistic harmony which is 'the one orderly product which our muddling race has produced'. If the novel's form (over which Forster can exert conscious control) is placed in the hands of its characters, then the characters themselves might emerge as the source of that internal order which the author himself will later perceive with surprise.

Such a narrative strategy traces its origin ultimately to the New Testament, in which Christ is both the central character and the source of spiritual, historical and aesthetic order. Wordsworth adopts a related strategy in *The Prelude*; its central character becomes the poet who can comprehend his own spiritual growth and express it in an ordered work of art.[20] Poetic tradition also offers the convention of the embodied Muse, the female figure who intercedes from within the text in the relations between poem, poet and external world. Wallace Stevens, who like Forster almost certainly assimilates this convention from Wordsworth, channels formal order in *The Idea of Order at Key West* through a woman within the work. She is 'the single artificer of the world / In which she sand', a world which becomes, in its widest sense, identical with the poem. Her song draws upon the inarticulate disorder of the sea, which 'was never formed to mind or voice', but the song, transformed by the infusion of artistic order, can be understood by a human audience. It is 'the maker's rage to order words of the sea' which creates the possibility for communication through art.[21] By associating the creation of artistic order with a figure inside the poem, Stevens inextricably links the idea of order in *Key West* with the human image of a woman singing beside the sea.

Stevens's strategy is suggestively parallel to Forster's undertaking. Like the sea in *Key West*, Mrs. Wilcox in *Howards End* 'cannot put things clearly' (p. 73). Mrs. Wilcox is the 'great wave' in Margaret Schlegel's life, a wave which

> had strewn at her feet fragments torn from the unknown. A curious seeker, [Margaret] stood for a while at the verge of the sea that tells so little, but tells a little, and watched the outgoing of this last tremendous tide. (p. 102)

Mrs. Wilcox in her reticence both represents and characterizes an inherited human understanding, tracing back perhaps to the sea, which culminates in a dependence upon Margaret's capacity for expression:

> "Indeed, you put the difficulties of life splendidly," said Mrs. Wilcox, withdrawing her hand into the deeper shadows. "It is just what I should have liked to say about them myself." (p. 73)

Margaret can express an echo of what Mrs. Wilcox might have wished to say, just as the woman in *Key West* can sing 'beyond the genius of the sea'. Margaret's is the 'rage for order' in *Howards End*; she continually attempts to articulate principles of order and strategies for dealing with life. Whereas Forster, at least by 1949, comes to conclude that only works of art can possess internal order, for much of *Howards End* Margaret attempts to identify some single, ordering idea which will work in the real world of human relations.

The tendency to focus on Margaret's strategies for dealing with 'the difficulties of life' leads the reader away from the stylistic surface of the narrative and into a different level of underlying form. The voices of Margaret and of the narrator both express aspects of Forster's own sensibility, but Margaret gradually gains authority as the principal interpreter of meaning in the novel.[22] In this role, she articulates three successive ideas of order: proportion, reconciliation, and connection. She develops the first of these in conversation with Mrs. Wilcox; when ideals of conduct conflict with one another, 'proportion comes in', Margaret believes, 'as a last resource' (p. 73). Later she realizes that Mrs. Wilcox, in dying, has 'kept proportion' (p. 102). But keeping proportion involves a balancing of ideals, values and courses of action; it is a passive rather than an active process. Margaret quickly finds herself anxious not merely to balance, to choose sensibly among opposites, but to merge those opposites into something whole. Writing to Helen after Mrs. Wilcox's death, Margaret suggests a new strategy, in discussing the relation of the unseen to the seen: 'Our business is not to contrast the two, but to reconcile them' (p. 104). Margaret's shift from keeping proportion between conflicting claims to reconciling them leads her into greater activity, and she hopes 'that for the future she would be less cautious, not more cautious, than she had been in the past' (p. 107).

Margaret's strategy of reconciliation is eventually broken down, however, just as proportion was, by its inadequacy as a consistent guide to human conduct. Meeting Leonard Bast for the second time, Margaret recognizes that extremes so irreconcilable exist that it is futile to attempt their union,

> so wide and so widening is the gulf that stretches between the natural and the philosophic man, so many the good chaps who are wrecked trying to cross it. (p. 115)

But as the goal of reconciliation is shaken, Leonard himself unintentionally provides a third idea for ordering human relations. 'I'm connected with a leading insurance company', he announces, pretentiously, to Mr. Wilcox. He 'fails to see the connection' between the Schlegels' amusement at his social demeanour and their admiration of his night-long walk through Surrey. Margaret picks up the word: 'We hoped there would be a connection between last Sunday and other days' (pp. 142–4). Later she seizes upon this idea of 'connection' and turns it into her last openly asserted strategy for dealing with life. When Henry Wilcox – who sees no link between passion and business – surprises her with an 'isolated' kiss (p. 184), her idea crystalizes:

Only connect! That was the whole of her sermon. Only connect the prose and the passion, and both will be exalted, and human love will be seen at its height. Live in fragments no longer. Only connect, and the beast and the monk, robbed of the isolation that is life to either, will die. (p. 187)

Margaret has advanced from the passive attempt to keep proportion among opposite values, through the impossibly idealistic task of trying to reconcile them; now she wants merely to try to establish connections between them. She has been living amid the 'fragments torn from the unknown' that Mrs. Wilcox left behind; now, connecting her life to Henry's in marriage – he is one of the largest of those fragments – emerges as part of her new sense of purpose.

The idea of connection preoccupies Margaret for much of the novel, yet it finally fails her in practice, like proportion and reconciliation before it. In the novel's penultimate crisis, Margaret is unable to make Henry see any connection between his own affair with Jacky and Helen's with Leonard: 'He had refused to connect, on the clearest issue that can be laid before a man, and their love must take the consequences' (p. 331). Yet this consequence undermines the original purpose of connection, which was to create an order in which 'human love will be seen at its height'. Forster foreshadowed this crisis when Margaret first articulated the idea of connection:

Mature as [Henry] was, she might yet be able to help him to the building of the rainbow bridge that should connect the prose in us with the passion. . . .
But she failed. (pp. 186–7)

In the past, when one of Margaret's strategies has failed her, she has replaced it rapidly with another. But in the final chapters of the novel, after her crisis of connection with Henry, neither connection nor any other strategy for dealing with the 'difficulties of life' is mentioned.

The idea of connection has some claim to be regarded as the central ordering principle of the novel. It appears, for one thing, in the epigraph: '*Only connect . . .*'. *Howards End* is in large part about the Schlegel sisters' attempts to make connections with members of the economic classes immediately above and below their own; about Margaret's attempts to help others make connections between warring elements within themselves; and about Forster's attempts to reconnect the life of the intellect with the life of the earth. But the main achievement of *Howards*

End criticism in the past thirty years has been to suggest that the first two of these attempts at connection fail explicitly within the text, and that the third succeeds only by authorial sleight of hand. The result of this line of argument has been, increasingly, to regard *Howards End* as a hopelessly flawed novel, not merely second in quality to *A Passage to India* but perhaps less successful than Forster's earlier novels as well.

I think that these difficulties can be partly circumscribed by regarding connection as lying somewhere just outside the thematic centre of the book. It is the last and most realistically promising of Margaret's ordering strategies, but it is finally no more successful than the others. Forster is apparently aware, at least in the passage which foreshadows Margaret's failure, of the strategy's inadequacy; Peter Widdowson has suggested that the epigraph hints at a more plaintive 'if we could only connect . . .' as well as echoing Margaret's confidently imperative sermon.[23] By the end of the novel she has spoken the word so forcefully and so often, however, that even Henry at last subconsciously picks it up. Speaking to Charles about his refusal to let Margaret stay with Helen at Howards End, Henry argues that 'this question is connected with something far greater, the rights of property itself' (p. 326). Since Forster clearly believes that the question is connected with something far greater than the rights of property, Mr. Wilcox's assertion serves to reveal the danger of mis-appropriation inherent in any attempt to put spiritual principles into words. Mr. Wilcox clearly believes, like Lionel Trilling, that the events of the story are primarily about England's fate, the rights of property, and rightful and wrongful heirs. But Forster, like Margaret, believes in the superiority of the unseen and the private to the seen and the institutional. This belief leads to the paradox that the centre of the novel must remain unseen and inaccessible to language; any idea that can be articulated in words becomes immediately inadequate, inevitably susceptible to reduction and institutionalization.

III

The problem of hinting at a centre of meaning which remains inaccessible to language becomes particularly acute at the conclusion of *Howards End*; much of the novel's strength lies in its continual series of detours around an unseen centre, as narrative strategies and intellectual themes are repeatedly tried out and then rejected. But this process of deferral cannot continue indefinitely; as Frank Kermode remarks, it is 'one of the great charms of books that they have to end'.[24] Forster must finally somehow suggest the geography of the unseen world, must render 'the voiceless language of sympathy' (p. 9) in the elusive but nonetheless communicable language of fiction.

Partly this centre is suggested by the patterns of recurrent motifs and symbols in the novel, which combine to create what Forster himself calls 'rhythm', Stuart Gilbert 'leitmotif', and Joseph Frank 'spatial form' in the modern novel.[25] Forster's use of phrases – 'to see life steadily and see it whole' – and physical objects – the house itself, the wisp of hay – as structural elements again anticipates Joyce; this aspect of the novel has received widespread critical attention.[26] But the leitmotifs are also metonymies for a continuous undercurrent which runs through the novel, breaking to the surface most explicitly during Margaret's meditation, after Leonard's death, on the failure of her marriage:

> At such moments the soul retires within, to float upon the bosom of a deeper stream, and has communion with the dead, and sees the world's glory not diminished, but different in kind to what she has supposed. She alters her focus until trivial things are blurred. Margaret had been tending this way all the winter. Leonard's death brought her to the goal. (p. 332)[27]

Margaret has failed in creating connection; her personal strategies have all ended in confusion. But she becomes swept up here at the end in a larger life process, one personified earlier in Mrs. Wilcox, with whom Margaret now has 'communion'. Margaret herself has 'been tending' all winter to become more and more like the older woman, whose earlier description is echoed here:

> she and daily life were out of focus: one or the other must show blurred. And at lunch she seemed more out of focus than usual, and nearer the line that divides daily life from a life that may be of greater importance. (p. 76)

This deeper life is also represented in the novel by the earth itself. In the scene immediately after Margaret's meditation upon Leonard's death, when Henry tells her what the verdict at the inquest will be, 'Margaret drove her fingers through the grass. The hill beneath her moved as if it were alive'. For the rest of the novel Margaret remains in contact with the earth, and 'all through that day and the next a new life began to move' (p. 334). The unseen centre of the novel seems to be located in 'a deeper stream' which also moves through and quickens life itself.

Mrs. Wilcox is the first in a series of older fictional women who are intimately in touch with this deeper stream: Mrs. Moore in *A Passage to India*, Mrs. Ramsay in *To the Lighthouse*, Dilsey in *The Sound and the Fury*. Critics have found Mrs. Wilcox in her realistic role inadequate to support the symbolic weight Forster attaches to her, but I think that he has rendered her more realistically than is generally realized.[28] It is symbolically important that she be dignified and reticent in contrast to the initially volatile and voluble Margaret, but Forster offers a realistic explanation for her possession of such qualities: Mrs. Wilcox was brought up in the Quaker faith, with its attendant disciplines of communal silence and empathetic awareness. The sermons of the rector in her husband's church – inadequate attempts to put spiritual principles into words, like Margaret's 'sermon' on connection – 'had at first repelled her, and she had expressed a desire for "a more inward light"' (p. 90). But she will not quarrel with Henry, for his money has enabled her to remain at Howards End, where she retains contact with the source of her strength in earth's deeper stream: 'Henry had saved it; without fine feelings or deep insight, but he had saved it' (p. 205). Yet Ruth's loyalty to her husband eventually leads her, like her Biblical namesake, to isolation in an alien land.[29]

The novel only retrospectively reveals the special poignancy of her final weeks. When she learns that Margaret is to lose her house, Ruth cries out that civilization can't be right 'if people mayn't die in the room where they were born' (p. 83). Perhaps aware that she herself is dying, she suddenly proposes taking Margaret down to Howards End. Startled, Margaret puts her off; they return to Wickham Place, and Margaret 'watched the tall, lonely figure sweep up the hall to the lift. As the glass doors closed on it she had the sense of an imprisonment' (p. 85). After a brief hesitation, Margaret changes her mind, pursuing Mrs. Wilcox to the station, 'convinced that the escapade was important, though it would have puzzled her to say why. There was a question of imprisonment and escape' (p. 86). As they speak at the station, Mrs. Wilcox evokes the house, meadow and sunshine of Hertfordshire, saying 'you will never repent joining them'. When Margaret answers 'I shall never repent joining you', her friend replies, out of the unity of the deeper stream, 'It is the same' (p. 86). But it is too late. Mr. Wilcox and Evie appear, Mrs. Wilcox is carried off back into London 'between her husband and daughter' (p. 87), imprisoned by her own loyalty and Margaret's fatal hesitation. Much later, in another context entirely, we learn what follows: 'When [Henry's] first wife was seized, he had promised to take her down into Hertfordshire, but meanwhile arranged with a nursing-home instead' (p. 283). She dies in London, never having returned to the house and country of her birth.

Margaret clearly represents Ruth Wilcox's first encounter with the world of intellectual liberalism and art, with the 'Schlegel' or 'Bloomsbury' millieu. Ruth quickly identifies this world as one more likely to see an 'inward light', to make contact with the deeper stream of life, than the world of the Wilcoxes. Her friendship with Margaret, Forster tells us,

> may have had its beginnings at Speyer, in the spring. . . . Perhaps it was she who had desired the Miss Schlegels to be invited to Howards End, and Margaret whose presence she had particularly desired. (p. 64)

She repeatedly admires Margaret's ability to express herself (pp. 68, 73, 76), inviting her the second time to Howards End because 'I want to hear what you say about it, for you do put things so wonderfully' (p. 83). Mrs. Wilcox is subconsciously seeking a Muse or an artist in Margaret, someone like the woman at Key West – or like Viriginia Woolf – who might translate her own 'voiceless language of sympathy' with the earth into a humanly understandable artistic order. Later novels – *Ulysses* and *To the Lighthouse* – will explore the capacity of artistic sensibility to contact, inherit and articulate the continual processes of nature which run through and quicken life. But Margaret never reaches Howards End during Ruth's lifetime, and the rest of the novel suggests the process by which – as one early reviewer expressed it – 'we see the house quietly, subtly, actively, setting to work to deliver itself into the hands of its proper possessor'.[30] The genius of place, unable to work any longer through Ruth Wilcox, sets out itself to work directly upon Margaret's capacity for spiritual understanding. As the influence of the house grows upon her, Margaret – rather than becoming Muse or artist – grows to be more and more like Mrs. Wilcox herself, until their identities merge and become almost indistinguishable.[31]

This process demands change and growth in Margaret unmediated by any living human example. She unconsciously begins to acquire Mrs. Wilcox's instinct to 'separate those human beings who will hurt each other most' (p. 22); in the chapter which begins with Margaret's sermon on connection (pp. 186–7), her main action is to *separate* Henry and Helen in order to keep them from quarreling openly (p. 193). In a later conflict, she reveals a growing tendency to value people more than principles, particular human ends more than abstract means:

> I have no use for justice. . . . Nor am I concerned with duty. I'm concerned with the characters of various people whom we know, and

how, things being as they are, things may be made a little better. (p. 228)

After her marriage 'she began to "miss" new movements, and to spend her spare time re-reading or thinking'. Her friends attribute the change to her marriage, 'yet the main cause lay deeper still'; she 'was passing from words to things' (p. 262). As she moves closer to the spirit of the elder Mrs. Wilcox, she loses the verbal facility which her friend so greatly admired.

Ruth Wilcox had been particularly anxious for Margaret to spend a night at Howards End; when Margaret finally does so, she makes lasting contact with the elder woman's spirit and with the 'deeper stream' of life. Margaret has come to the house on this occasion to trick and trap Helen; the moment of arrival is her spiritual nadir, and her sister seems at first unwilling to forgive her for 'a greater crime than any that Helen could have committed – that want of confidence that is the work of the devil' (p. 293). But gradually the presence of their own furniture and the spirit of place labor to repair the damage; 'each minute their talk became more natural' (p. 297), and at last they realize that though 'explanations and appeals had failed', they cannot be parted 'because their love was rooted in common things' (p. 299). The inadequacy of language to express matters of the spirit is further underlined when, in the following chapter, Margaret breaks with Henry over his stubborn refusal to see his own sin in Helen's and forgive her. Margaret chooses to spend the night at the house with Helen against Henry's express command, but despite the crisis in her marriage it is a 'night of peace' (p. 315).

Mrs. Wilcox personifies for Margaret the deeper unity in life which can generate such peace, a unity of which she is becoming increasingly aware:

> I feel that you and I and Henry are only fragments of that woman's mind. She knows everything. She is everything. She is the house, and the tree that leans over it. (p. 313)

Margaret has altered her earlier image for Mrs. Wilcox's spiritual legacy – 'fragments torn from the unknown' – to emphasize her new focus on the initially 'unknown' unity from which the fragments were torn. As the evening gives way to night and the sisters go to sleep in the house, Forster offers his fullest attempt to evoke this level of deeper unity in the language of the novel:

The present flowed by them like a stream. The tree rustled. It had made music before they were born, and would continue after their deaths, but its song was of the moment. The moment had passed. The tree rustled again. Their senses were sharpened, and they seemed to apprehend life. Life passed. The tree rustled again . . .

The peace of the country was entering into her. . . . It is the peace of the present, which passes understanding. Its murmur came "now," and "now" once more as they trod the gravel, and "now," as the moonlight fell upon their father's sword. They passed upstairs, kissed, and amidst the endless iterations fell asleep. (p. 315)

Forster attempts to convey Margaret's discovery of this peace by echoing its 'endless iterations' in the rhythm and quiet simplicity of his prose. But the persistently echoing 'now' also foreshadows the novel's imminent crisis. After a long series of delays and complications, Margaret has at last completed her delayed trip to Hertfordshire; she has found her home at the precise moment when she will need the strength she can draw from such rootedness in the earth.

In the hours following Leonard's death the next morning, Margaret assumes fully Ruth Wilcox's mantle of quiet calmness:

She moved through the sunlit garden, gathering narcissi, crimson-eyed and white. There was nothing else to be done; the time for telegrams and anger was over, and it seemed wisest that the hands of Leonard should be folded on his breast and be filled with flowers. (p. 330)

This moment echoes Ruth's creation of peace and stillness after the quarrel between Charles and Aunt Juley, a moment which began in the same garden with an insistence upon the inadequacy of things that can be phrased:

"Charles dear," said a voice from the garden. "Charles, dear Charles, one doesn't ask plain questions. There aren't such things." They were all silent. It was Mrs. Wilcox.

She approached just as Helen's letter had described her, trailing noiselessly over the lawn, and there was actually a wisp of hay in her hands. (p. 22)

In the wake of an unexpected crisis, Margaret now shows a similar calmness and ability to create order; she has achieved these qualities by moving away from the expression of theories and strategies. 'It seemed wisest', not to attempt any general statement, not to express anything in words, but rather to perform an action, a gesture, as the quiet Mrs. Wilcox might have done. Because she is now in contact, through Howards End, with life's 'deeper stream', Margaret has at last found the ability both 'to see life steadily and see it whole'.[32]

IV

While the novel sweeps Margaret on toward triumphant contact with the deeper unity of life, however, Forster is also attempting to tie up the loose ends of his plot. As he observed seventeen years later in *Aspects of the Novel*, novels become 'feeble at the end' because the novelist 'has to round things off, and usually the characters go dead while he is at work'.[33] After Leonard's death, he allows Margaret a similar meditation on the plot she finds herself involved in:

> Out of the turmoil and horror that had begun with Aunt Juley's illness and was not even to end with Leonard's death, it seemed impossible to Margaret that healty life should re-emerge. Events succeeded in a logical, yet senseless, train. People lost their humanity, and took values as arbitrary as those in a pack of playing-cards. It was natural that Henry should do this and cause Helen to do that, and then think her wrong for doing it; natural that she herself should think him wrong; natural that Leonard should want to know how Helen was, and come, and Charles be angry with him for coming – natural, but unreal. In this jangle of causes and effects, what had become of their true selves? Here Leonard lay dead in the garden, from natural causes; yet life was a deep, deep river, death a blue sky, life was a house, death a wisp of hay, a flower, a tower, life and death were anything and everything, except this ordered insanity, where the king takes the queen, and the ace the king. (pp. 329–30)

Life and death, in other words, are present everywhere except in the too palpably 'natural, but unreal' causes and effects of a literary plot. Forster tries to keep Margaret above this 'ordered insanity' by letting her share his awareness that the demands of plot are temporarily taking over; the final visionary chapter is an attempt to evoke a world beyond the denouement, where 'healthy life' has once again been able to 're-emerge'. After the ravages of plot pass by, Forster tries to draw upon Margaret's contact with the deeper stream of life to restore 'humanity' to the characters, so that our final impression of them will not be through 'deadness'. Though he is not entirely successful, Forster recognizes that the modern novelist who wants to create believable people must finally break the 'senseless' logic of a plot which arises from incident, and generate closure out of a deeper, spiritual current which runs through and vitalizes character.

The order created in the novel's final chapter seems to derive from Margaret, but is not ascribed to any articulated theory of proportion, reconciliation, connection or the like. Rather, she insists, 'No doubt I have done a little towards straightening the tangle, but things that I can't phrase have helped me' (p. 339). Helen and Henry are living with her at Howards End because 'no better plan had occurred to her' (p. 335). She is 'growing less talkative' (p. 336) and worrying about things that Ruth Wilcox must once have worried about:

> Every summer she would fear lest the well should give out, every winter lest the pipes should freeze; every westerly gale might blow the wych-elm down and bring the end of all things, and so she could not read or talk during a westerly gale. (pp. 335–6)

This vision of her life beyond the time frame of the novel turns on the auxilliary verb 'would', which can also refer to habitual action in the past; the passage might stand unchanged as a description of Mrs. Wilcox's life before the novel began. The novel describes a period of crisis during which the characters lost touch with the deeper stream of life; thinking of the previous year, Margaret realizes that 'one usen't always to see clearly before that time. It was different now' (p. 336). The period of transition in *Howards End* corresponds to Wordsworth's personal crisis in *The Prelude*, when he 'Lost sight' of the stream of poetic imagination, 'bewildered and engulphed', only later to give it 'greeting as it rose once more / In strength'.[34] Wordsworth's stream is essentially the same as Margaret's; arising from the earth, the current of poetry and life is itself unbroken and continuous, though human perception may not always be able to trace its course. Like the tree outside *Howards End*, 'it had made music before they were born, and would continue after their deaths'.

Margaret's final moment of vision in the novel reveals to her most fully the power and continuity of this deeper stream. The moment itself arises from an apparently accidental social blunder; Dolly, 'anxious to contribute' as she takes her leave, says 'It does seem curious that Mrs. Wilcox should have left Margaret Howards End, and yet she get it, after all' (p. 342). Dolly's unthinking revelation is an example of what Frank Kermode calls 'peripeteia', or narrative irony, 'a disconfirmation followed by a consonance', which 'respects our sense of reality' in arriving at 'the discovery or recognition by an unexpected and instructive route'.[35] When Margaret questions her husband later about Dolly's remark, he tells her the 'very old story' of Mrs. Wilcox's note:

> When she was ill and you were so kind to her, she wanted to make you some return, and, not being herself at the time, scribbled 'Howards End' on a piece of paper. I went into it thoroughly, and, as it was clearly fanciful, I set it aside, little knowing what my Margaret would be to me in the future.

In response,

> Margaret was silent. Something shook her life in its inmost recesses, and she shivered. "I didn't do wrong, did I?" he asked, bending down. "You didn't, darling. Nothing has been done wrong." (p. 342)

At this moment, Margaret discovers a completely unexpected consonance between past and present, one which reveals that the current of unity and order in her life is far stronger than she had supposed. Her final words to Henry suggest that the power of earth's 'deeper stream' is so great that nothing could possibly have been done wrong. This sudden revelation is an example of what Forster called, in the title of another story, 'The Eternal Moment'. Such a moment retrospectively reorganizes the past, reshaping it into a new form; as J. B. Beer writes, though without specific reference to Margaret's experience here, it is the moment 'that gives meaning to all the others'.[36]

Forster foreshadows this moment much earlier when he affirms that Margaret originally knew nothing of Ruth's unconventional bequest: 'She was to hear of it in after years, when she had built up her life differently, and it was to fit into position as the headstone of the corner' (p. 102). This Biblical phrase appears first in the Psalms: 'The stone which the builders refused is become the head stone of the corner' (Psalms 118:22 KJV). It is echoed frequently by Christ and his apostles (Matthew 21:42, Mark 12:10, Acts 4:11, 1 Peter 2:7) because it offers a metaphor for Christ's power to rewrite history, to reshape the materials of the past into a new order.[37] In *Howards End*, the metaphor ultimately ascribes a similar power over history to Forster's secular version of spiritual unity. Margaret's inheritance of Howards End is the headstone which the 'builders' of England – Henry and Charles – originally 'set aside', but which a deeper power than theirs finally restores to its proper place. Even Margaret's marriage, which she had thought to be part of her own effort at making 'connection' with another social class, now seems to have been the work of a deeper process and merely one necessary preliminary to a larger goal. In the moment of discovery, Margaret's life is shaken 'in its inmost recesses' by the awareness of this greater power. Her contact with life's deeper stream at Howards End has fulfilled Mrs. Wilcox's intuition that she might grow to acquire a capacity, corresponding to the elder woman's own, to transmute the life of the earth into order and peace in human relations. The moment of self-understanding confirms Margaret's role and identity, just as Wordsworth's vision of 'a mighty mind' on Snowdon confirms his poetic vocation.[38]

While the final chapter affirms Margaret's place in life's over-arching continuity, it also acknowledges the possibility of local loss. London is 'creeping', and Howards End may be merely an anachronistic survival, its way of life soon to be swept away by the modern world (p. 339). Forster makes the pun inherent in the name of the house explicit during an earlier discussion about Mrs. Wilcox's brother Tom, the last of the Howards: ' "I say! Howards End – Howard's Ended!" cried Dolly' (p. 203). The Howard family has entirely died out (Ruth's children and grandchildren seem to represent a pure strain of Wilcoxism), but the name of their home remains as an explicit *memento mori*, recalling a lost tradition of contact with the earth which was once passed on without wrenching difficulty from generation to generation. In adopting this name as the title of his novel, Forster invokes a still broader range of meanings. An 'end', according to the *OED*, can mean 'a piece of broken, cut off, or left; a fragment, remnant'. The house is one of the 'fragments torn from the unknown' which Mrs. Wilcox has left behind in Margaret's life; this particular fragment has, in fact, been quite explicitly 'left' to her. As a verb, 'to end' can mean 'to put (corn, hay, etc) into (a barn, stack, etc); to "get in" '; and the novel concludes, fittingly, with a harvest.

Helen's final speech immediately follows Margaret's culminating moment of vision, defining and articulating Margaret's awareness of life's deeper stream in terms of the annually recurring harvest:

"The field's cut!" Helen cried excitedly – "the big meadow! We've seen to the very end, and it'll be such a crop of hay as never!" (p. 343)

Margaret has now also seen 'to the very end' of her own world; her moment of revelation clearly is meant to coincide with the moment when

Tom's father, cutting the big meadow in narrowing circles, reaches 'the sacred centre of the field' (p. 335). Helen's joy is the visible sign of the unseen spiritual power, rooted in the earth, from which Margaret has drawn together the final order in the lives of the characters. But this conclusion serves a still larger purpose in the structure of novel. In terms of the cyclical harvest, the novel began some years earlier on the day immediately after the one on which it ends: while Helen is writing her first letter, Mrs. Wilcox 'came back with her hands full of the hay that was cut yesterday' (p. 4). *Howards End* is thus, like *The Prelude*, circular in design. It begins and ends during haying season at the house, finally returning to its origin in both time and place after a long circuitous journey.[39] Ultimately, the circular structure creates a frame which suggests an identification between the house and the novel itself. The entire novel is finally enclosed, like the characters, within the surrounding frame of the house, which organizes the space within the novel just as Margaret's vision organizes its time. The house within which order can be created becomes a symbol for art, the 'one orderly product which our muddling race has produced', and a central part of the 'civilisation' which is 'the chief justification for the human experiment'.[40]

The problem with the final chapters of *Howards End* is not one of conception but of execution. Forster fails to convince most of his readers that the concluding unity emerges from life's deeper stream rather than from the artificial manipulation of the author; the final social order seems to proceed too much from the writer's will and too little from inevitable tendencies in the characters themselves. In 1910 Forster knew very little about the worlds of Henry Wilcox and Leonard Bast, and even less about that of heterosexual attraction. He rendered these aspects of the story by means of what he calls the writer's 'valuable faculty of faking'.[41] But most readers seem inclined to agree with Katherine Mansfield, who wrote in 1917 that

> I can never be perfectly certain whether Helen was got with child by Leonard Bast or by his fatal forgotten umbrella. All things considered, I think it must have been the umbrella.[42]

In Forster's own terms

> The test of a round character is whether it is capable of surprising in a convincing way. If it never surprises, it is flat. If it does not convince, it is a flat pretending to be round.[43]

The testimony of a large number of readers suggests that Leonard and Henry are flat characters 'pretending to be round'. Because Forster has insufficient sympathy for either to render their life with the fullness which his structural conception demands, the final victory of unity and order sometimes seems a triumph over cardboard goblins.[44]

But Forster's originality in employing visionary form and closure set the stage for the experiments of other modernist writers. Forster was almost alone among his Bloomsbury friends in his high regard for Lawrence; he praises him with very few qualifications in *Aspects of the Novel*. Despite widely different backgrounds, both novelists write out of a Romantic literary tradition which – most characteristically in Wordsworth's turning to Nature – attempts to locate a centre for spiritual, moral and artistic order in the life of the earth. Forster and Lawrence engage in a running dialogue of symbols: the 'rainbow bridge that should connect the prose in us with the passion' of *Howards End* (p. 186) becomes Lawrence's visionary rainbow that promises a connection between new heaven and new earth;[45] Forster transmutes that image in turn into the 'overarching sky' of *A Passage to India*.[46]

Forster's and Lawrence's characters, too, are often versions of one another. Margaret Schlegel foreshadows Ursula Brangwen; the complexity of modern life forces the growth of both women to be intellectual as well as physical and spiritual – qualities which alone sufficed in earlier generations. Mrs. Wilcox and Miss Avery hint at the older world, rooted in the earth, which Lawrence evokes more vividly in the first half of *The Rainbow*. If Margaret had left Henry Wilcox at the end of the novel, as Ursula later leaves Skrebensky, *Howards End* would have anticipated *The Rainbow* even more closely and perhaps been truer to its own internal logic. But Forster could not erect a positive final vision over a ruin of personal relations, whereas Lawrence was willing to celebrate Ursula's growth beyond a relationship which he saw to be flawed and inadequate. The relationship of Margaret and Helen looks ahead further to that of Ursula and Gudrun in *Women in Love*; in both novels the elder sister moves toward creating order in personal relations, finding what will suffice, while the younger sister moves toward the idealization of absolutes. In Rupert Birkin and Gerald Crich, Lawrence recreates Forster's opposition of Schlegels and Wilcoxes, but suggests more explicitly the futility of an attempt at union between the world of intellect and the world of business. Forster, in turn, echoes the ending of *Women in Love* in *A Passage to India*; in each novel, the final scene centres on a failure in the struggle to achieve male friendship across spiritual barriers. For both writers, this movement beyond visionary closure emerges from a less optimistic vision of the prospects for human relations.

Forster himself understood less clearly the relation between Joyce's work and his own. Yet several elements in the structure of *Howards End* prefigure similar elements in *Ulysses*: a funeral occurs early in both novels, a child is born late; the imperfectly realized character and world of Leonard Bast are like rough sketches for those of Leopold Bloom; and both novels move from a concern with the larger social world toward a final return home to the private sphere.[47] In both *Howards End* and *Ulysses*, fluctuations in the narrative surface ultimately lead toward a deeper underlying level of unifying form, but the deeper stream in *Ulysses* works more effectively because it is embodied in a more complex tissue of myth and imagery. In Molly Bloom, Joyce conflates the mythic Ruth Wilcox, the articulate Margaret Schlegel, and the sensual Jacky Bast into a single character who is both realistically convincing and symbolically representative of the deeper stream of life.[48] *Howards End* even more closely prefigures Virginia Woolf's *To the Lighthouse* in the relation between the older and younger central female characters: Mrs. Ramsay leaves behind 'fragments torn from the unknown' in Lily Briscoe's life just as Mrs. Wilcox does in Margaret's; significantly, however, Lily refuses in her search for order the way of marriage and chooses instead the way of art. In both novels the central struggle is to wrest some new order from a world bereft of the older stabilities and certainties that the elder women represented. Taking together these thematic and structural parallels to the work of Lawrence, Joyce, and Woolf, I think that *Howards End* emerges to a surprising degree as the prologue to a significant strain in the modernist novel as a whole.

3

The Rainbow and the Flood of Consciousness

I

D. H. Lawrence almost certainly read *Howards End* between its publication in 1910 and the beginning of his own work on what was to become *The Rainbow* and *Women in Love*. Forster's novel was favourably reviewed, widely discussed, and sufficiently rooted in Edwardian conventions to enjoy considerable popular success. Lawrence mentions it several times in his letters;[1] *The Rainbow*'s structure and symbolism suggest that he both understood Forster's aims and worked to avoid Forster's failures. 'You *did* make a nearly deadly mistake glorifying those *business* people in *Howards End*', Lawrence wrote to Forster several years later. 'Business is no good.'[2] Like his heroine, Forster seems to undermine his own aesthetic and humanistic values out of fairness to those who guarantee his income; Lawrence, in contrast, was freed by birth and poverty from any such constraint. In *The Rainbow*, he reworks Forster's antinomies of prose and passion, business and art, into broader contrasts between mind-consciousness and blood-intimacy, between male and female principles, between the life of the spirit and the life of the body. Ursula's culminating rainbow vision retrospectively unites these contrasts, promising that man's relationship with nature will never again be nearly drowned beneath a flood of consciousness like that which has innundated the modern world. This promise arises not from God, but from a process of Wordsworthian interchange between mind and external world; Ursula's vision reaches back through the flood to reconnect consciousness with an earlier, unconscious life lived in harmony with the earth. As he worked on the multiple versions of his novel, Lawrence strengthened this ending by rendering with increasing fullness the life and passing of that earlier, rural world which Forster was content merely to hint at in the histories and portraits of Ruth Wilcox and Miss Avery.

Lawrence wrote *The Rainbow* backwards into this earlier world from its ending, which makes it perhaps the most clearly end-determined novel in English literature. He began work on a new novel in 1913, shortly after his elopement with Frieda Weekley, and after completing his auto-biographical fiction *Sons and Lovers*. Although this early manuscript has not survived, evidence indicates that it consisted almost entirely of material which ultimately became the basis of *Women in Love*.[3] Even the title by which Lawrence referred to this draft – *The Sisters* – seems more a description of *Women in Love* than of *The Rainbow* as we now know it. But by September 1913 he is writing to his advisor Edward Garnett that 'The Sisters has quite a new beginning – a new basis altogether.'[4] It was beginning to grow backward. In January 1914, after Garnett had read this new version and sent it back to Lawrence in Italy with his comments, Lawrence replies that

> I agree with you about the Templeman episode. In the scheme of the novel, however, I *must* have Ella get some experience before she meets her Mr. Birkin . . . tell me whether you think Ella would be possible, as she now stands, unless she had some experience of love and of men. I think, impossible.[5]

Templeman and Ella were early names for Skrebensky and Ursula; the second half of what now stands as *The Rainbow* was thus generated by the need to explain Ursula's character. But in the process of writing those chapters, Lawrence seems to have felt the need to go further and further back for his explanation; Will and Anna are generated to provide a context for Ursula's growth, Tom and Lydia to provide one for Anna's. In January 1915 Lawrence realized that the story had grown beyond the bounds of a single volume, and split it into *The Rainbow* and *Women in Love*. The great opening pages of *The Rainbow* were probably the last part of that novel to be written.[6] Thus *Women in Love* was not written as a sequel to *The Rainbow* – although it was rewritten extensively after *The Rainbow* was completed – but was rather its elder sister in conception. *The Rainbow* emerges from this account as a quest backward for origins, an end-determined attempt to discover the history that will lead to its close.

This account of the novel's composition as currently understood is considerably at odds, however, with the record of critical response to its structure. F. R. Leavis inaugurated a tradition of dissatisfaction with the novel's ending which has been nearly as pervasive – but without as much justification – as the critical discomfort with the conclusion of *Howards End*. Leavis finds 'something oddly desperate about that closing page and a half' in *The Rainbow*; the 'confident note of prophetic hope in the final paragraph' is 'wholly unprepared and unsupported, defying the preceding pages'. Leavis thinks this local problem less disturbing, however, than 'signs of too great a tentativeness in the development and organization of the later part [of the novel]; signs of a growing sense in the writer of an absence of any conclusion in view'.[7] It is of course odd that a novel whose conclusion was the first part written should give such an impression, but Leavis has been by no means alone in his judgment. 'The last paragraph of *The Rainbow* has annoyed almost everyone', Alan Friedman summarized accurately in 1966.[8] Most critics also follow Leavis in finding the entire second half of the novel weak and inconclusive, although only Friedman goes so far as to suggest that this apparent structural weakness was part of a conscious strategy, that Lawrence deliberately planned *The Rainbow*, 'from first page to last page', to 'provide, inevitably, for the absence of any conclusion'.[9] The history of the novel's composition suggests that, rather, Lawrence deliberately planned its opening to provide inevitably for its close.

Examined in this light, *The Rainbow* reveals a surprising degree of careful formal structuring. Its sixteen chapters divide quite clearly into four groups of four. The novel's first quarter opens with the wedding of Tom and Lydia and focuses on their marriage; the second quarter opens with the wedding of Will and Anna and focuses on their marriage in turn. The novel's second half divides evenly into the two major phases of Ursula's growth: her passages from childhood to adolescence and from adolescence to young adulthood. Lawrence interweaves the two halves of the novel by ending the first half with the beginning of the new world – Ursula's – in 'The Child', and opening the second half with the end of the old world – Tom Brangwen's – in 'The Marsh and the Flood'. He further ties the two halves together by providing structural parallels between Anna's experience and Ursula's. The two chapters titled 'The Widening Circle' designate Ursula's first and second major periods of growth; they occupy second place in the third and fourth quarters of the novel, and correspond thematically to the two earlier chapters – 'Childhood of Anna Lensky' and 'Girlhood of Anna Brangwen' – which chart the two similar stages of development in Ursula's mother, although the greater complexity of modern experience demands that Ursula's growth spill over into additional chapters in each of the novel's final two quarters. The two chapters which describe the two phases of Ursula's relation with Skrebensky – 'First Love' and 'The Bitterness of Ecstasy' – occupy third place in the third and fourth quarters of *The Rainbow*. The final chapter in each of these quarters describes a reaction to failure with Skrebensky – the first, in 'Shame', which Lawrence evaluates as a false direction for Ursula; and the second, in 'The Rainbow', which he presents as a positive one. Finally, the second half of the novel – which critics find particularly weak in structure – opens with a flood and ends with the vision of a rainbow. This extensive thematic organization reflects Lawrence's effort, orchestrated with considerable success, to bring the two halves of *The Rainbow* together in aesthetic unity. Critics have failed to recognize this unity largely because it rests upon conventions and structures that are still new to the novel.

More than any of the other modernists, Lawrence writes out of Biblical and Romantic traditions that provide models for understanding the form and closure of his major visionary novel. Though critics have not generally discussed the ending of *The Rainbow* in these contexts, much excellent work has already been devoted to placing Lawrence in relation to Romanticism and to the Bible.[10] But it is the openly hostile T. S. Eliot – oddly enough – who seems first to have unintentionally identified Lawrence's essential relation to these two traditions. In a 1931 review of John Middleton Murray's book on Lawrence, *Son of Woman*, Eliot identifies in Lawrence's work

a peculiarity which to me is both objectionable and unintelligible. It is using the terminology of Christian faith to set forth some philosophy or religion which is fundamentally non-Christian or anti-Christian.[11]

But such use of Christian tradition is not original to Lawrence; it appears earlier in the Romantic poets – Blake, Wordsworth, Shelley – in images and rhetorical figures such as Wordsworth's appropriation to secular ends, in the Prospectus to *The Recluse*, of the great apocalyptic marriage of Revelation.[12]

Lawrence directly continues this Romantic practice of secularizing religious terms and symbols to provide literary correlatives for deeply felt emotion and experience. Eliot, who cared little for the Romantics and less for Lawrence, nonetheless identifies quite accurately (though negatively) Lawrence's particular secular philosophy as

his hopeless attempt to find some mode in which two persons – of the opposite sex, and then as a venture of despair, of the same sex – may be spiritually united . . . the whole history of Lawrence's life and of Lawrence's writings . . . is the history of his craving for greater intimacy than is possible between human beings.

For Eliot in 1931, 'the love of two human beings is only made perfect in the love of God'.[13] But for Lawrence, as for most of the modernists, the loss of any certain belief in God forces the whole quest for spiritual unity in human life to rest upon human relations alone, as Rupert Birkin, Lawrence's spokesman in *Women in Love*, argues:

> The old ideals are dead as nails . . . there remains only this perfect union with a woman – sort of ultimate marriage – and there isn't anything else . . . seeing there's no God.[14]

Thus the language and symbolism of religious tradition, already made available to describe secular experience in Romantic poetry, become for Lawrence modes in which to attempt a new gospel rooted in interpersonal relations and sexual love.

II

Like the mythological and historical systems of Blake and Yeats, Lawrence's intellectual system – which has been outlined in detail by Graham Hough, H. M. Daleski, and others – replaces a religious tradition that seems to have become spiritually and imaginatively bankrupt. On the first page of *The Rainbow* the church spire is to the Brangwen farmer 'something standing above him and beyond him in the distance'; by the last page Ursula sees 'the old church-tower' as 'standing up in hideous obsoleteness'.[15] Midway between these two perspectives, however, Anna Brangwen sees the Cathedral as 'a great involved seed, whereof the flower would be radiant life inconceivable' (p. 198). Lawrence does not simply reject Christianity; he wants, rather, to rewrite it in his own image. The religious world provides, in embryonic form, images and prefigurations of the new Lawrentian gospel; as Eliot irritably observed, Lawrence persistently adapts the terms and symbols of Christianity to sexual relationships. Tom Brangwen grows up feeling an 'innate desire to find in a woman the embodiment of all his inarticulate, powerful religious impulses' (p. 14). When Tom and Lydia at last achieve a mutual relationship after two years of marriage, Tom wants 'to mingle with her, losing himself to find her, to find himself in her'; their final understanding is 'the baptism to another life' (pp. 90–1). Will Brangwen, when first married to Anna, feels himself in 'a new world', imagining that he and his wife are alone within it like Adam and Eve (pp. 140, 143, 146).

In describing sexual relationships, Lawrence extends this adaptation of Biblical language beyond Romantic practice; but in describing the relations between man and nature, he duplicates Romantic models precisely. Before the dawn of modern consciousness, the Brangwens lived in unconscious harmony with nature: 'They knew the intercourse between heaven and earth, sunshine drawn into the breast and bowels' (p. 2). Despite the Biblical phrases Lawrence weaves into his description, this intercourse between man and nature is more essentially Wordsworthian than Biblical. As in Wordsworth, God is absent from any mediating role between man and nature; nature alone exhibits

> That mutual domination which she loves
> To exert upon the face of outward things,
> So moulded, joined, abstracted, so endowed
> With interchangeable supremacy,
> That men, least sensitive, see, hear, perceive,
> And cannot choose but feel.[16]

Just as, in *The Prelude*, Nature both shapes the mind and is herself shaped by interaction with man, so Lawrence gives the Brangwens an active role in a process of 'interchangeable supremacy' and 'mutual domination' between man and the natural world. The soil 'became smooth and supple after their plowing'; mounting their horses, they 'held life between the grip of their knees', and harnessing them at the wagon they 'drew the heaving of the horses after their will' (p. 2). In language almost identical to Wordsworth's, Lawrence writes, 'so much exchange and interchange had they with these, that they lived full and surcharged' (p. 3). Later, Anna will find in the Brangwen house 'a deep, inarticulate interchange which made other places seem thin and unsatisfying' (p. 100). Yet in all its fullness, this life in nature is not fully human; the Brangwens exist as Wordsworth did in boyhood 'when like a roe, I bounded o'er the mountains', living 'with glad animal movements' in a pre-conscious world where nature 'was all in all'.[17] Neither the boy Wordsworth nor these early men in *The Rainbow* possess self-consciousness or identity in the modern sense.

As consciousness dawns, Lawrence's characters persistently find their internal experience echoed back from the external world; they live in 'the mighty world / Of eye, and ear, – both what they half create, / And what perceive'.[18] The uneasy birth of consciousness in Tom and Lydia is embodied in the night of Tom's proposal, when

> all the sky was teeming and tearing along, a vast disorder of flying shapes and darkness and ragged fumes of light and a great brown circling halo, then the terror of a moon running liquid-brilliant into the open for a moment, hurting the eyes before she plunged under cover again. (p. 44)

The Brangwen fall into human knowledge is reflected externally in the 'terror' of the moon and the 'vast disorder' of the sky; this vaguely malevolent universe with which the first chapter closes is radically different from the Edenic natural world evoked in its opening pages. In this new world, Tom needs the relation with his wife to sustain him; when she withdraws into her pregnancy, he feels 'like a broken arch thrust sickeningly out from support. For her response was gone, he thrust at nothing' (p. 60). Unlike his fathers, he no longer possesses his self-sufficient place in an unconsciously apprehended natural order.

In his isolation, Tom tries to escape from the nearly unendurable burden of self-consciousness. On the night of Lydia's labour, Tom quiets his step-daughter Anna by taking her out to the barn with him to feed the animals; alone together after he 'hung the lantern on the nail and shut the door', they find themselves 'in another world'. The lantern illuminates this world, like Wordsworth's moon on Snowdon and Saul's flash of light on the Damascus road, but this is not a new world like theirs; it is the surviving heart of the old life of The Marsh. As Tom sets to work, Anna is imperceptibly altered by a process of mutual interchange with the natural surroundings: 'a new being was created in her for the new conditions' (p. 74). The new relation she establishes here with Tom offers a temptation, which he never fully understands, to retreat from the difficult new semi-conscious relation with Lydia back into a lost innocence which Anna as a child and the old world of The Marsh together represent. But the strain of his unresolved need for the older certainty is too great to be fairly placed upon the child; when at last Tom comes to terms with Lydia, Anna is

> no longer called upon to uphold with her childish might the broken end of the arch. Her father and her mother now met to the span of the heavens, and she, the child, was free to play in the space beneath, between. (p. 92)

Yet as late as Anna's wedding, Tom still regrets the lost link with the innocent past that she – like Dorothy for Wordsworth in *Tintern Abbey* – has come to represent for him.

No one can retreat from consciousness back into an unconscious unity with nature. One must learn to see, instead, that consciousness itself is still connected to that larger unity, to 'something far more deeply interfused' in both Nature 'and in the mind of man', something which 'impels / All thinking things, all objects of all thought, / And rolls through all things'.[19] In a well-known letter to Edward Garnett,

Lawrence describes his attempt in *The Rainbow* to abandon 'the old stable ego of the character', not to return to earlier modes of rendering external reality, but in order to penetrate still further beneath character into the subconscious layers of the psyche. Lawrence demands of his reader a new willingness to sense the 'non-human, in humanity', at a level where 'the individual is unrecognisable', merely a brief state of the common 'radically-unchanged element',

> as diamond and coal are the same pure single element of carbon. The ordinary novel would trace the history of the diamond – but I say 'diamond, what! This is carbon'. And my diamond might be coal or soot, and my theme is carbon. . . . don't look for the development of the novel to follow the lines of certain characters: the characters fall into . . . some other rhythmic form.[20]

Alan Friedman aptly christens this 'other rhythmic form' in observing that 'if Joyce's technique is the stream of consciousness, Lawrence's technique is . . . a stream of the unconscious'.[21] The unconscious in human nature, like carbon in soot and diamond, exists at a level below individual identity; similarly, just as carbon remains unchanged over time despite changes in the objects it constitutes, the stream of the unconscious runs connectedly through nature and human life from generation to generation. This 'carbon', Robert Langbaum writes, 'is the phase of identity that makes connection with the universe'.[22] Like the 'deeper stream' that Forster identifies in *Howards End*, Lawrence's conception emerges, as Herbert Lindenberger has observed, out of a continuing tradition which has attempted 'to render that mysterious life existing far below the level of everyday, social experience' in terms such as Wordsworth's 'underpresences', 'underpowers', 'undersoul', and 'underconsciousness'.[23]

It is not clear whether Lawrence knew *The Prelude*, although he places Wordsworth appropriately among those thinkers and leaders who 'established a *new* connection between mankind and the universe'.[24] Langbaum remarks that 'Lawrence was deeply read in Wordsworth and almost always refers to him with respect'.[25] The correspondences with Wordsworth in *The Rainbow* are so extensive that if Lawrence did not know *The Prelude*, he has accomplished something more remarkable than being influenced by it: he has, in effect, drawn upon the same traditions as Wordsworth and rewritten it. *The Rainbow* resembles *The Prelude* quite closely in its structural organization around moments of intense experience; the obvious differences between novel and autobiographical poem become less significant in light of Lawrence's focus on the level of carbon beneath separate characters and generations.[26] At the centre of the novel Will and Anna metaphorically cross the Alps and find – just as Wordsworth found – that the experience is anti-climactic. Anna remains on a 'Pisgah mount' of partial vision, unwilling to descend and continue the quest for a new world (p. 193); but *The Rainbow* itself does descend from the insufficient peak moments of 'Anna Victrix' and 'The Cathedral', to 'The Marsh and the Flood', and the reader finds – as Wordsworth found – that a larger vision of the whole lies unexpected in the wild flood of water below.

Lawrence's most central reworking of Biblical symbolism in *The Rainbow* is his use of the Flood to represent uncontrolled consciousness. Several years later, in *Psychoanalysis and the Unconscious*, he described the 'stream of consciousness' that other modernists seemed anxious to render as a

> stream of hell which undermined my adolescence! . . . I felt it streaming through my brain, in at one ear and out at the other. . . . Horrid stream![27]

Lawrence is primarily interested in rendering what lies beneath this stream, in an unconscious to be sharply distinguished from Freud's:

> The Freudian unconscious is the cellar in which the mind keeps its own bastard spawn. The true unconscious is the well-head, the fountain of real motivity. . . . We must discover, if we can, the true unconscious, where our life bubbles up in us, prior to any mentality.[28]

These two internal realms – consciousness and unconsciousness – are often difficult to distinguish, because Lawrence uses water imagery to describe both. The 'fountain of real motivity' corresponds to the level of 'carbon' beneath individual identity; like Forster's 'deeper stream', it lies somewhere beneath the 'stream' of consciousness, just as a subterranean water table runs far beneath all visible streams and rivers on the earth, yet is ultimately part of the same cyclical system.

Thus Lawrence writes that at first Tom Brangwen 'had naturally a plentiful stream of life and humour' (p. 14). But after conscious thought begins to stir within him, the internal stream becomes 'his troublesome current of life', which is only restrained by his love for Lydia 'so that it did not foam and flood and make misery'. When he establishes a close relationship with Anna, 'gradually a part of his stream of life was diverted to the child, relieving the main flood to his wife' (p. 78). The water imagery undergoes a similar alteration in successive descriptions of Will Brangwen, who appeals to Anna at first because of his contact with the subterranean realm of 'real motivity': 'Out of the rock of his form the very fountain of life flowed' (p. 125). But as his relationship with Anna rouses him to a state of semi-consciousness, he finds his stream strangely transformed to 'hidden water' into which he must throw himself 'to live or die' (p. 184). When he relaxes his will, he discovers that 'a vagueness had come over everything, like a drowning. And it was an infinite relief to drown' (p. 186). Will survives by immersing himself, as Stein recommends in Conrad's *Lord Jim*, in the destructive element of life, which for Lawrence is always consciousness. Will's survival by drowning figuratively within himself parallels Tom's destruction by drowning literally in the world outside; in the Lawrentian world, the stream of surface consciousness is always in imminent danger of breaking out of its channel, turning into a flood, and working untold damage.

The canal, built across the Brangwens' land in 'about 1840' (p. 6), works in the novel as a symbolic external projection – a Wordsworthian reflection back from the landscape – of modern man's stirring internal self-awareness. The canal is a product of rational endeavour; it serves trade and communication, providing for the most part a safe and functional channel for the stream of consciousness. But it is still potentially dangerous. During a severe rainstorm it breaks its banks and drowns Tom Brangwen, the last survivor of the old world of The Marsh. His death by water, in a state of semi-conscious drunkenness, parallels the Biblical destruction of the first world in God's uncontrolled consciousness of wrath at human failure. In Lawrence's secular reworking of this event, the Flood of modern human consciousness both literally and symbolically destroys the old pastoral life of the earth. Yet consciousness in *The Rainbow* is not altogether evil; like the Biblical Flood, it both destroys and purifies. It washes away the inadequate, preliminary stage of semi-conscious willfulness which Tom Brangwen shares with the early men of Genesis. Tom is sacrificed because, although partially roused from the 'drowse of blood-intimacy' (p. 2), he has refused the self-responsibility that consciousness entails. It will be two generations later before, in Ursula, the responsibilities of consciousness are fully faced.

III

In April 1914, when *The Rainbow* and *Women in Love* were still one novel, Lawrence wrote that the 'germ' of the work was the idea of 'woman becoming individual, self-responsible, taking her own initiative'.[29] This germ was modified in the event by *The Rainbow's* long reach backward in time, which shifts the novel's emphasis to include the historical process that led to woman's quest for individuality in the present century. But the ultimate focus of the whole psychological history upon Ursula remains. Having completed an autobiographical novel about his own struggle toward individuality and self-responsibility, Lawrence turns – more fully than Forster before him in the transition from *The Longest Journey* to *Howards End* – to a reworking of the same struggle from a female perspective. As in Joyce's movement from the autobiographical Stephen Dedalus to the quite antithetical figures of Leopold and Molly Bloom, Lawrence's recasting of himself in Ursula is an imaginative re-envisioning of the self as other, an exercise in sympathetic projection. But it also marks Lawrence's appropriation and redefinition of the Muse, the female figure who mediates in the artist's access to a realm of imaginative experience traditionally inaccessible to the male mind alone. Ursula is modelled partly on Frieda Lawrence; in purely biographical terms, the advent of Frieda into Lawrence's life evidently helped to provide the impetus that generated his two greatest novels.

At the heart of Lawrence's intellectual system is the belief that a satisfactory sexual relationship is a necessary foundation for successful creative work, but it is a system in which the woman must possess – as Frieda clearly did – her own sense of individuality, self-responsibility, and initiative. Anna Brangwen is an inadequate Muse because 'she relinquished the adventure to the unknown' and 'had not played her fullest part'; as a consequence, Will, who is a failed artist, finds that 'something undeveloped in him limited him, there was a darkness in him which he *could* not unfold, which would never unfold in him' (pp. 193, 192, 207). Lawrence's contrasting success in unfolding his own creative darkness seems owing in part to Frieda's success as a Muse; in addition to her effect on his subconscious creativity, which may only be conjectured, Lawrence credits her explicitly with various kinds of conscious assistance, such as suggesting the title of *The Rainbow*.[30] Feminist criticism may justly fault Lawrence for failing to take the next obvious step of conceding that, in any given relationship, the female might emerge as artist and the male as Muse, or – still more equitably – that each might be capable both of creative work and of providing inspiration to the other, either simultaneously or in oscillation. But even as it stands, Lawrence's casting of Ursula to represent Frieda within the novel works a radical transformation in the traditional nature of the Muse: she is brought down to earth, embodied in human flesh, given an individual history and a capacity for human growth. The modernist Muse no less than the modern woman must be capable of 'becoming individual, self-responsible, taking her own initiative'.

Ursula's role in *The Rainbow* suggests that Lawrence recognized more clearly than Forster how readily a Muse figure can be combined with a realistically conceived character. In *Howards End*, Margaret Schlegel ultimately retreats from her potential role as Muse by simply repeating the life of the elder Mrs. Wilcox, gaining contact with the subterranean unity of life at the cost of losing all power to articulate her understanding. Ursula, by contrast, develops into a character capable of mediating between an artist and life's deeper currents, helping to translate their voiceless power into human language. Lawrence's successful merging of Muse with character arises out of his interest in the subconscious: 'I don't so much care about what the woman *feels*', he wrote in the letter to Garnett, 'that presumes an *ego* to feel with. I only care about what the woman *is* – inhumanly, physiologically, materially . . . as representing some greater, inhuman will'.[31] In *The Rainbow*, Lawrence explores woman's evolving mediation between inhumanity and man.

Identity comes into this world from women. In the early pages of *The Rainbow*, the males are always 'the Brangwen men', or 'one of the Brangwen men', or 'they'. But in his first reference to the female sex Lawrence introduces a definite article – 'the woman wanted another form of life than this, something that was not blood-intimacy' – and then individual actions: 'she stood', 'she faced', 'she decided' (pp. 3–4). The man begins to acquire a social indentity in relation to her; she looks out from the front of the house, while 'her husband' looks back on the blood-intimacy of the farm (p. 3). The man's identity becomes increasingly specific as the woman's social awareness widens; comparison with the vicar's 'range of being' makes 'Brangwen' seem 'dull and local', and she realizes that though the vicar has no power over 'Tom Brangwen', yet he is Tom's master (p. 4). She mediates the male's development from 'one of the Brangwen men' to 'her husband' to 'Brangwen' to 'Tom Brangwen'. This female intercession in the male's acquisition of identity is again Wordsworthian, as when the Wordsworthian Muse in *The Solitary Reaper* enables the poet to speak of himself in the first person by reconnecting him to a human community. In Lawrence's world, this mediating role places the woman in 'the supreme position', making her 'the symbol for that further life which comprised religion and love and morality' (p. 13). Like Mrs. Wilcox in *Howards End*, whom her husband thinks of as 'steady',[32] the woman at The Marsh represents order and solidity; the men 'depended on her for their stability', and she stands for all they know of the divine: 'She was the anchor and the security, she was the restraining hand of God' (p. 13). But this traditional, unselfconscious female role becomes insufficient as the flood of modern consciousness gradually alters the conditions of life.

Anna Brangwen is a potential Muse figure, but she resists the experience of traditional religious vision. Looking at a stained glass window representing the lamb of resurrection,

> Suddenly she had a powerful mystic experience, the power of the tradition seized on her, she was transported to another world. And she hated it, resisted it. (p. 156)

She does not believe in conventional religion, yet she cannot win through to a true Lawrentian vision which would reshape the old religious forms to new secular ends. Her glimpse of the rainbow at the end of the 'Anna Victrix' chapter is a vision of something far off in the distance to which she has not attained:

> She was straining her eyes to something beyond. And from her Pisgah mount, which she had attained, what could she see? A faint, gleaming horizon, a long way off, and a rainbow like an archway, a shadow-door with faintly coloured coping above it. Must she be moving thither?

She sees the symbol of Lawrence's new heaven and earth, in which the whole daylight world will be remade: 'Dawn and sunset were the feet of the rainbow that spanned the day, and she saw the hope, the promise' (p. 192). But having come this far, Anna 'relinquished the adventure to the unknown'. She recognizes that 'through her another soul was coming' (p. 193); she will leave the quest for a new world as an inheritance to her daughter.

Anna's partial vision enables her, nevertheless, to see beyond the claims of conventional religion. The cathedral, which she and Will visit in the following chapter, only imitates the wider world of light and sky; it is 'spanned round with the rainbow' (p. 198) but clearly contained within it, 'a world within a world, a sort of side show' (p. 202). She is only briefly caught up in Will's ecstasy at 'the two-fold silence where dawn was sunset, and the beginning and the end were one' (p. 199). Here, the two feet of the rainbow – dawn and sunset – are drawn together to a single point, in the religious alpha and omega the light of the living day is lost in darkness. The cathedral represents religion's claim to contain all, 'beyond which was nothing, nothing, it was the ultimate confine'. But this claim fails in the light of Anna's larger knowledge; remembering the open sky 'where stars were wheeling in freedom', she 'claimed the right to freedom above her, higher than the roof' (p. 200). Within the cathedral itself, she finds allies in the carved gargoyle faces that mock at the structure's pretensions, like the goblins that Helen Schlegel hears amid the grandeur of Beethoven's Fifth Symphony in *Howards End*. Helen finds the goblins intensely disquieting; they come to symbolize 'panic and emptiness' for her, the presence of forces and evils in the world beyond her power to control.[33] For Will, too, Anna's delight in the gargoyles is 'the serpent in his Eden' (p. 201), awakening him to consciousness of the larger world outside. Religion is no longer an adequate source of meaning in the modern world, no longer 'a reality, an order, an absolute, within a meaningless confusion' (p. 202). Will is forced to admit to himself that 'there was much that the Church did not include' (p. 203), but like Anna, he 'lapses back for his fulfilment', busying himself with 'the church fabric and the church ritual', the 'form of service' (pp. 204–6). He settles for aesthetic order; in art and architecture the old world view 'completed and satisfied him. He did not care whether or not he believed' (p. 276). But his preservation of old rituals creates for his children 'at least this rhythm of eternity in a ragged, inconsequential life' (p. 279). Because he takes on this task, Ursula grows up familiar with the old religious terms and symbols that can ultimately be reshaped into a new order.

Lawrence wrote later in life of his deep familiarity, dating back to childhood, with the book of Revelation.[34] With appropriate complementarity he makes Ursula's 'favourite book in the Bible' the book of Genesis (p. 323); Muse and artist thus represent between them the beginning and the end, alpha and omega, the power of creative generation and the power to determine finished form. At the same time, Ursula's growth involves coming to share her creator's conviction that Christianity is simultaneously inadequate as a system of belief but invaluable as a source of language to describe the deepest levels of human experience. At the beginning of her development she finds that in church, quite simply, a 'visionary world came to pass'. It is a 'marriage of dark and light', sunset and sunrise brought together in unity, out of which 'the Voice sounded, re-echoing not from this world, as if the Church itself were a shell that still spoke the language of creation'. And the language it speaks tells a version of her own family history, the Genesis story of those 'giants in the earth' who resemble the early Brangwens, men deriving from a different line than Adam's and who perhaps 'had known no expulsion, no ignominy of the fall' (p. 274). The story is appropriate to Ursula's early adolescence, for she too has yet to fall into consciousness, away from harmony with the natural world.

Ursula's growth toward becoming a Muse begins with the dawning of self-consciousness. Her identity emerges as she discovers what is to become the principal struggle of her life, that struggle toward selfhood which Lawrence has announced as the germ of the novel. As she

> passed from girlhood towards womanhood, gradually the cloud of self-responsibility gathered upon her. She became aware of herself, that she was a separate entity in the midst of an unseparated obscurity, that she must go somewhere, she must become something.

She discovers it a 'torment indeed, to inherit the responsibility of one's own life'. Immediately the 'religion which had been another world for her' begins to alter; it

> now fell away from reality, and became a tale, a myth, an illusion, which, however much one might assert it to be true an historical fact, one knew was not true – at least, for this present-day life of ours. (p. 281)

Appropriately, when she next enters a church, she finds that 'the place re-echoed to the calling of secular voices' (p. 294), the voices of workman engaged – as her father has been engaged for many years – in repairing the ancient and decaying physical fabric of religion.

As the first phase of her relationship with Anton Skrebensky awakens her sexuality and sense of self, Ursula moves further away from conventional religion. She no longer pays attention to the church service; it 'passed unnoticed by her'. But she turns of her own separate will to the book of Genesis and reads the story of Noah. As the object of this conscious search for meaning, the story is inadequate:

> Ursula was not moved by the history this morning. Multiplying and replenishing the earth bored her. Altogether it seemed merely a vulgar and stock-raising sort of business. (pp. 323–4)

It is, of course, the business of her Brangwen ancestors, but her devaluation of their work merely extends Tom Brangwen's own earlier realization, at the time of Anna's marriage, that 'anybody could have done it' (p. 124). With the birth of consciousness, multiplying and replenishing the earth no longer offer adequate fulfilment. Noah and his sons emerge from this new perspective as 'sub-tenants under the great Proprietor', and Ursula imagines herself as a nymph, able to

> have laughed through the window of the ark, and flicked drops of the flood at Noah, before she drifted away to people who were less important in their Proprietor and their Flood.

Ursula's ironic deflation of Noah is, for Lawrence, an appropriate response to the Biblical episode's claims to represent final truth. But she must also grow to understand the Bible's real value as a repository of language and symbolism that can be reshaped to fulfil a continuing, though continually changing, human need for symbolic correlatives to subconscious experience.

As the first step in this process, she becomes aware – with Skrebensky's help that she is a romantic (pp. 209, 325); romanticism retains the emotional intensity of religious experience but translates it into secular terms. Later, under Winifred Inger's influence, she learns to see traditional religion from a secular perspective:

> They took religion and rid it of its dogmas, its falsehoods. Winifred humanised it all. Gradually it dawned upon Ursula that all the religion she knew was but a particular clothing to a human aspiration. The aspiration was the real thing, – the clothing was a matter almost of national taste or need. . . . Religions were local and religion was universal. Christianity was a local branch.

In religion, as in the ministry of Wordsworth's Nature, there are 'the two great motives of fear and love' (p. 340). Religion has become merely one aspect of a larger secular system, although Winifred parts company with Lawrence in her belief that the larger system is purely scientific and mechanistic. In Lawrence's judgement, Skrebensky and Winifred are both more limited than Ursula, but both can offer necessary help in her process of growth and self-definition.

A large part of Ursula's struggle, however, ultimately involves learning to distinguish between experience that will aid her growth toward selfhood and experience that will provide temptations to turn aside from her true path. Lawrence suggests early in her acquaintance with Skrebensky that he will figure primarily as a temptation which Ursula must struggle to overcome. When Ursula first meets him, she feels 'as if she were set on a hill and could feel vaguely the whole world lying spread before her (p. 288). This moment parallels the temptation of Christ, when Satan takes him up the mountain and offers him the kingdoms of the world below. But just as Satan has no power to make good on his offer of a world which lies only in the gift of God, so the promise Skrebensky holds out will prove to be ultimately illusory. Ursula will find that she has more power in herself to discover the outside world than Skrebensky can offer; in the end she 'knew him all round, not on any side did he lead into the unknown' (p. 473). As her self-sufficiency increases, she discovers that 'she found herself very rich in being alone, and enjoying to the full her solitary room' (p. 459). A sense of identity replaces her need to contact the world through the experience of someone else, because 'self was a oneness with the infinite. To be oneself was a supreme, gleaming triumph of infinity' (p. 441). Skrebensky no longer can offer any temptation for her; only a man with a sense of self as strong as her own will be able to extend her experience further than she has arrived by herself.

Between her two periods of involvement with Anton Skrebensky, Ursula encounters a different temptation in a marriage proposal from Anthony Schofield. Visiting his farm, she perceives that it is 'like the Garden of Eden', a version of the old world of The Marsh. Anthony Schofield still lives in an unawakened blood-intimacy, in a world like that from which Tom Brangwen began to stir two generations earlier in Ursula's family. Ursula becomes poignantly aware of this barrier between them: 'Her soul was an infant crying in the night. He had no soul. Oh, and why had she? He was the cleaner' (p. 416). Soulless and selfless, he is 'one with' the natural scene and cannot see it, whereas she can both be herself and achieve oneness with it through the mediation of perception: 'she saw it, and was one with it. Her seeing separated them infinitely' (p. 417). Anthony has failed to grow up into the modern world as the Brangwens have; he is an anachronism, tempting Ursula to return to an Eden she cannot ever return to, because she has fallen into consciousness.

By the end of the novel, Ursula has acquired a strong enough sense of identity and self-responsibility to perform the central task of the modern Muse: that of mediating between the blood-intimacy of nature and the mind-consciousness of the modern world. She is capable of simultaneously seeing the world and being at one with it; she possesses the potential to translate inarticulate meaning into humanly comprehensible order. In the great scene beneath the moon at the end of the novel's penultimate chapter, Ursula – like the woman in Wallace Stevens's *Idea of Order at Key West* – actively channels the inarticulate power of nature into a current capable of inspiring an artist to evoke that power in the human language of consciousness. Like the woman in *Key West*, she walks the 'foreshore alone after dusk'. The sea, in its swinging, definite motion, its strength, its attack, and its salt burning, seemed to provoke her to a pitch of madness, tantalizing her with vast suggestions of fulfilment.

But 'for personification' of these suggestions comes only Skrebensky, 'whose soul could not contain her in its waves of strength' (p. 477). Skrebensky is not an artist, and the experience for him more closely resembles electrocution than inspiration. As in the scene beneath the moon in the first phase of their relationship, she seems here 'a beam of gleaming power' (p. 319). And, also as in the earlier scene, the power of moon and salt sea coursing through her seems to burn and corrode him (pp. 318–20, 478–80). Skrebensky cannot contain and shape into conscious art the vast inhuman power that she commands. The scene becomes a *Key West* gone wrong; the Muse generates a destructive bolt of lightning rather than providing Stevens's subtly modulated current of poetic inspiration. The parallel between poem and novel is extended by Lawrence's repeated turn, in this chapter, from the world of primal darkness in which the lovers meet to the world of man-made light (pp. 447, 451); but because the Muse's message is not received, the novel cannot achieve the poem's final vision of harmony between the darkness and the lights. After Skrebensky leaves, Ursula finds that 'there was now no moon for her, no sea' (p. 480), somewhat as for the woman in *Key West* 'there never was a world for her / Except the one she sang, and singing, made'.[35] But at this point in *The Rainbow* Ursula is left in a desolation without exception; no new world in art has been made for her because her power has not been perceived as song.

IV

The last chapter of *The Rainbow* begins quietly in this mood of defeat. Ursula, finding herself with child, tries with her conscious mind to abandon her semi-conscious quest for selfhood. 'What did the self, the form of life matter?' she thinks. 'Only the living from day to day mattered, the beloved existence in the body, peaceful, complete, with no beyond' (p. 483). She is tempted to surrender, as Anna did, the quest for the unknown that lies beyond woman's traditional roles as wife and mother. Was not the 'life that was given' enough 'for her, as it had been for her mother?' (p. 484). In this mood Ursula writes to Skrebensky, asking him to take her back, 'as if from her deepest, sincerest heart. She felt that now, now, she was at the depths of herself'. But she is not at the depths of herself; she is still trapped in consciousness, only writing 'as if' from her heart. She imagines a false conventional ending for the novel, thinking that 'she should join him and her history would be concluded forever'. But the calm this decision engenders is 'unnatural', and gradually she is aware of 'a gathering restiveness, a tumult impending within her' (p. 485). As always in Lawrence's universe, her internal tumult will ultimately find itself projected upon the external world, answered back from a Wordsworthian landscape that is partially shaped by the unconscious self behind her perceiving eye.

Like Wordsworth on Snowdon, she walks out on a day of mist and rain, 'seeing the colliery and its clouds of steam for a moment visionary in dim brilliance, away in the chaos of rain. Then the veils closed again' (p. 485). She sees 'the pale gleam of Willey Water through the cloud below' and the 'great veils of rain swinging with slow, floating waves across the landscape' (pp. 485–6). The experience that follows functions exactly like a Wordsworthian spot of time, one that will have 'A renovating virtue, whence, depressed / By false opinion and contentious thought . . . our minds / Are nourished and invisibly repaired'.[36] After walking for a long time, wet and far from home, she finds that she 'must beat her way back' to 'stability and security' through the 'fluctuation' of 'rain and waving landscape'. This necessity reflects her present figurative distance from what are, for her, true stability and security; in her fluctuating attempts to conciliate Skrebensky, she has alienated her conscious mind from her true unconscious self, and now she must beat back a long circuitous journey home.[37] Like the Wordsworthian Muse – like Lucy and the Solitary Reaper – she is 'a solitary thing' against the landscape (p. 486). But as a self-conscious modern Muse she will also encounter, like Wordsworth the poet, an overwhelming image for the power within herself that she has sought to abandon and deny.

In her heart is 'a small, living seed of fear'. Then 'suddenly she knew there was something else. Some horses were looming in the rain, not near yet. But they were going to be near'. Lawrence insists explicitly on the connection between these horses and her internal condition: 'she knew the heaviness on her heart. It was the weight of the horses' (pp. 486–7). Much critical debate has centred upon whether the horses are really present in the landscape or whether they are a kind of visionary hallucination on Ursula's part. But this way of framing the issue misses the essential point. The horses are simultaneously present in the landscape *and* a projection of her own heaviness and fear. She both perceives and half-creates the world around her; like Wordsworth's Nature, the landscape she experiences is shaped partly by the emotion she projects upon it, and partly by its own separate being.

Ursula first thinks that she is strong enough in her conscious will to evade the horses: 'she would circumvent them. She would bear the weight steadily, and so escape. She would go straight on, and on, and be gone by' (pp. 486–7). She hopes to escape just as she has hoped to escape her own subconscious passional being by marrying Skrebensky. But Lawrence suggests the impossibility of this goal in the paradox of her attempt to 'circumvent' the horses by going 'straight on'. She believes that the conscious will is the straight path through her self, that the sexual and sensual world is at the margins, visible 'like the eyes of wild beasts, gleaming' outside the 'circle of consciousness' (p. 437).[38] It seems to her now that

> The way was open before her, to the gate in the high hedge in the near distance, so she could pass into the smaller, cultivated field, and so out to the highroad and the ordered world of man. (p. 488)

But the horses return, enclosing her – as her passionate response to Skrebensky has – a second time, and all at once she recognizes that 'it was the crisis' (pp. 488–9). The restive passion that the horses represent is closer to the centre of her self than her conscious will. To pass them she must alter her course and her point of view. With this realization she is finally able to escape, not by going straight on, but by climbing up a tree and swinging over a hedge.

Ursula's experience with the horses projects into the external world her internal confrontation with the subconscious realm of passionate 'blood-intimacy'. As she lies exhausted and wet, safe on the other side of the hedge, she discovers that she has reached the real depths of herself:

> she lay as if unconscious upon the bed of the stream, like a stone, unconscious, unchanging, unchangeable, whilst everything rolled by in transience, leaving her there, a stone at rest on the bed of the stream, inalterable and passive, sunk to the bottom of all change. (p. 489)

Ursula has finally found her way to the bed-rock carbon, long hidden beneath her stream and flood of consciousness. This moment of stillness 'whilst everything rolled by in transience' resembles Wordsworth's boyhood experience when, skating between 'shadowy banks', he 'stopped short' to find that 'still the solitary cliffs / Wheeled by me – even as if the earth had rolled/With visible motion her diurnal round!'[39] For Ursula, as for the young poet, the world still echoes the rapid motion she has suddenly abandoned; she has reached the level beneath individual identity where the self within and the world without unite in creating the world she perceives. Later, when she lies at home ill with a fever from her experience, she still feels 'in some way like the stone at the bottom of the river, inviolable and unalterable, no matter what storm raged in her body' (p. 490).

Much earlier, at her Uncle Fred's wedding, Ursula had a proleptic vision of these 'depths of the underworld, under the great flood' (p. 316). Now she has reached them within herself. In another age Tom Brangwen was capable of reaching this level 'at the bottom of his brain', of experiencing moments when 'his heart sunk to the bottom' (pp. 79, 74). Will Brangwen briefly glimpsed this deeper realm during his sexual passion for Anna, seeing external reality as merely 'the rind of the world' which had suddenly 'been broken away entire' to reveal 'the permanent bed-rock' of 'one's own being' (p. 146). But only in Ursula has a character finally struggled her way down to this region from a state of fully roused consciousness. She has arrived beneath the conscious 'stream' of her relation with Skrebensky, which had 'covered her, flowed over the last fibre of her' (p. 447); arrived beneath the 'dark stream' of civic intercourse that governs public life (p. 448); and arrived beneath the 'undercurrent of darkness' in her family (p. 450). She has not merely survived, like her father, by immersing herself in the destructive element of consciousness; she has got beneath it, becoming aware in the process of the relation between consciousness and the unconscious.

From Ursula's point of view, the first flood of modern consciousness that killed Tom Brangwen is a dimly remembered event which destroyed the old world of unconscious blood-intimacy, just as for the writers of Genesis the Flood would have been a watershed far back in history that ended a mythic era of universal origins and giants in the earth. Now that Ursula has discovered the stream bed beneath this modern flood, a member of the Brangwen family is at last rooted again in the earth, able to control and guide the stream of consciousness within herself. She has achieved the self-control that she only thought she had reached, in reacting with despair to her failure with Skrebensky, at the beginning of the final chapter. But the despair has been, as for Wordsworth in *The Prelude*, a necessary precondition for true self-knowledge and understanding. Because this Lawrentian stream bed of carbon at the bottom of consciousness lies beneath individual indentity, she is at first able to define herself from the new perspective only by negation; thus she repeats in her illness:

> I have no father nor mother nor lover, I have no allocated place in the
> world of things, I do not belong to Beldover nor to Nottingham nor to

England nor to this world, they none of them exist, I am trammelled
and entangled in them, but they are all unreal. (p. 492)

The bed-rock of Lawrentian carbon exists undifferentiated in all things;
in taking her place within this vast continuum, Ursula must at first give
up her sense of selfhood.[40] But like Christian salvation, the process is one
of losing herself to find herself. She is acting out her earlier intellectual
realization that 'selfhood was a oneness with the infinite' (p. 441); the self
which finally emerges will be stronger for having recognized its
rootedness in the universe.

As she begins to recover, she thus begins to glimpse – like Wordsworth
and the Christian visionaries before her – new heaven and new earth:
'soon she would have her root fixed in a new Day . . . a new sky and a new
air'. She falls asleep 'in the confidence of her new reality', sleeps
'breathing with her soul the new air of a new world', and 'when she woke
at last it seemed as if a new day had come on the earth' (p. 492). Again,
Lawrence's use of the phrase 'as if' is crucial. The world has not in reality
been changed yet, but Ursula, out of the intensity of her internal victory,
achieves a prophetic vision of what will ultimately come to pass. In his
reading of these final pages, H. M. Daleski ignores the 'as if' and contends
of Ursula that 'being made new herself, it is her facile assumption that she
will find the world changed to measure'. This apparent weakness leads
him to agree with Leavis that the final note of prophetic hope is
'unprepared for and unsupported'.[41] But the objection misses the
essential nature of visionary experience. Paul after his experience on the
Damascus road and Wordsworth after his vision on Snowdon return to
the everyday world, in which the new world they have glimpsed has still
to be achieved. Similarly, once the final visionary moment of *The
Rainbow* passes away, Ursula will again find herself in a world unchanged,
as the opening of *Women in Love* makes sufficiently clear. But here in a
brief moment of intense apprehension she is able to see the earth as it
ideally might be, transformed and created anew; translated beyond
herself in the visionary experience, she sees the world of possibility
flickering beneath the world of everyday life.

The final vision, as it unfolds, is explicitly framed in apocalyptic
language; as Ursula recovers, 'she sat to watch a new creation' (p. 493).[42]
She completely rejects 'the old, hard barren form of bygone living', while
in 'everything she saw she grasped and groped to find the creation of the
living God' (p. 494). She is looking for invisible signs of the new heaven
and earth in the visible creation, among 'the things that are made'
(Romans 1:20). Like Margaret Schlegel in *Howards End*, she is forced to

acknowledge an ugly, creeping civilization that seems destined to
frustrate the promise of renewal:

> she saw the hard, cutting edges of the new houses, which seemed to
> spread over the hillside in their insentient triumph, the triumph of
> horrible, amorphous angles and straight lines, the expression of
> corruption triumphant and unopposed.[43]

Unlike Forster, Lawrence makes no attempt to play down the power of
this corruption; it fills Ursula with 'a nausea so deep that she perished as
she sat' (p. 494). But the pattern of Biblical symbolism that Lawrence has
woven into the fabric of the novel allows him to offer a more dramatic
promise of final hope than Forster was able to provide.

This promise is embodied in the oldest symbol for the covenant, the
ancient sign of divine restraint and natural order:

> She saw a band of faint iridescence colouring in faint colours a portion
> of the hill . . . she looked for the hovering colour and saw a rainbow
> forming itself. (p. 494)

Reworking his Biblical symbolism in the Romantic secular tradition,
Lawrence makes this culminating event a purely natural phenomenon;
Ursula sees a rainbow 'forming itself', not a rainbow placed in the
heavens by God. It exists and acquires its significance out of a creative
interchange between the observer and the natural world. Ursula's vision
of the rainbow promises that the process of mutual interchange between
mind and nature, which creates the world as we know it, will never again
be nearly drowned beneath a flood of consciousness. As we rebuild the
world in the aftermath of this flood, she envisions that 'new, clean, naked
bodies would issue to a new germination, to a new growth'; she sees 'in the
rainbow the earth's new architecture, the old, brittle corruption of houses
and factories swept away' (p. 495). This final vision is partially
anticipated in Will's vision of 'the discarded rind of the world' (p. 146),
and in Anna's earlier distant vision of the rainbow (p. 192). But Anna's
vision was purely personal, including no image of transformation for the
larger world of humanity; and Will's vision was purely one of that larger
world's being swept away, including no personal glimpse of the rainbow.
Only Ursula is granted the full visionary promise because only she has
discovered her oneness with the infinite, discovered the place of her own
identity in a larger universal pattern of Lawrentian unity and
redemption.

The novel ends with Ursula's final prophetic hope of 'the world built up in a living fabric of Truth, fitting to the over-arching heaven'. In quite similar language, Wordsworth concludes *The Prelude* by envisioning a new world created out of the relation between mind and nature. This world is located within 'the mind of man', which 'becomes / A thousand times more beautiful than the earth', rising

> above this frame of things
> In beauty exalted, as it is itself
> Of quality and fabric more divine.[44]

For Wordsworth, the mind of man is ultimately of 'quality and fabric more divine' than nature, potentially capable of achieving an order like Lawrence's 'living fabric of Truth'. Like Plato's ideal city, Wordsworth's new heaven and new earth have become a paradise within, probably impossible to realize in the external world. But for Lawrence at the time of writing *The Rainbow*, men and women may still be able to join with nature in creating a new order on earth, incorporating both mind-consciousness and blood-intimacy; the rainbow's arch reaches 'the top of heaven', but it also 'stood on the earth'.

In Lawrence's new symbolic scheme the visible rainbow represents only half of the complete circle of experience. It stands for the conscious hope of men and women, the promise that 'would quiver to life in their spirit', the half of the circle that extends from earth up to heaven. But the full circle includes the half that extends from the surface of the earth down into the unconscious world of blood-intimacy, the world in darkness and in the body, the half of the circle that is 'arched in their blood' (p. 495). Together, the two arches combine in the 'widening circle' that Lawrence has used as a repeated image for Ursula's growth. Ursula's final rainbow vision is a sign that her growth toward selfhood is completed, a testimony to her place among the Lawrentian elect, the saved. She will belong to the promised new world in which human sensuality and spirituality are joined, rooted in the earth but fitting to the over-arching heaven.

The rainbow is, finally, a symbol for Lawrence's art, an art that he also wants to create out of a union between earth and sky, blood and spirit. He sharply distinguishes this new aesthetic from that older one represented in the etherialized cathedral arch, in which the rainbow form is cut off from the true rainbow's invisible connection with the blood-bound half of the circle. He also distinguishes the widening Lawrentian circle of experience from another old but no longer adequate symbol of unity.

Early in the novel, during one of the first meetings between Tom Brangwen and Lydia, Tom had looked down at her wedding ring, thinking to himself that 'it excluded him: it was a closed circle'. Shortly after, the thought comes to Lydia that she 'would have to begin again, to find a new being, a new form' (p. 34). In the course of composing the novel, Lawrence had at one point thought of calling it *The Wedding Ring*;[45] but for the author as well as for his characters, the widening circle that includes the visible rainbow replaces the old image, the old form, of the closed and exclusive ring. Men and women can no longer unite in marriage to shut out the larger world of humanity beyond. Ursula will finally marry, like her parents and grandparents, but her marriage will only be possible beyond the confines of a single work of art. Though thematically complete in itself, *The Rainbow* is, finally, only half of a new and larger aesthetic form, the widening circle that includes both this novel and *Women in Love*.

4

Unweaving the Wind: *Penelope* and *Claritas* in *Ulysses*

I

In August 1921, while working on the final chapters of *Ulysses*, James Joyce wrote to Frank Budgen that '*Penelope* is the clou of the book'.[1] Marilyn French has observed that 'paradoxically it is this chapter with its symbolic character that nails the book down to solid earth',[2] but his use of the French 'clou' in an English sentence also suggests that Jeems Joker is invoking a characteristic pun: *Penelope* is both nail and clue to the book as a whole. My goal in this chapter is to suggest how *Penelope* retrospectively shapes and informs the rest of *Ulysses*. Like Leopold Bloom, however, I have found that the 'longest way round is the shortest way home',[3] and before I turn to *Penelope* itself I would like to explore the evolving formal structure of *Ulysses* as a whole.

Critical debate has long sought to define form in *Ulysses* by assigning the book to one or another of various fictional genres; the two dominant perspectives see *Ulysses* as either a realistic novel of character or as a mythic novel of symbolic correspondences, although the history of *Ulysses* criticism is full of readers who combine and realign these perspectives in complex ways.[4] Matters are further complicated because Joyce himself never offers an unqualified statement, in his own persona and untouched with irony, of his views on literary form. A. Walton Litz suggests, however, that the theory of aesthetic apprehension described in Joyce's early notebooks and fictions provides a unified model for our gradual experience, as readers, of form in *Ulysses*:

The sequence – *integritas, consonantia, claritas* – is a movement from cognition to recognition to satisfaction. First we must understand the integrity and symmetry of the work, which involves seeing it in relation to other works and tracing the relationship of part to part: it is here that our knowledge and experience of the various traditional genres comes

77

into play. But finally, when our experience of the different parts and their relationship is fused into a single image, the unique meaning of the work stands forth in individual clarity.[5]

In other words, *Ulysses* finally transcends categorization in any traditional genre, or combination of genres, that the reader attempts to impose on the novel out of an external experience with other works. But unlike genre, form – conceived as an internal property of the work itself – cannot be transcended in a work of art that exists in time and space; it can only exist on unperceived levels or cohere in unexpected ways. I want to pursue Litz's suggestion that the aesthetic theory presented in *A Portrait of the Artist* can help identify such a level of unifying form in *Ulysses*, one at which the novel's warring formal elements – such as myth and realism – cohere in a transcendent unity or *claritas*.

The principal objection to seeking such authority from *Portrait* for a reading of Joyce's work has been articulated most clearly by S. L. Goldberg, who argues that

> it is always dangerous to judge a writer's work by his own theories – we tend, only too easily, to beg the most relevant questions; and these dangers are particularly acute when, as in Joyce's case, the theories appear as an integral part of a complex work of art.[6]

In his own lengthy analysis of Joyce's aesthetic theories, Goldberg confines himself to following them 'towards the preoccupations and the forms of [Joyce's] imagination'. But Goldberg's concern that the theories are endangered by their presentation in a work of art clearly proceeds from his viewing *Portrait*, as well as *Ulysses*, purely as a dramatized novel of character in which Stephen's perspective cannot in any sense be identified with that of his creator. Northrop Frye offers a useful rebuttal to this view in arguing that *Portrait* combines confessional autobiography with the traditional novel form: 'when we find that a technical discussion of a theory of aesthetics forms the climax of Joyce's *Portrait*, we realize that what makes this possible is the presence in that novel of another tradition of prose fiction'.[7] The aesthetic theory is perhaps the most undiluted element of autobiography in the book; according to Ralph Rader, Joyce encouraged Stuart Gilbert to present it as 'the functioning aesthetic of *Ulysses*', and he worked on the theory in his notebooks both before and after *Portrait* appeared.[8]

For Goldberg, the principal internal weakness in Stephen's theory – reason enough to assert that it cannot be Joyce's own – is Stephen's failure to account for the *meaningfulness* of art, those subtle relations with life that others have tried to explain with terms like "imitation," "universality," "revelation," "express," "symbol," and so on.[9]

But all of these terms for describing meaning in art arise from aesthetic theories with orientations quite different from Stephen's, from models which attempt to describe aesthetic meaning as possible only in an art that imitates, universalizes, reveals, expresses, or symbolizes 'subtle relations with life'. Stephen's view belongs rather to what M. H. Abrams has called 'objective' aesthetic theory, which isolates the work of art from the external universe, audience and artist, 'analyzes it as a self-sufficient entity constituted by its parts in their internal relations, and sets out to judge it solely by criteria intrinsic to its own mode of being'.[10] The work of art is an autonomous world, not meaningless, but whose meaningfulness emerges from 'its parts in their internal relations', without reference to the world of human life beyond its boundaries. Stephen once 'thought' that *claritas* might be

the artistic discovery and representation of the divine purpose in anything or a force of generalisation which would make the esthetic image a universal one, make it outshine its proper conditions,

but he no longer thinks so; he now defines all three conditions for aesthetic apprehension as internal properties of the work itself: *integritas* is its wholeness, *consonantia* its harmony, and *claritas* 'the scholastic *quidditas*, the *whatness* of a thing'. *Claritas* is what makes it 'that thing which it is and no other thing'.[11] Perception of *claritas* is perception of a unique formal meaning within the work itself, isolated from its relationship with the external world.[12]

The discussion of literary form in *Portrait* actually predicts *Ulysses* with considerable accuracy:

The simplest epical form is seen emerging out of lyrical literature when the artist prolongs and broods upon himself as the centre of an epical event,

much as we find Stephen, the dramatized version of Joyce, brooding in the opening of *Ulysses*, though unaware that he is to be at the centre of an epical event; 'and this form progresses till the centre of emotional gravity is equidistant from the artist himself and from others', which permits the creation of the second character, Bloom. At this point the narrative is no longer purely personal. The personality of the artist passes into the narration itself, flowing round and round the persons and the action like a vital sea.

This sea of narration parallels the sea of Dublin which Bloom must navigate; it becomes more and more perilous until, at his final return home, it suddenly subsides. Stephen sees such a progression in 'that old English ballad *Turpin Hero* which begins in the first person and ends in the third person'. *Ulysses* dramatizes this grammatical process: Stephen is the first person, artist and author, hero of Joyce's preceding autobiographical fiction; Bloom is the second person, the other whose contact with the artist is the subject of the plot; Molly is the third person, essentially unknown to the dramatized artist, with whom the epic ends:

> The dramatic form is reached when the vitality which has flowed and eddied round each person fills every person with such vital force that he or she assumes a proper and intangible esthetic life.

Molly alone is fully filled with the vital force of 'a proper and intangible esthetic life' because she is the only character left awake when the dramatic form is reached.[13]

From the reader's perspective, the result of this epical evolution is that

> The personality of the artist, at first a cry or a cadence or a mood and then a fluid and lambent narrative, finally refines itself out of existence, impersonalizes itself.

The increasing impersonalization of Joyce's epic narrative culminates in *Ithaca*; the purely dramatic form of *Penelope* is completely new to the novel and not a return to the form of the initial chapters, as some critics have argued. In the early chapters stream of consciousness is filtered through novelistic narrative; in *Penelope*, Molly's thoughts appear directly, without apparent mediation. In *Penelope*, as in the works of a mature dramatic artist like Shakespeare,

> The esthetic image in the dramatic form is life purified in and reprojected from the human imagination. The mystery of esthetic like that of material creation is accomplished. The artist, like the God of the creation, remains within or behind or beyond or above his handiwork, invisible, refined out of existence, indifferent, paring his fingernails.

This final goal is a state of Keatsian negative capability in which the artist's presence in the work is completely subsumed within and reprojected outward through the vitality of the characters. *Penelope* stands as a clear indication that Joyce never abandoned his plan, outlined in *Portrait,* to achieve this goal through the formal progression of epic narrative from lyric to drama; the process of writing *Ulysses* was predicated upon a kinetic evolution of form. This evolution is not equivalent to meaninglessness or formlessness; it does imply, however, that the book's transcendent form will lie not in a static vision, but in a unified principle of change.

According to the aesthetic theory of *Portrait,* the reader's perception of formal unity in *Ulysses* should emerge in conjunction with his aesthetic response:

The instant wherein that supreme quality of beauty, the clear radiance of the esthetic image, is apprehended luminously by the mind which has been arrested by its wholeness and fascinated by its harmony is the luminous silent stasis of esthetic pleasure.

That is, the reader's experience of formal meaning in *Ulysses,* his perception of *claritas,* in analogous to the radiance 'felt by the artist when the esthetic image is first conceived in his imagination'. The text engages the reader in an essentially creative process of completing meaning and form which the artist has left trembling on the verge of completion: as perceiver 'you make the only synthesis which is logically and esthetically permissible. You see that it is that thing which it is and no other thing'.[14] The reader achieves aesthetic pleasure by seeing the novel's form momentarily fused into what Litz calls 'a single image', at which point 'the unique meaning of the work stands forth in individual clarity'.

I would like to propose Penelope's web as a suggestive 'single image' for the organization of *Ulysses.* In the *Odyssey,* Penelope, waiting and hoping for Odysseus's return, continually puts off her suitors; in the words of their spokesman Antinous, she 'gives hope to all, and makes promises to every man . . . but her mind is set on other things'. Seeming to concede Odysseus's death, she still begs that they allow her to postpone remarriage until she finishes weaving a 'shroud for the hero Laertes'. For three years she deceives them by weaving the web in the daytime and unweaving it at night, but in the fourth year she is discovered and forced to finish the web against her will.[15] The relationship between this story and the form of *Ulysses* rests in part on a similarity between the artistic processes involved. In weaving, one set of parallel threads, called the warp, is set up lengthwise with alternate threads pulled out slightly in opposite directions from the plane in which all would lie stretched if undisturbed. A shuttle carrying another thread, the woof, is passed through the 'shed' thus formed in the warp; the threads of the warp are then reversed, each pulled out in the opposite direction, and the shuttle passed back again through the new shed from the opposite side of the web. Variation in the pattern of the fabric can be achieved by varying the colour or thickness of threads in either warp or woof, by varying the number of times the woof or filling thread is passed through each shed, or by setting up the warp with the shed formed according to some pattern other than a simple alternation of threads.[16] Weaving may thus be an extremely simple craft or an extremely advanced one, depending on the degree of complexity aimed at in the choice of pattern; Penelope's skill is attested by Antinous: 'Athene hath given her beyond women, knowledge of all fair handiwork, yea, and cunning wit, and wiles'.[17]

Ulysses dramatizes a metaphorical relationship between weaving and language, just as it dramatizes the grammatical progression of forms that Stephen describes in *Portrait*. Language, like weaving, proceeds according to basic patterns of repetition which anyone can master and employ competently; but also like weaving, it is capable of complex artistic elaboration in the hands of a skilled master. As *Ulysses* proceeds to chronicle Leopold Bloom's day in Dublin, the reader perceives an increasing complexity of narrative and artistic form, just as during each day observers would have seen the extension and elaboration of Penelope's web. A number of critics have spoken of the 'web of allusions' in *Ulysses*; Michael Groden observes that Joyce's 'late revisions built up the "web" of the book's realistic details. The great increase in the number of minor leitmotifs interconnected different parts'.[18] But Groden also observes that Joyce made comparatively few draft revisions in the early chapters of the book; since he might easily have made far more than he did, he seems to have deliberately intended to create the effect of progressively increasing rhetorical complexity.

This complexity culminates in *Ithaca*, the style of which Edmund Wilson characterized in 1931 as 'the most opaque and uninviting medium possible'.[19] Many critics have shared his view that the characters nearly vanish here behind the web of Joyce's narrative. Indeed, if *Ithaca* were the last chapter in the book, it might be difficult to dispute readings that see *Ulysses* as a protracted stylistic experiment which evolved beyond the author's control, or as a triumph of nihilism which defeats all attempts to read in any positive meaning.[20] Earlier humanist readers helped to set up this difficulty by assuming that the end of *Ulysses* centres exclusively on

Stephen's meeting with Bloom.[21] But *Ithaca* is followed by *Penelope*, which introduces a radical reversal of the book's previous movement in the direction of increasing narrative and stylistic complexity. According to Joyce's Homeric parallel, Molly Bloom's soliloquy represents the night-time phase of Penelope's activity; it is the time when she unweaves her work of the day, revealing her secret desires and intentions. Similarly, *Penelope* unweaves the movement of *Ulysses* away from dramatized human experience and positive meaning; the chapter restores such meaning, and reveals that the entire book so far has seemed to progress, like Penelope's web, toward an end entirely opposite to that which actually occurs.

II

This model for the structure of *Ulysses* identifies the formal strategy that Frank Kermode calls 'peripeteia', or narrative reversal, which compels the reader of a complex fiction to 'reach the discovery or recognition by an unexpected and instructive route'.[22] In its abrupt switch from a pattern of weaving to one of unweaving, *Penelope* becomes the 'clou' of the book, both the nail that holds *Ulysses* together and the clue to how this structural binding is achieved. But like its Biblical counterpart Revelation, *Penelope* is symbolic in design, and hence has generated numerous differences in interpretation. In attempting to identify the 'discovery or recognition' – the *claritas* – which emerges in *Penelope*, I have found it useful to seek signposts throughout the novel that help to indicate the 'unexpected route' Joyce is taking toward his denouement. *Ulysses* differs from conventional fictions in the extent to which Joyce self-consciously sets up the work's peripeteia by means of internal allusions and imagery; in particular, three of the novel's characters – Molly, Mulligan, and Stephen – seem to represent symbolic elements in the formal pattern that the image of Penelope's web suggests.

Molly Bloom appears as a fully realized character only in *Penelope*, where, unweaving the narrative and stylistic web which has concealed her from sight, she reveals herself to the reader. But as several readers have sensed, her voice is also present at another level in the artistic design of the preceding seventeen chapters. Arnold Goldman conceives of *Penelope* 'as a process which goes on all the time during the novel, not just in Molly Bloom between waking and sleeping'.[23] James Maddox, too, hears Molly's voice throughout *Ulysses*:

It is as if the only sound left, Molly's voice, has been a low murmur – like the sound of the sea accompanying Stephen's abstrusiosities in "Proteus" – which we hear clearly for the first time now that the men have left the scene.[24]

Maddox also sees unweaving as a connection between Molly and Penelope, arguing that the web Molly unweaves by night is both 'the woolly jacket she wove for her dead son' which has become a 'death shroud surrounding her marriage', and 'the intricate tapestry of rationality which the two men have woven during the day'.[25] But Maddox does not connect these two insights. In terms of the Homeric parallel, the web that Molly unweaves in the night must be one that she herself – and not the two men – has woven during the day. What Goldman and Maddox seem to hear is Molly's voice, woven into the 'intricate tapestry of rationality' built up into the first seventeen chapters; it is the voice of artistic process, the moving line of music that binds up the woof of words into the warp of reason.

In a complementary insight, Hugh Kenner suggests that the *Penelope* chapter 'would appear to show us how the Muse behaves without Homer: a great feminine welling of lore and opinion and gossip and feeling'.[26] This identification of Molly with the Muse, like the identification of Molly with Penelope, expands Molly's role beyond her personal appearance in the final scene and acknowledges her symbolic presence in the formal structure of the whole novel. Joyce suggests this symbolic extension of Molly's voice within the novel itself in her professional role as Dublin's 'vocal muse' (p. 135). In *Penelope* we at last hear the voice of the Muse alone because the artist has refined himself out of the narrative; what remains is the pure voice of artistic inspiration, the welling up of poetic potentiality from the springs of everyday life. This change in voice is prepared for dramatically by the artist's having disappeared into the night in the preceding chapter, destination and purpose unknown; it is carried out structurally by the disappearance of narrative intrusion and the emergence of a single voice speaking in solitude. At the same time, Molly's identity with the Muse, like her identity with Penelope, does not diminish her own existence as a realistic character, but rather extends and universalizes her purely human response to experience by recognizing it as the source of artistic process.

Like Penelope, Molly has spent her day weaving an elaborate camouflage, a mask, a concealment and confusion of her purposes; her role as the artist's Muse extends this process of self-falsification to the narrative fabric of *Ulysses* as a whole. From the reader's perspective, the first seventeen chapters build up a vast web which conceals the weaver; in the last chapter that web is unwoven and the woman behind it gradually appears. To employ temporarily a different metaphor, one might say that during the day the star of Antinous seems ascendant, and appears to govern even Penelope's words and actions. The suitors can justify their position in her home only by a rigorous denial that Odysseus might still be alive, and Penelope herself seems to accede in that denial: 'Now that the goodly Odysseus is dead' she says; and the web itself is a shroud. But her nightly unweaving of the shroud is a rejection of death and denial, and an affirmation of faith, life and love. Her actions undermine both her own daytime mask and the apparent ascendancy of Antinous. Yet at the same time both the web and the unweaving of it are her own work; the shroud whose progress represents the daily success of denial and death is the unwilling labour of the same hands that voluntarily unweave it in a nightly affirmation of life. Negation cannot create even images of death by itself; Antinous must unconsciously try to warp Penelope's creative power to serve his own ends.

In the narrative elaboration of language in *Ulysses*, forces of rationalistic negation act out a similar struggle to usurp the creative powers of art. Joyce provides two versions of Antinous, both with alliterative names that suggest comic book villainy: Malachi Mulligan and Blazes Boylan. Both are physical usurpers, Mulligan of Stephen's home and Boylan of Bloom's bed; but Boylan's role is almost exclusively a physical one, whereas Mulligan also represents more dangerous forces of intellectual negation that attempt to usurp the place of the artist – as Antinous dispossesses Telemachus – and control the Muse's power over language and artistic process. Mocker and Muse are thus symbolically opposed: Mulligan dominates the opening of *Ulysses*, just as Molly Bloom dominates the close; the initials of his nickname, Buck Mulligan, are the reverse of hers, much as Dog is the substitute for God in the black mass; Buck and Molly also look somewhat alike: 'stately, plump' would describe either with equal accuracy. The two figures are simultaneously similar and antithetical, male and female versions of energetic sexual potency. But it is also clear that Mulligan's will works to defeat his creative capacity. He is neither father nor artist, whereas Penelope and Molly are both mothers and artists – one a weaver, the other a professional singer. Mulligan sterilizes his sexuality through masturbation and contraception; he squanders his potential artistic creativity in insulting mockery and satiric parody.

As a medical student, Mulligan is a fitting apostle of scientific knowledge and scientific nihilism. He opens *Ulysses* with an act of parodic creation analogous to Frankenstein's, using scientific parodies of religious language to conjure up the body of Christ in a shaving bowl; he simultaneously performs the sorcery of conjuring the virgin – in this case Stephen – who appears at the foot of the stairs. But Mulligan's creation is mere wind of words without substance; he rejects both a father's physical and believer's spiritual power to make the word flesh. He can summon Stephen but did not make him, and he knows with scientific detachment that the bowl contains merely lather. As in this scene, his language throughout *Ulysses* is largely language cut off from any serious purpose: 'idle mockery' Stephen calls it (p. 21). Idly in *Scylla and Charybdis* Mulligan begins a play 'in three orgasms' about masturbation which unites his interests in onanism and parody; it also reveals his lack of interest in sustained labour and artistic possibility (p. 216). Mulligan and Antinous will attempt to weave their interests and world view parasitically into artistic labours already under way, but will not or cannot perform acts of artistic creation themselves.

It is the presence of Mulligan's mocking and denying spirit among other presences within Joyce's imagination that necessitates most of the stylistic difficulty of *Ulysses*. Mulligan's abdication of the scientifically inexplicable and rationally illogical human power to control the meaning of language leaves him – and his heirs in recent theories of linguistic signification – with no recourse save to treat all speech and writing as an elaborate game, an autonomous process in which anything that can be said mocks both audience and speaker. Unchecked, he would multiply mere words for words' sake in a spiralling linguistic chaos where all positive intentions and purposes could become lost, and man destroy himself in a collective inability to achieve any mental construction of reality. But running counter to this potentially destructive spirit in *Ulysses* is the final affirmative voice casting its influence backward, retrospectively revealing its share in the fabric of the whole. The Muse weaves her voice into the narrative web to placate and deceive her suitors; her strategem seems an acquiescence in their eventually inevitable victory, but actually serves to stave off that victory and preserve her own freedom.

To the eyes of rational scientific observation, the web's union of rationalistic warp and poetic woof seems to promise a marriage of Antinous and Penelope, of Mulligan and Molly, of reason and the Muse, in which reason at last will rule. But from the secret perspective of Penelope, the Muse of Joyce's creative inspiration, the web's perpetual incompletion promises the redemption of destructive male rationality by creative female art; as long as the creative process continues, the destructive potential of reason will be neutralized, daily woven up into a 'luminous silent stasis' of aesthetic form. T. S. Eliot was ultimately responding to this redemptive promise in recognizing that Joyce's use of myth gave him 'a way of controlling, of ordering, of giving a shape and a significance to the immense panorama of futility and anarchy which is contemporary history'.[27] Futility and anarchy find their place in the pattern; they do not rise up to destroy the creative process.

The artist's role in this struggle of opposing forces is dramatized in *Ulysses* in the character of Stephen Dedalus. As the day progresses he moves slowly but steadily away from Mulligan's influence and toward Molly's. He is the only character in the book who thinks self-consciously about artistic and linguistic processes; he is also the only character who uses the image of weaving metaphorically in attempts to give shape to his experience and thought. He first does so in thinking of Mulligan's verbal sterility:

> Words Mulligan had spoken a moment since in mockery to the stranger. Idle mockery. The void awaits surely all them that weave the wind. (p. 21)

Here the weaving image identifies Mulligan's language as mere words, purposeless rhetoric, and establishes the identification of such rhetoric with wind which will become thematic in *Aeolus*.[28] At this point Stephen assumes that an artist can do nothing with such material, such futility and anarchy: 'the void awaits surely all them that weave the wind'. But four pages later, in the next chapter, Stephen employs this image somewhat differently as the temporary culmination of a lengthy mental digression from the history lesson he is teaching:

> Had Pyrrhus not fallen by a beldam's hand in Argos or Julius Caesar not been knifed to death? They are not to be thought away. Time has branded them and fettered they are lodged in the room of the infinite possibilities they have ousted. But can those have been possible seeing that they never were? Or was that only possible which came to pass? Weave, weaver of the wind. (p. 25)

This invocation of the process Stephen had earlier condemned seems to mark a slight, perhaps unconscious change in his attitude toward the power and purposes of art. The questions he had just been asking are rationally unanswerable; to that extent they seem mere waste of breath, like Mulligan's idle mockery. If nothing can be made out of nothing, the weaving of such thoughts together can lead only to the void. But what if the artistic process of weaving itself can contribute some positive meaning to the patterning of initially meaningless material? This question does not arise consciously in Stephen's mind; the image of the weaver seems rather to appear here without connection to what came before. It is an intuitive welling up of creativity in response to rational bafflement; a summoning up of artistic process like Homer's invocation of the Muse.

This invocation yields a sequence of immediate results: Stephen interrupts his history lesson, turns the class to a recitation of *Lycidas*, and when his own thoughts resume it is to formulate an answer to his earlier questions: 'it must be movement, then, an actuality of the possible as possible'. The answer is framed in rational terms, but it has apparently been woven into this pattern through the mediation of an essentially creative and rationally inexplicable power. Inspiration has provided a synthesis where rational dialectic had failed; the process of creative affirmation which will reveal itself clearly only in *Penelope* has here intervened to weave Stephen's thoughts together in a moment of epiphany. All the major characters of *Ulysses* experience such moments, but only Stephen seems to be moving toward conscious control of the process involved.

In the paragraphs leading up to this moment, Stephen's mind circles around an awareness of this creative process through a sequence of images and phrases borrowed from William Blake. Weldon Thornton identifies the main source of these allusions as 'A Vision of the Last Judgment', in which Blake writes that

> Fable or Allegory are a totally distinct & inferior kind of Poetry. Vision or Imagination is a representation of what Eternally Exists, Really & Unchangeably. Fable or Allegory is Form'd by the daughters of Memory. Imagination is surrounded by the daughters of Inspiration, who in aggregate are call'd Jerusalem.

This passage challenges the Platonic claim that reason and philosophy have access to a realm of ideal forms which reality imitates at one remove and poetry at two; Blake contends that visionary poetry directly represents not merely reality, but the ideal forms themselves. In explaining Blake's contrast between the lesser 'Daughters of Memory' and the greater 'Daughters of Inspiration' Thornton quotes Arthur Symons, who argues that to Blake 'observation was one of the daughters of memory, and he had no use for her among his Muses, which were all eternal, and the children of the imagination'. Thornton also glosses

Stephen's weaving imagery with a statement from Blake's *Jerusalem*: 'the Daughters of Albion Weave the Web / Of Ages and Generations'.[29] Blake distinguishes – like Coleridge in his separation of fancy and imagination – between two kinds of mental process: memory, fable, observation on one hand, and inspiration, imagination, vision on the other. This distinction resembles the contrast between Penelope's daily and nightly activities: in the daytime she seems to join the daughters of Memory in weaving 'the Web / Of Ages and Generations'; but in unweaving it at night she reveals her true identity as one of the daughters of Inspiration, Blake's Muses, the children of the imagination. Stephen never meets Molly in *Ulysses*, but part of his necessary growth as an artist involves learning to hear and recognize in himself the voice of the process she represents.

Stephen's second extended use of weaving imagery is in *Scylla and Charybdis*:

– As we, or mother Dana, weave and unweave our bodies, Stephen said, from day to day, their molecules shuttled to and fro, so does the artist weave and unweave his image. And as the mole on my right breast is where it was when I was born, though all my body has been woven of new stuff time after time, so through the ghost of the unquiet father the image of the unliving son looks forth. In the intense instant of imagination, when the mind, Shelley says, is a fading coal, that which I was is that which I am and that which in possibility I may come to be. (p. 194)

Here Stephen speaks of both weaving and unweaving; his understanding of artistic process has expanded to comprehend both phases of Penelope's activity, though Joyce seems deliberately to keep her image out at the borders of Stephen's consciousness. But 'mother Dana', the Celtic goddess of plenty and fertility, represents here a life process exactly analogous to weaving as a symbol of art; she is credited with a biological patterning, a weaving of molecules in endless motion which create in aggregate an impression of cohesion, unity, identity. Such an explanation of life is purely mythical, an unscientific personification of an unobservable power. Mother Dana's resemblance to Molly Bloom suggests that Molly, in her symbolic role as Gea-Tellus (p. 737), is present in all life, just as in her symbolic role as Muse she is present throughout *Ulysses*. Stephen's first two sentences in this passage are similes; he is careful to compare biological and artistic inspiration as though they were two separate things. But the union of both processes in Molly Bloom suggests a merging of tenor and vehicle in what is essentially a single power; the springs of art are identical with the springs of life. It is this identity of Mother Dana with the Muse which ultimately enables Stephen to speak of the artist's life and work as parallel results of the same process.

What is unique in the artist is his ability to draw upon that inner life process consciously, to work with it and shape it, to 'weave and unweave his image'. In 'the intense instant of imagination', this life process welling up inside enables him to project his own consciousness into that of an external object, in Aristotelian terms to find 'in the world without as actual what was in his world within as possible' (p. 213). Stephen decided earlier in the day with the aid of this process itself that the history of external reality is 'an actuality of the possible as possible'; earlier in *Scylla and Charybdis*, he has defined the opposite of history – 'what might have been' – as 'possibilities of the possible as possible' (p. 193). Art is neither of these, neither mere actuality nor mere possibility; it is rather the bringing of consciousness into consonance with reality through the mediation of the Muse, through the intervention of that process of inspiration which quickens both imagination and life.

One of Joyce's achievements in *Ulysses* is to have found an internal fictional consonance with the modern 'futility and anarchy' which he found without in the world as actual; the result is a work of art into which representations of that futility and anarchy are woven as parts of a larger whole. In a metaphorical reversal of vehicle and tenor entirely appropriate to the essential unity of the process involved, Eliot spoke of this achievement as 'a step toward making the modern world possible for art'.[30] Art redeems actuality by showing its consonance with possibility; the construction of artistic possibilities is inherently creative rather than destructive, affirmative rather than negative. But in Eliot's view, this redemptive function of art has become a difficult one, for Joyce as for all modern artists. The modern world has become increasingly complex, the winds of futility and anarchy increasingly strong; to incorporate such actualities into the web of art and establish their consonance with fictional possibilities, artists have had to weave ever more elaborate and innovative patterns. In *Ulysses*, numerous contradictory winds of words released in Dublin, Ireland, the whole modern world, are gradually woven up into the still pattern of art. The spirit of Mulligan and Antinous would compel the completion of this web, making the novel's characters and human meaning disappear behind an opaque fabric of words. The sinister sense of the word web describes the effect of the fabric that is woven while their daily influence prevails; it is a snare, an entanglement, designed only to trap and destroy. But this web of wind never reaches completion, never becomes the final goal of artistic process; the Muse's nightly unweaving of her daily work still promises that 'her mind is set on other things'. Each day's external conditions contribute to the pattern of art, but the Muse begins each day with a fresh receptivity to potential changes in those conditions.

Joyce's symbolic development of Molly, Mulligan and Stephen thus helps to shape the evolving formal pattern of the novel. The analogy with weaving suggests that the form of *Ulysses* contains two elements and a dramatically rendered process: a warp of rationality and a woof of words, woven together by an artist listening for and following the voice of creative possibility. Rationality, like the warp, is ordered but artistically incomplete; words, like the threads of woofing, are in themselves artistically meaningless, but capable of producing meaning when an inspiriting process brings them into conjunction with an organizing structure. The different narrators of *Ulysses* correspond to variations in the colour or consistency of the woof, the different ordering strategies to variations in the warp; the process of bringing these two elements together results from a cooperation of artist and Muse, of will and potential artistic order.[31] But the final chapter departs from this formal structure, unravels it, in order to suggest an undiluted version of the artistic potential that binds up the whole.

III

In an often-quoted sentence from a letter to Harriet Weaver, Joyce claims that *Ithaca* 'is in reality the end as *Penelope* has no beginning, middle or end'.[32] This statement is actually a non-sequitur: the lack of internal temporal structure cannot prevent a part from functioning in the temporal structure of a larger whole. But the statement does suggest Joyce's awareness that in *Ithaca* he had completed the web of allusion and narrative which is the form of the first seventeen chapters. *Penelope* is not part of this web, but is Joyce's attempt to render into English prose the voice of creative inspiration, of potentiality, which flowed before and throughout *Ulysses* and will continue after its close. It is this process of creativity in life and art which is timeless; in *Penelope* itself Joyce can only offer a fragment of the infinite whole. Like any fragment of prose, *Penelope* necessarily possesses some temporal structure, although Joyce has made it resemble unstructured process as closely as he can by the virtual elimination of stops and other punctuation. But this fragment of essentially unmediated creative process is sufficient to reverse the meaning of the earlier pattern of *Ulysses*, just as Penelope's nightly unweaving of her daily work reverses our perception of her intentions.

Within this all-encompassing peripeteia in *Ulysses* Joyce offers numerous smaller ones, syncopations in the rhythm of the narrative. At least one of these smaller syncopations parallels the larger strategy. At the end of *Nausicaa*, as at the end of *Ithaca*, Bloom summarizes the events of his day as a prelude to sleep (pp. 380, 728-9). And in *Nausicaa*, as in *Ithaca*, Bloom's final drifting off into sleep is followed by the emergence of a proximate female voice:

> Because it was a little canarybird bird that came out of its little house to tell the time that Gerty MacDowell noticed the time she was there because she was as quick as anything about a thing like that, was Gerty MacDowell . . . (p. 382)

This partial prefiguration of the end of *Ulysses* is itself a false end; Bloom is asleep but not yet at home, and Gerty's natural female share in creative process is crippled both by her obsessive awareness of time and by the absence of Molly's initial 'yes', which affirms external reality and saves the creative process from solipsism. But despite these differences, the end of *Nausicaa* bears a structural resemblance to the end of *Ulysses*, and hence the chapter after *Nausicaa* – *Oxen of the Sun* – offers a symbolic prefiguration of the future that will follow the book as a whole.

Oxen of the Sun revolves around two events external to the actions of Bloom and Stephen: a crack of thunder which heralds the coming of rain to end a long drought in Dublin (p. 394), and the birth of Mina Purefoy's child (p. 406). These events seem to possess special power in the structure of *Ulysses*. Richard Ellmann remarks that 'the thunderstorm as a vehicle of divine power and wrath moved Joyce's imagination so profoundly that to the end of his life he trembled at the sound'.[33] Here in *Oxen of the Sun*, Joyce describes the thunder in language that echoes Stephen's definition of God as a shout in the street (p. 34):

> A black crack of noise in the street here, alack, bawled, back. Loud on left Thor thundered: in anger awful the hammer-hurler . . . as the god self was angered. (p. 394)

In terms of the Homeric parallel, this moment is a prefiguration of apocalypse: Apollo destroys Odysseus's men for their sacrilege in eating the sacred cattle; in *Ulysses*, 'the god that was in a very grievous rage . . . would presently lift his arm and spil' the souls of Mulligan's consorted crew 'for their abuses' (p. 396). As Biblical allusion, the moment also recreates the beginning of the Flood; Mulligan's denial of life is a sacrilege which condemns him to the ultimate fate of Penelope's suitors, Odysseus's sailors, and Noah's sinning contemporaries. But closely following the apocalyptic warning in *Oxen of the Sun* is the new birth, the promised renewal of human life. Rain falls immediately, ending the 'drought' and 'barrenness' (p. 396), so that when the characters leave the hospital, they find that 'the air without is impregnated with raindew moisture, life essence celestial' (p. 423). As in Eliot's *Waste Land*, the world has been waiting for rain; in *Ulysses* that rain actually comes, making possible fertility and generation.

The cataclysmic end foretold in *Oxen* is thus, like Biblical apocalypse, temporarily deferred; the thunderclap and birth become prefigurations of a greater cataclysm and rebirth beyond the end of *Ulysses*. One of the novel's largest structuring patterns is Biblical: *Ulysses* proceeds from the genesis of Mulligan's mock-creation in *Telemachus*, though the birth of the son and the word in *Oxen*, to the revelation of *Penelope*. Like the Biblical Revelation, *Penelope* predicts the end of the world we have known in the preceding pages, just as Penelope's faith in her husband's return predicts the end of her years of waiting; but faith can predict and envision only events, not times: 'of that day and hour knoweth no man, no, not the angels of heaven, but my Father only' (Matthew 24:36). Joyce makes explicit in *Ulysses* what Kermode finds implicit in the form of all fictions: the use of a Christian temporal model in which the meaning of each moment is derived from its relation to an envisioned end.

The event which, in Kermode's terms, purges Leopold Bloom's life 'of simple chronicity, of the emptiness of *tock-tick*, humanly uninteresting successiveness', is clearly his wife's adultery on 16 June 1904, an event which makes that day 'a significant season, *kairos* poised between beginning and end'.[34] Critical consensus in recent years has gradually reached the conclusion that Molly's affair with Blazes Boylan is her first adultery, and that Bloom's list of her lovers in *Ithaca* is a purely imaginative compound of his own jealousy and fantasies.[35] That list is thus the final and most complete concealment of Molly behind the book's narrative and allusive web, one which it has taken readers and critics fifty years to unravel. The new consensus, in addition to restoring much of Molly's long-stained honor, has discredited earlier theories that *Ulysses* is merely meant to represent an 'ordinary day' in the life of the Blooms. This change has renewed critical interest in seeing Leopold and Molly as realistic rather than symbolic characters, as people engaged in a struggle with growth and change in themselves and in each other rather than as static human pieces manipulated according to Joyce's cosmic scheme.

Yet the importance of Molly's first adultery, now that we have learned to read it rightly, also appears in Joyce's symbolic manipulation of his fictional chronology. Milly Bloom reached puberty on September 15, 1903, probably the same day that Mina Purefoy's baby was conceived, 'a period of 9 months and one day' before 16 June. During this nine months Bloom has noticed

> a limitation of activity, mental and corporal, inasmuch as complete mental intercourse between himself and [Molly Bloom] had not taken place.

Her daughter's fertility seems to have conceived in Molly's mind a movement away from Bloom and toward adultery, as part of a complex awareness of her own

> limitation of fertility inasmuch as . . . there remained a period of 10 years, 5 months and 18 days during which carnal intercourse has been incomplete.

Odysseus was missing on his travels for only ten years; on the Homeric calendar, Bloom is some five and one-half months overdue, which has led to

> various reiterated feminine interrogation concerning the masculine destination whither, the place where, the time at which, the duration for which, the object with which in the case of temporary absences, projected or effected. (p. 736)

Molly's prerogative to ask such questions is in part suggested by its being leap year, as in the year of her engagement and marriage sixteen years before; Joyce reinforces this chronological suggestiveness by setting the book in the fourth leap year of the Bloom's marriage, in the fourth year of the century, and on the sixteenth day of the month. The four year cycle also recalls the length of time during which Penelope was able to deceive her suitors by weaving and unweaving her web. Joyce's extensive temporal organization focusing on this day helps to confirm that the meaning of *Ulysses* lies not in its presentation of simple Dublin chronicity, but in its presentation of a season, *kairos*, in which the characters may create significance and change.

Molly's soliloquy is therefore significant both in its symbolic role as a revelation of the novel's structure, and in its realistic role as a revelation of Molly's psychological response to her situation. These two kinds of significance support each other in *Penelope* and evolve toward the novel's final moment of vision together. The chapter begins its structural reversal of the novel's previous direction with Molly's immediate ability to win the reader over into hearing out what she has to say for herself. For hundreds of pages our sympathies have been engaged with Bloom; all we know so far of his wife is that she is domineering, lazy, uneducated (from her brief appearance in *Calypso*) and that she has probably been unfaithful to the hero earlier in the day (from narrative hints and from Bloom's preeminent obsession). Yet for most readers Molly is able to defeat this accumulated skepticism – partly, of course, through our relief at meeting a genuine human voice again after struggling through the web of style imposed between reader and characters in the penultimate chapters of the book. But almost at once the force of her personality imposes its own demands upon the reader's capacity for sympathy and interest. Joyce's choice of Molly to manage the vast concluding peripeteia of *Ulysses* confirms the importance of her character in the structure of the novel, but the convincing mixture of compassion and irony with which she is drawn as a character is also largely responsible for the extent to which the symbolic structure succeeds.[36]

IV

In turning now to *Penelope* itself, I want to look closely at the movement and texture of its opening 'sentence' in order to explore this evolving relationship between Molly's character and the novel's symbolic form. As the movement of her mind unweaves the narrative and allusive web of the novel, it repeatedly duplicates on a smaller scale the larger pattern of progression and reversal; formal analysis of a part can therefore predict and suggest, as in Biblical exegesis, the structure of the whole.

Penelope's opening 'yes' plays a formal role in part analogous to the key signature of an aria; it defines the dominant tone of Molly's mind by providing the note of affirmation to which her soliloquy continually recurs and with which it will conclude. But the initial 'yes' is also the answer to an ungiven question, which presumably either preceeds it in Molly's thoughts, or which – more likely – is so strongly present at a level immediately below her stream of consciousness that she feels no need to put it to herself in words. In either case the initial word contributes to the sense of beginning in *medias res*; as readers we feel that we are breaking in on a process which, like life and art, has been going on before we arrived at the scene. But what is the question to which 'yes' is the answer? The first succeeding clause helps to narrow the range of possibility by providing a reason for the answer: 'Yes because he never did a thing like that before as ask to get his breakfast in bed with a couple of eggs' (p. 738). Molly adduces her affirmative answer from Bloom's behaviour; the ungiven question is clearly about her husband, and almost certainly concerns some change she has observed in him.[37]

In the course of her first sentence, this absent question gradually emerges as Molly's central concern. Her next clause qualifies the word 'never' in the first – 'since the *City Arms* hotel' – and begins a long digression that serves, however, the important structural purpose of connecting Molly's memory with Stephen's and Bloom's (and the reader's) through the figure of Dante Riordan, whose presence in Joyce's fictional world extends all the way back to the early pages of *Portrait*. This digression is followd by a second, again conjured up by the first qualifying clause – 'since the *City Arms* hotel when he used to be pretending to be laid up with a sick voice' – on Bloom's deficiencies as an invalid, in particular, and on the constitutional tendency of men to exaggerate pain and illness, in general. But this second digression is interrupted by an abrupt change in thought from illness to Bloom's sexual activity:

> of course the woman hides it [illness or pain] not to give all the trouble they do yes he came somewhere Im sure by his appetite (p. 738)

This thematic shift seems to refer back to something she has thought about earlier; 'Im sure' suggests a sudden resolution of previous uncertainty. Because it refers to nothing given in the chapter so far, the clause 'yes he came somewhere Im sure by his appetite' seems to function in parallel with the first clause of the chapter and to derive from the absent initial question.

This interest in Bloom's sexual activity becomes the dominant theme in the early stages of her soliloquy. Molly's mind now goes to work at figuring out the circumstances of the orgasm that she guesses Bloom has had since she last saw him: 'anyway its not love or hed be off his feed thinking of her'. She intuits the lies and omissions in his narration of the day's events: maybe 'it was one of those night women if it was down there he really was and the hotel story he made up a big pack of lies to hide it' (pp. 738–9). Molly's perceptions about her husband's sexual activity are quite accurate; her second guess that Bloom has had a sexual experience 'on the sly' with 'some little bitch or other' may even conjure up Gerty MacDowell in the reader's mind. But she does not give any thought at all to the possibility that Bloom's orgasm was merely onanistic. I think that this blind spot arises from her current preoccupation with adultery; she needs to imagine Bloom's guilt in attempting to assuage her own. This need is so great that it temporarily overcomes possessive jealousy: 'not that I care two straws who he does it with' she insists (p. 739); but the jealousy will emerge more strongly later for having been suppressed here.[38]

Assuming Molly's adultery with Boylan to be her first provides both a starting point for the monologue and an explanation of its structure. Her preoccupation with adultery suggests that she feels subconsciously guilty; since she refuses to entertain guilt consciously, she projects her own motivations and actions onto her husband:

> yes because he couldnt possibly do without it that long so he must do it somewhere and the last time he came on my bottom when was it the night . . . (p. 740)

This clause is again one which functions in parallel with the first clause of the chapter in referring back to an unknown question. Since Molly's ability to suppress internal moral qualms clearly depends in some measure upon Bloom's response to her adultery, I would guess that the absent initial question takes some such form as this: Will my life with him be changed now? ('yes because he never did a thing like that before') or Will he help to justify me by also being unfaithful? ('Yes he came somewhere I'm sure . . . yes because he couldn't possibly do without it that long').

She knows that Bloom is aware of her adultery; in the morning, he made and mentioned his plans for the day in order to give Molly a clear afternoon and evening: 'he has an idea about [Boylan] and me hes not such a fool he said Im dining out and going to the Gaiety' (p. 740). This conscious complicity recalls for Molly the pattern of their sexual life for the past ten years, which has been a curious mixture of joint fantasies about Molly's making love with other men and various kinds of non-coital stimulation and orgasm. In justifying her adultery, she finds the limited sexual activity in her marriage both immoral and inadequate: 'you can feel him trying to make a whore of me what he never will . . . no satisfaction in it pretending to like it till he comes then finish it off myself anyway'. But even after these efforts at self-justification, the first direct reference to her adultery is significantly flat:

> anyhow its done now once and for all with all the talk of the world about it people make its only the first time after that its just the ordinary do it (p. 740).

Despite this effort at understatement, Molly never loses sight of the central fact that she has finally acted instead of merely imagining action. Bloom's mind, capable of the Christian view that adultery in one's heart and in one's actions are equivalent, is able to reach equanimity by lumping Boylan together in his notorious catalogue with other men whom he and Molly have imagined as her lovers; Molly, with her superbly literal mind, is totally unable to maintain such confusions of fantasy with reality.

Molly's guilt, insecurity and uncertainty develop much more vividly in the course of the page that follows this initial, oblique confrontation with the afternoon's implications. She veers off into thinking of how much she enjoys a more innocent sexual activity – kissing – but she remembers a slightly more intimate early encounter (being touched on the bottom) only in the context of a subsequent interrogation in the confessional. Molly's nature is ardently sensual, but her values are those of middle class respectability; she supresses and condemns her impulses toward deviant sexual activity, or attempts – as here in her speculation on the sexual lives of priests – to implicate others in similar deviance (p. 741). But again abruptly and with no transition, one of her most immediate anxieties wells up: 'I wonder was he satisfied with me.' Beneath the unblushing directness of her thoughts lie deep insecurities about how she is perceived and whether she is accepted by the others in her world.

Characteristically, she counters the challenge of such insecurity by mentally taking the offensive:

> I wonder was he satisfied with me one thing I didn't like his slapping me behind going away so familiarly in the hall though I laughed I'm not a horse or an ass am I (p. 741)

But her having laughed rather than take issue at the time betrays her nervous unwillingness to risk losing even the little companionship and sympathy Boylan can provide; she wonders 'is he awake thinking of me or dreaming am I in it'. After a digressive series of recollections sparked by the way he smelled, she recalls that 'he had all he could do to keep himself from falling asleep after the last time'. Then the dominant chord emerges, again in structural parallel with the first line of the chapter: 'yes because I felt lovely and tired myself and fell asleep as sound as a top the moment I popped straight into bed'. In the immediate context, this statement responds to her uncertainty about whether Boylan was 'satisfied with me'; sleepiness is adduced as evidence of sexual satiation, at least. But in the context of structural patterning in the chapter thus far, the evidence of Bloom's present sound sleep becomes a further proof of his sexual activity during the day. She does not know about his nap on the beach in *Nausicaa*, but the reader now knows that the Blooms were simultaneously though separately napping at around nine p.m. after experiencing different forms of sexual release.

Molly's conscience was first awakened when, without warning, potential apocalypse interrupted her slumber:

> that thunder woke me up as if the world was coming to an end God be merciful to us I thought the heavens were coming down about us to punish when I blessed myself and said a Hail Mary like those awful thunderbolts in Gibraltar and they come and tell you theres no God what could you do if it was [the world ending] running and rushing about nothing only make an act of contrition (p. 741)

This is the same thunder the other characters heard in *Oxen of the Sun*, symbolically foreboding the end of the world and God's judgment of sinners, but literally forerunning the life essence of rain and the birth of a child. The depth of Molly's remembered fear more accurately measures the extent of her guilt that anything she has yet expressed; she fears a vengeful heaven 'coming down about us to punish', for adultery among other sins, but she realizes that even if the end of the world were imminent she could do no more to ward off judgment than she has done: say a Hail Mary, make an act of contrition, and trust in God. This simple faith of Molly's, which is representative of the flesh, stands in ironic contrast to the agonies of religious conscience which Stephen suffers as representative of the mind.

Yet Molly does not fully regain her equilibrium for some time after this recollection. She experiences a series of abrupt shifts in thought, apparently in an attempt to suppress the guilt which the thunderclap has stirred, before memory of the afternoon's activities with Boylan wells up in explicit detail. The memories are not altogether positive; she recalls 'that determined vicious look in his eye', and remembering her rudimentary efforts at birth control ('I made him pull it out and do it on me') leads to new concerns:

> nice invention they made for women for him to get all the pleasure but if someone gave them a touch of it [child bearing] themselves theyd know what I went through with Milly nobody would believe (p. 742)

Her fear of pregnancy leads to a far less admiring view of Mr. Purefoy than we received in *Oxen of the Sun*:

> Mina Purefoys husband . . . filling her up with a child or twins once a
> year regular as the clock always with a smell of children off her . . . last
> time I was there a squad of them falling over one another and bawling
> . . . not satisfied till they have us swollen out like elephants

But then, unexpectedly although typically, Molly reverses herself:

> swollen out like elephants or I dont know what supposing I risked
> having another not off him [Boylan] though still if he was married Im
> sure hed have a fine strong child but I dont know Poldy has more spunk
> in him yes thatd be awfully jolly (p. 742)

From here to the end of her first sentence, Bloom is the controlling
presence in her thought. What has happened? The thought of conceiving
a child, as long as it was associated with Boylan, was almost entirely
negative; but when associated with Bloom, the idea becomes 'awfully
jolly', even though in her experience pregnancy is a matter of emotional
and physical risk. The idea of childbearing mediates the movement of her
thought from Boylan to Bloom, a pattern reduplicated in the structure of
the chapter as a whole.

Several critics have traced the gradual movement of Molly's mind over
the course of the soliloquy from early acceptance to final rejection of
Boylan, and, simultaneously, from initial indifference to ultimate
acceptance of Bloom. I want to accept such readings without repeating in
full the textual evidence from which they derive.[39] Although Molly's
mind takes one step backward for every two ahead, the general direction
of this shift in attitude remains clear. The first sentence predicts such a
progressive structure; near its close, Molly asserts of Bloom:

> that I could quite easily get him to make it up any time I know how . . .
> I know plenty of ways ask him to tuck down the collar of my blouse or
> touch him with my veil and gloves on going out 1 kiss then would send
> them all spinning (p. 743)

A page later, the final appearance for many pages of the 'yes because'
chord signals an explanation of her power over him, generalized in its
application to all husbands and all wives: 'what do they ask us to marry
them for if were so bad as all that comes to yes because they cant get on
without us' (p. 744). Molly's confidence that she can get Bloom back if
she wants to makes her receptivity to the idea of having his child more
significant; no fear of failure will prevent her from attempting a

reconciliation if her preliminary movement towards Bloom here in the first sentence finally prevails. The paradox embodied in this chapter is that Molly's act of adultery is what ultimately leads to her renewed interest in her husband; at its realistic level, the soliloquy reveals the complex mental process by which this renewal is accomplished.

At the symbolic as well as at the realistic level, the pattern of Molly's soliloquy thus far offers a model for the recurring patterns of the whole chapter. The pattern is, in the first place, musical: a dominant theme, often introduced in the first sentence by the words 'yes' and 'because', recurs at different intervals in slightly different forms. Between these appearances of the main theme are variations – what I have up to now called digressions – but variations which are not purely digressive because they derive from the main theme and supplement it. The soliloquy continually circles around Molly's adultery and her estimation of Bloom's response; her own attitude toward her adultery is continually modified by the emergence and incorporation into consciousness of latent anxieties and doubts. The main theme of her soliloquy always reappears abruptly, unexpectedly, without immediately apparent connection to what came before. This structural pattern is analogous to the process of weaving: each variation has a place in the whole pattern; each reemergence of the dominant theme is like the sudden return of the shuttle across the loom. But the return is always slightly more than a simple repetition. Weaving is progressive as well as cyclical; each return of the shuttle is to a point slightly ahead of the one reached by the previous return.

Such a temporal model resembles the Yeatsian gyre, which envisions history as a spiral in which each age achieves both progress and a cyclical repetition of the past. In the Yeatsian model two such spirals operate simultaneously, one expanding outward while the other is closing inward.[40] This model actually resembles the form of *Ulysses* quite precisely; the process of unweaving in *Penelope* liberates and expands its materials, whereas the weaving of the earlier chapters contracts and limits them. One can envision the process by which *Penelope* unravels the web of *Ulysses* as an outward spiral, in contrast to the downward spiral (or whirlpool) which is associated in *Scylla and Charybdis* with Mulligan, and which would draw all experience in toward one dark goal.[41] The expanding gyre and the unravelling web also resemble the 'widening circle' that Lawrence incorporates into the form of *The Rainbow* to suggest the pattern of Ursula's experience. In *Ulysses* the final full stop of *Ithaca*, like a conventional novelistic ending, draws our experience of the novel in to one still centre; but on that point the whole novel turns, massively, and initiates its counter-movement outward toward Molly's final, culminating vision. Molly unweaves the web of infidelity she has woven during the day; at the same time, the creative process she represents unweaves the narrative web of the novel, radically changing the reader's perception of its final direction and shape.

V

In unweaving and finally reversing her daytime movement away from her husband, Molly's mind ranges backward and forward through her experience, invoking both recollection of the past and imagination of the future. But as the final moment of vision approaches, her focus is increasingly fixed on the future. At the end of sentence seven she fantasizes about a future affair with Stephen in idealized terms which do not coincide at all with what we know of him: she thinks he would be young and clean, like the 'fine young men' bathing at Margate (but Stephen is a hydrophobe), and she concludes that he cannot be a 'stuck up university student' because 'otherwise he wouldn't go sitting down in the old kitchen with him [Bloom] taking Epps cocoa' (but Stephen is clearly an intellectual snob despite this odd adventure) (p. 775). Nevertheless, Molly's idealized picture of Stephen provides a striking contrast to her realistic knowledge of Boylan, and leads at the beginning of sentence eight to the strongest negative of the chapter:

> no thats no way for him has he no manners nor no refinement nor no nothing in his nature slapping us behind like that on my bottom because I didnt call him Hugh the ignoramus that doesnt know poetry from a cabbage . . . of course hes right enough in his way to pass the time as a joke sure you might as well be in bed with what with a lion God Im sure hed have something better to say for himself an old Lion would (p. 776)

Stephen has helped to slay Boylan in Molly's mind; but Stephen did not stay in Eccles Street and will not return, opening the possibility for Bloom to emerge as the most desireable lover after all:

> of course a woman wants to be embraced . . . no matter by who so long as to be in love or loved by somebody if the fellow you want isnt there (p. 777)

Her shared past with Bloom suggests that he alone can be the 'fellow' she wants who isn't there; like Penelope, she is still waiting for her husband's return.

Penelope is as enigmatic as the rest of *Ulysses* in its refusal to explain exactly what is wrong with the Blooms' marriage, or to assign the blame to either Molly or Leopold for their prolonged separation. But the thought of Stephen carries Molly inexorably back to the origin of that separation:

> well its a poor case that those that have a fine son like that [Stephen] theyre not satisfied and I none ... it wasnt my fault ... that disheartened me altogether I suppose I oughtnt to have buried him in that little woolly jacket I knitted crying as I was but give it to some poor child but I knew well Id never have another our 1st death too it was we were never the same since O Im not going to think myself into the glooms about that anymore (p. 778)

This passage is moving because Molly is still uncertain if she was right to let her loyalty to one lost child prevail over an instinctive, anonymous charity toward the living. As a symbolic manifestation of the life process, Molly is unthinkingly faithful to the life that goes on, but as a realistic character she is individuated from that process by her personal capacity to experience human suffering. Molly also perceives this experience as one she shares with her husband: 'our first death . . . we were never the same since'. For a page she resumes her fantasy about Stephen to get herself out of the 'glooms', but then announces, abruptly, that she will 'just give him [Bloom] one more chance'. She will make his breakfast and try to seduce him in the morning. But she will not try to pretend that today's infidelity – a possibility they have often discussed – has not occurred: 'I'll let him know if thats what he wanted that his wife is fucked yes and damn well fucked too up to my neck nearly not by him' (p. 780). Bloom's participation in her guilt is now clear to her: 'its all his own fault if I am an adulteress'. His neglect and his encouragement of her sexual fantasies are entirely to blame for an act which she seems now thoroughly to regret having committed. Adultery has not solved any of her most serious problems, but its failure has forced her to perceive that her hope of happiness lies elsewhere.

Molly's final vision follows and confirms her decision to attempt some form of reconciliation with her husband. It begins with her wish to bring home flowers; flowers function throughout the novel as a punning symbol for Bloom, even in her conscious awareness:

what did I tell him [Mulvey] I was engaged for fun to the son of a
Spanish nobleman named Don Miguel de la Flora and he believed that
I was to be married to him in 3 years time theres many a true word
spoken in jest there is a flower that bloometh (p. 759)

Molly recognizes her marriage to Bloom as the fulfillment of that
unconscious prophecy; her mind's return to him thus conjures up an
associative deluge of flowers in the novel's final pages. She herself is
caught up in the deluge; on Howth Head Bloom called her 'a flower of the
mountain', prefiguring her eventual assumption of his name (p. 782).
Molly also uses flower symbolism to measure an inner debate about the
mood she should adopt in the future. One of the music-hall songs running
through her mind is called 'Shall I Wear a White Rose or Shall I Wear a
Red?' (p. 781). In the language of flowers, a white rose means charm and
innocence; a red, love and desire.[42] As the final vision begins she is
thinking partly of receiving Stephen, who now seems to be an object of
maternal solicitude to her rather than a potential lover: 'whatll I wear
shall I wear a white rose or' she begins, and then breaks off. But sixty lines
later, at the final moment when she fuses the memory of Bloom's proposal
on Howth with the memory of her first sexual experience with Mulvey on
Gibraltar, she completes the allusion: 'or shall I wear a red yes' (p. 783).
The line of song has hung suspended for the whole interval; the entire
vision passes through her mind in a single moment, and the affirmative
tag after 'red' confirms her final choice of love and desire.

The vision is organized around Molly's memory of Bloom's marriage
proposal on Howth Head. Like Wordsworth's experience on Snowdon,
Molly's vision occurs on a mountain top – or at least a commanding hill –
a setting M. H. Abrams characterizes, in speaking of Wordsworth, as 'the
traditional place for definitive visions since Moses had climbed Mount
Sinai'.[43] Joyce emphasizes the importance of this location by giving
Molly an earlier, parallel romantic experience with Lieutenant Mulvey
high up on the Rock of Gibraltar. Both Gibraltar and Howth are
surrounded by water, and both look down on cities; both events also
occur at midday: Molly has her first sexual experience with Mulvey in
'broad daylight' (p. 761) on Gibraltar, and Bloom tells her that 'the sun
shines for you today' (p. 782) on Howth. She is recalling a past when she
felt no need for concealment or self-consciousness, when she could reveal
her heart in sunlight rather than secretly in the night, as now. Her vision
is also, like Wordsworth's, a *remembered* experience. Wordsworth did not
perceive the visionary significance of his experience on Snowdon at the
time that it occurred, but only later, in the process of recovery from an

intervening personal crisis. Like Wordsworth's, Molly's memory is one that is transfigured and reshaped to visionary significance in the moment of recollection. Molly's giving of herself to Bloom is not merely a memory but also a prophecy; the whole monologue progresses toward a prefigured repetition of that event. The vision transforms memory by ascribing significance for the future to a moment in the past.

Joyce does not give the Blooms a reconciliation scene in the novel, but the Homeric parallel suggests that it will occur: Odysseus does return home, and Penelope accepts him as her husband. James Maddox suggests that

> the relationships among the three central characters remain vague at the end of *Ulysses* because Joyce is interested there - as he is interested throughout - in projecting the myriad possibilities contained within the moment, not in pointing to one inevitable event.[44]

But the final vision promises something more specific than simply 'myriad possibilities'. It offers hope for a reconciliation, although it leaves fulfillment in the hands of the characters themselves rather than in the enforced domination of the author. The point is not that Bloom will now make love to Molly and conceive a son - neither event actually occurs - but that the possibility for both has been created. Bloom and Molly are mistaken about Stephen; he is not their son, or a proper substitute, but the contact with Stephen seems to have led both to recognize their need for another child and to have freed them from the paralyzing need for the son who is lost. The narrative irony in this recognition is that Bloom's meeting with Stephen is probably only made possible by Molly's adultery, which prevented him from returning home earlier and which intensified his loneliness, isolation, and need for human contact. The undifferentiated passage of *chronos* has yielded to *kairos*, a season in which the Blooms can change the pattern of their lives. But the characters remain living in the reader's mind in part because Joyce does not insist that they *will* take advantage of their opportunity - only that they are free to do so.

Several critics have asserted that Molly ceases to be a real character in these final pages because she has been fully assimilated into her symbolic role as earth-goddess or life process.[45] Such readings ignore the Biblical tradition of vision as an experience in which an individual can be temporarily translated from a physical to a spiritual plane; in this final moment, Molly is translated from her realistic role as a character to her symbolic role as the source of creative process in art and life. But in this translation she also retains her human identity, so that she is simultaneously individual and archetype, at once Molly and the Earth, Molly and Penelope, Molly and the Muse. Visionary experience transfigures but does not disfigure the individual. Thus Molly's vision incorporates a double past: tonight she remembers the moment on Howth, but in the moment on Howth she also paused to remember her earlier past in Gibraltar: she 'wouldnt answer first only looked out over the sea and the sky I was thinking of so many things he didnt know of' (p. 782). The past Bloom does not know of is the unique history of personal experience which individuates her as a character from the life process which is about to unite her with Bloom, and of which she is a part.

By recalling her past in this moment of potential self-surrender, Molly forces the moment to be personal as well as archetypal, making her engagement an act of union rather than of submission. She gives herself without giving up herself, finally fusing her personal past with the archetypal present:

> Gibraltar as a girl where I was a Flower of the mountain yes when I put the rose in my hair like the Andalusian girls used or shall I wear a red yes and how he [Mulvey] kissed me under the Moorish wall and I thought well as well him [Bloom] as another (p. 783)

Time is transcended here to make Molly's acceptance of Bloom concurrent and identical with her earlier acceptance of Mulvey. Her past experience as a character is not subsumed but is incorporated in her submission to the life process; she accepts Bloom but remains an individual strongly committed to maintaining her own integrity and sense of self. In the final passage it is clearly Bloom who submits to Molly, not Molly to Bloom. She 'asked him with my eyes to ask again', and when he does so, 'first I put my arms around him yes and drew him down to me' (p. 783). Molly is in full control of the timing and actions of this moment; in the final embrace, it is Bloom who is passively drawn down and incorporated into the life process of the earth and the woman beneath him.[46]

The final moment of vision of *Ulysses* simultaneously resolves personal tensions in Molly's mind and symbolic tensions in the structure of the novel; the ending ultimately breaks down the division between character and form without destroying the significance of either. Such attempts to connect character with form in modern literature can give rise to surprisingly similar features in dissimilar genres; once again, Wallace Stevens's *The Idea of Order at Key West* suggests clarifying parallels. The woman in *Key West* sings beside the sea; Molly's voice emerges on the shore of the Dublin sea that Bloom has navigated. Both singers shape and humanize forces of nature that are in themselves 'inhuman' and inarticulate, 'never formed to mind or voice'. Stevens makes no attempt to incorporate the words of the woman's song into his poem, whereas Joyce, in *Penelope*, has tried to render a fragment of the creative utterance itself. But like the singer of *Key West*, Molly is finally revealed to be 'the single artificer of the world / In which she sang'. Molly's translation of life process into human language creates the whole world of the novel in which she appears; as Muse, as Penelope, she weaves and unweaves the web of *Ulysses*. In the novel, as in the poem, the interchange between character and nature is reciprocal: 'the sea, / Whatever self it had, became the self / That was her song, for she was the maker'.[47] The life process represented by the sea breathes into and quickens the world of art and its people, so that, as Stephen asserted in *Portrait*,

> the vitality which has flowed and eddied round each person fills every person with such vital force that he or she assumes a proper and intangible esthetic life.[48]

In ordering her universe, Molly retrospectively fills the novel's form and characters with the vital force she draws from the natural world.

Characters, even Muse figures, have no real life beyond the works of art in which they live; the narrator of *Key West* understands of the singer that 'there never was a world for her / Except the one she sang and, singing, made'. Molly and Bloom will forever remain on the verge of reconciliation, like the lovers on Keats's Grecian Urn who can never kiss, 'though winning near the goal'.[49] But the characters take on a new life in the mind of the reader, whose impulse is to complete the meaning and form that Joyce has left trembling on the verge of completion. In *Key West*, Stevens moves beyond the encounter with visionary experience to suggest a narrative response to such experience, one which I think parallels the reader's response to *Penelope*. When the 'singing ended', the narrator becomes conscious of perceiving an enhanced order in the external world:

> The lights in the fishing boats at anchor there,
> As the night descended, tilting in the air,
> Mastered the night and portioned out the sea,
> Fixing emblazoned zones and fiery poles,
> Arranging, deepening, enchanting night.

The man-made fishing boats and lights are harmonized with the sea and night; 'the maker's rage to order words of the sea' enables man to find an ordered place in the natural world. Like the song in *Key West*, Molly's soliloquy emerges out of primordial process in order to change our perception both of 'ourselves and of our origins'. The maker's 'rage for order' is identical with Molly's unselfconscious impulse to articulate, catalogue, and reformulate her experience; both utterances create humanly perceptible order that the Universe cannot make alone.

Molly's kinship with the woman of *Key West* suggests the persistence of the modernist impulse to reveal the ordering *claritas* of a work of art through a character within that work. Joyce himself repeats his use of a concluding, visionary female monologue in *Finnegans Wake*. Anna Livia Plurabelle, like all the characters in the *Wake*, is an archetypal aspect of the life process itself. She is less realistic and more fully realized as a symbolic figure than Molly Bloom, but both soliloquies are spoken by wakeful women while their husbands sleep. Anna Livia is identified with the river Liffey, which passes through Dublin during the course of the final monologue; in its passing the river finally dies into the arms of her father the sea, but the passage promises her reincarnation through the water cycle as newborn rain. The water cycle becomes a figure for life process and for the creative process running through the whole novel, starting with the first word, 'riverrun', which in the circular structure of the book is also the last.[50] In *Finnegans Wake*, Christian temporal structure is incorporated into a cyclical Viconian progress and return, so that the creative tension between the two formal models mirrors the relation between the individual life that ends in death and the process of life itself that never ends.

5

To the Lighthouse: Reshaping the Single Vision

I

E. M. Forster once observed of Virginia Woolf that she believed in reading a book twice:

> The first time she abandoned herself to the author unreservedly. The second time she treated him severely and allowed him to get away with nothing he could not justify. After these two readings she felt qualified to discuss the book.[1]

Woolf was probably almost alone among her contemporaries in applying such a habit of double readings to *Ulysses*. She first encountered the novel in 1918, when Joyce approached the Woolfs through T. S. Eliot about the possibility of publishing it at the Hogarth Press.[2] The incomplete version Woolf saw at this time was more traditional in form and style than the book ultimately published in 1922; in 1918 *Ulysses* certainly contained no chapters resembling *Ithaca* and *Penelope* as we now know them. In an essay written a year later on 'Modern Fiction', Woolf's public response to this version was guardedly enthusiastic. The early chapters of *Ulysses* were being serialized in the *Little Review*; with 'such a fragment before us' her judgements are 'hazarded rather than affirmed', but she believes that Joyce's intention.

> is of the utmost sincerity and that the result, difficult or unpleasant as we may judge it, is undeniably important. . . . The scene in the cemetary, for instance, its sudden lightning flashes of significance, does undoubtedly come so close to the quick of the mind that, on a first reading at any rate, it is difficult not to acclaim a masterpiece. If we want life itself here, surely we have it.[3]

This response follows quite conscientiously the policy of fairness on a first reading; even later, she always spoke of *Ulysses* more respectfully in public than in private.

Her diary and letters reveal, however, that far from abandoning herself to the author 'unreservedly', she felt an uneasy annoyance with Joyce from the first. She describes *Ulysses* as 'monotonous' and 'boring', condemns 'the directness of the language, and the choice of incidents, if there *is* any choice, but as far as I can see there's a certain sameness', and objects strenuously to Joyce's apparent preoccupation with scatology.[4] Yet in 1920, while she was momentarily stuck in writing *Jacob's Room*, she nervously 'reflected how what I'm doing is probably being better done by Mr Joyce'.[5] In August 1922 she began *Ulysses* for the second time, now prepared to judge Joyce seriously:

> I should be reading Ulysses, & fabricating my case for & against. I have read 200 pages so far – not a third; & have been amused, stimulated, charmed interested by the first 2 or 3 chapters – to the end of the Cemetery scene; & then puzzled, bored, irritated, & disillusioned as by a queasy undergraduate scratching his pimples. And Tom [Eliot], great Tom, thinks this on a par with War & Peace!

But she observes that 'I may revise this later. I do not compromise my critical sagacity'.[6] In the end, she remains critical:

> I finished Ulysses, & think it a mis-fire. Genius it has I think; but of the inferior water. The book is diffuse. It is brackish. It is pretentious. It is underbred, not only in the obvious sense, but in the literary sense.[7]

She concedes, however, that 'I have not read it carefully', tacitly acknowledging at least the complexity and difficulty of Joyce's achievement. Only a day later, she read an American review of *Ulysses* which 'analyzes the meaning; & certainly makes it very much more impressive than I judged'.[8] Her anxious vacillation about Joyce suggests a depth of response to his work which she accorded to no other contemporary (with the possible exception of Proust), and which very few among his contemporaries accorded to Joyce.

Woolf was less deeply troubled by Lawrence, but her responses to his novels sometimes suggest a similar ambivalence. In a letter written while she was reading *Women in Love*, she remarks that she

> can't help thinking that there's something wrong with Lawrence, which makes him brood over sex, but he is trying to say something, and he is honest, and therefore he is 100 times better than most of us.[9]

In a review of *The Lost Girl*, which she did not much like, she suggests that on the basis of his other work 'we might have to allow him the praise, than which there is none higher', of being an 'original' writer, because his work is 'disquieting'.[10] It is not clear that she ever read *The Rainbow*. Given her objections to the obscenity in *Ulysses*, she may simply have avoided a book considered so pornographic that it was suppressed upon publication, although she was probably aware that her friends Clive Bell and Lytton Strachey were involved in the public opposition to this act of censorship.[11] In November 1917 she was subjected to having long passages from *The Rainbow* quoted aloud to her by Lady Ottoline Morrell, so that she at least possessed a degree of second-hand familiarity with the text.[12] Lady Ottoline's enthusiasm for Lawrence waned considerably after she was satirized as Hermione in *Women in Love* three years later, but Woolf's respect seems to have increased for the same reason; reading *Women in Love* in July 1921, she writes that Lady Ottoline is 'there to the life'.[13]

Woolf's relationship with her friend E. M. Forster was, in its own way, as complicated as her responses to Lawrence and Joyce. Her diaries reveal clearly that he was the person whose professional opinion of her writing she most respected.[14] Yet her essay on 'The Novels of E. M. Forster' is gently but firmly critical of Forster's fiction; it also suggests how much she herself learned from what she perceived to be his failures. In the work of the greatest writers, she argues, one finds a 'combination of realism and mysticism' unified in a 'single vision'. If the writer's mind 'has completely mastered its perspective', the 'paraphernalia of reality have at certain moments to become the veil through which we see infinity'. The writer achieves this mastery 'not by performing some miraculous conjuring trick at the critical moment', but by

> putting us into the right mood from the very start and by giving us the right materials for his purpose. . . . Thus when the moment of illumination comes we accept it implicitly . . . the thing we are looking at is lit up, and its depths revealed. It has not ceased to be itself by becoming something else . . . the object which has been so uncompromisingly solid becomes, or should become, luminously transparent.

She believes that Forster attempts but fails to achieve this transparency of the world of fact upon the world of vision, so that 'we doubt both things – the real and the symbolical: Mrs. Moore, the nice old lady, and Mrs. Moore, the sibyl. The conjunction of these two realities seems to cast doubt upon them both', and instead of seeing 'one single whole we see two separate parts'.[15]

This goal of the single vision, the simultaneous presence of real and symbolic worlds, seems to me to be fully achieved in *To the Lighthouse*. From the start Woolf provides the materials and creates the mood necessary to make Lily Briscoe's culminating vision believable, so that 'when the moment of illumination comes we accept it implicitly'. The final moment in turn irradiates and transforms the novel as a whole, changing its fabric into a thin veil through which we glimpse, fleetingly but unmistakably, a world beyond our own.[16] Yet Woolf creates this remarkable achievement in visionary form despite, and partly because of, special obstacles and problems. As a woman writing in a predominantly male literary tradition, she must continually transform inherited literary conventions which assume that the artist is a man. In *To the Lighthouse*, she turns this necessity for reshaping convention into a source of narrative strength rather than a liability; as the novel moves toward its final moment of vision, Woolf explores and redefines the roles of artist and Muse from a female perspective.[17]

She begins this process of redefinition with an extraordinary portrait of the conventional relations between female inspiration and male achievement. Mrs. Ramsay, modelled on Woolf's mother Julia Stephen, is a traditional Muse figure. Her beauty and capacity to create social order have inspired poets, although she does not read their poems:

> Alas! even the books that had been given her and inscribed by the hand of the poet himself: "For her whose wishes must be obeyed" . . . "The happier Helen of our days" . . . disgraceful to say, she had never read them.[18]

Like Mrs. Wilcox in *Howards End*, Ursula in *The Rainbow*, Molly Bloom in *Ulysses*, and the woman in *The Idea of Order at Key West*, Mrs. Ramsay is in touch with the creative process which runs through and quickens both life and art. Just as Molly begins *Penelope* with the assent to this process that ultimately underlies and shapes the form of *Ulysses*, Mrs. Ramsay opens *To the Lighthouse* with an inaugural speech – 'Yes, of course, if it's fine tomorrow', – that is strongly (and, from Mr. Ramsay's perspective, even naively) affirmative. But because the author of *To the Lighthouse* is a woman, the presentation of Mrs. Ramsay also offers, for perhaps the first time in literature, an extended and believable inside view of what the Muse herself sees, hears, and feels. Her contact with the creative process is associated, as for other Muse figures, with water and the sea. But in *To the Lighthouse* we listen to the sea through the ears of the Muse herself; she hears

> the monotonous fall of the waves on the beach, which for the most part beat a measured and soothing tattoo to her thoughts and seemed consolingly to repeat over and over again as she sat with the children the words of some old cradle song, murmured by nature, "I am guarding you – I am your support." (p. 27)

Mrs. Ramsay's experience parallels Wordsworth's recollection of the river Derwent, which in his childhood 'loved / To blend his murmurs with my nurse's song', and 'sent a voice / That flowed along my dreams'.[10] As a woman and a Muse, however, Mrs. Ramsay still hears in maturity the special message of consolation that remains for the male poet only in fragmentary memories from childhood.

But the price paid for continuing receptivity to such messages is that this sea which 'for the most part' offers consolation also

> at other times suddenly and unexpectedly . . . had no such kindly meaning, but like a ghostly roll of drums remorselessly beat the measure of life, made one think of the destruction of the island and its engulfment in the sea, and warned her whose day had slipped past in one quick doing after another that it was all ephemeral as a rainbow – this sound which had been obscured and concealed under the other sounds suddenly thundered hollow in her ears and made her look up with an impulse of terror. (pp. 27–8)

The Muse is here in touch with a power in nature that counters and undermines Romantic consolation. This power changes the rainbow – an affirmative symbol for both Forster and Lawrence – into a simile for the transience of human activity; it turns nature's message into a sound that thunders 'hollow' in her ears, like the meaningless echo that speaks in the Marabar caves of *A Passage to India*. As a Muse, Mrs. Ramsay's task is to transmit the consolation of nature into human language and order, while shielding others from this counter-message of terror by taking up its burden and keeping it to herself.

Her role in marriage offers her largest challenge in this double task. Just as Socrates needs to enshrine the irrational philosophic love taught by the woman Diotima at the heart of his rational intellectual life, Mr. Ramsay needs the love and consolation of his wife to carry on his philosophic work. In the scene that reveals most clearly the dynamics of this relationship, Mr. Ramsay arrives at the window demanding sympathy; Mrs. Ramsay

> braced herself, and, half turning, seemed to raise herself with an effort, and at once to pour erect into the air a rain of energy . . . into this delicious fecundity, this fountain and spray of life, the fatal sterility of the male plunged itself. (pp. 58–59)

As in Lawrence and Stevens, the relationship between the male and the Muse is explicitly sexual, associated with imagery of water, illumination and electricity.

The nature of Mr. Ramsay's occupation helps to explain his unusually urgent need for the creative renewal that a Muse figure like Mrs. Ramsay can provide. Andrew's explanation to Lily of Mr. Ramsay's philosophic work – 'subject and object and the nature of reality . . . think of a kitchen table . . . when you're not there' (p. 38) – places him in the British empiricist tradition of Hume and Berkeley; it is a tradition peculiarly conducive to doubts about the reality of the concrete universe. Mrs. Ramsay has the power to bring him out of his philosophic skepticism and to recreate for him the reality of this world:

> she assured him, beyond a shadow of a doubt, by her laugh, her poise, her competence . . . that it was real; the house was full; the garden blowing. If he put implicit faith in her, nothing should hurt him. (p. 60)

Her sympathy does not merely console; it is an effectual act, like the power of divine fiat in a theocentric universe, which creates the world of life for him. Mr. Ramsay is an agnostic by temperament and rational belief (p. 308); Mrs. Ramsay too, though from somewhat different motives, is a religious skeptic: 'How could any Lord have made this world?' she asks herself, thinking of injustice, death and suffering (p. 98). But in a world without God, for Woolf as for Arnold, Forster, and Lawrence, human relations bear the full strain of the human need for meaning and order; in place of the divinity he has rejected, Mr. Ramsay is compelled to 'put implicit faith' in the creative power of his wife alone.

Viewing this relationship of man and Muse from the female perspective, however, Woolf is able to see the traditionally unseen cost of the male's creative renewal. The result of the Ramsays' interaction is that the male is 'restored, renewed' (p. 60), but afterward Mrs. Ramsay 'seemed to fold herself together, one petal closed in another, and the whole fabric fell in exhaustion upon itself' (pp. 60–1). Mrs. Ramsay also feels 'dissatisfaction' in sensing her central importance to him, because 'she did not like, even for a second, to feel finer than her husband' (p. 61). She wants to believe the convention that the Muse is something less than an equal partner in the male's achievement; it distresses her when 'people said he depended on her' (p. 62). But the novel suggests that she is even more successful at her work than her husband is at his. She does not expend all her creative energy for his benefit alone, but has become a kind of professional meaning-maker, weaving her power to create order into the entire social fabric. The dinner party at the end of the novel's first section is her greatest triumph in this medium; she brings together the guests who originally 'all sat separate' (p. 126), gradually 'merging and flowing and creating' a unified occasion out of their unconnected identities.

The special poignancy of Mrs. Ramsay's social art lies in its transcience, which sets it apart from male achievements like her husband's second-rate, but published, philosophy. As she leaves the room at the end of the dinner party, 'it had become, she knew, giving one last look at it over her shoulder, already the past'. The moment of order depends entirely upon the Muse's presence to sustain it; 'directly she went a sort of disintegration set in' (p. 168). But it consoles her to think that 'wound about in their hearts, however long they lived she would be woven' (p. 170). This imagery associates her, as Molly Bloom is associated, with Penelope the weaver; in this role, Mrs. Ramsay stays at home awaiting her husband's return while he is off voyaging through strange seas of thought alone. She has spent the free intervals of her day knitting a stocking as a gift for a child both chronically ill and poor; the stocking thus gradually acquires a value symbolic of her skill in life at knitting up the ravelled sleeve of care, creating a shield of love and order between others and the terror she sometimes hears in the sea.[20] Now she realizes that as long as she lives in memory she will possess the power of shielding and consoling others, 'wound about in their hearts', just as memories of nature preserved from childhood possess that power for Wordsworth. In this mood Mrs. Ramsay experiences 'that community of feeling with other people' which arises from the hidden unity of life; she realizes 'that practically (the feeling was one of relief and happiness) it was all one stream' (p. 170), just as Margaret Schlegel ultimately senses the 'deeper stream' beneath everyday reality in *Howards End*.[21]

The relationship between Mr. Ramsay's world of rationally apprehended fact and Mrs. Ramsay's world of intuitively apprehended vision is figured symbolically in the novel by the central image of the lighthouse itself. Critics have differed markedly over what the lighthouse symbolizes; in treading this ground, it is well to remember Woolf's assertion to Roger Fry that

> I meant *nothing* by The Lighthouse. One has to have a central line down the middle of the book to hold the design together. I saw that all sorts of feelings would accrue to this, but I refused to think them out, and trusted that people would make it the deposit for their own emotions – which they have done, one thinking it means one thing and another another.[22]

But most interpretive differences have pointed toward a consistent explanation, even if it is one that Woolf herself refused to work out consciously. Readers persistently associate the lighthouse with one or the other of the Ramsays – some identifying it with the husband, others with the wife. Mr. Ramsay bears a clear figurative resemblance to the lighthouse tower; Mrs. Ramsay sees him 'as a stake driven into the bed of a channel upon which the gulls perch and the waves beat . . . marking the channel out there in the floods alone' (p. 69). But such a stake possesses no light of its own; the light of the lighthouse is associated, rather, with Mrs. Ramsay:

> Often she found herself sitting and looking . . . until she became the thing she looked at – that light, for example . . . it seemed to her like her own eyes meeting her own eyes . . . for she was stern, she was searching, she was beautiful like that light. (pp. 96–7)

The lighthouse itself is a union of the stake and the beam of light, an intersection of male and female, fact and vision, time and eternity, *chronos* and *kairos*.[23]

The lighthouse thus functions as a unifying image, like Penelope's web for Joyce and the rainbow for Lawrence, in bringing together male rationality and female creativity. The symbol also bears a slight diagrammatic similarity to the cross that the modernists rejected, but differs from the cross in the substitution of a long, moving beam of light for the shorter arm. This change seems to arise from the influence upon modern imagery of the Romantic lamp, the subjective eye irradiating and transforming the world of the objective landscape.[24] On the beam's first appearance in the novel Mrs. Ramsay is sitting in the window, having just finished reading a story to James, when she saw in his eyes, as the interest of the story died away in them, something else take its place; something wondering, pale, like the reflection of a light, which at once made him gaze and marvel. Turning, she looked across the bay, and there, sure enough, coming regularly across the waves first two quick strokes and then one long steady stroke, was the light of the Lighthouse. It had been lit. (p. 94)

This beautifully managed moment focusses the novel's complex use of light imagery to figure human vision. The light of the lighthouse, reflected from James's eyes, both replaces and parallels his interest in the story Mrs. Ramsay has been reading. But the light itself calls up a new subjective response in his eyes, generated from within; at the same time, Mrs. Ramsay experiences by reflection the same succession of perception and wonder, followed by a confirmatory turn of her head which sends her gaze out directly to meet the lighthouse beam and commingle with it.

The window in which Mrs. Ramsay sits is like the window atop the lighthouse; like the tower standing amid the wind and waves, Mr. Ramsay supports the whole material establishment – house, wife, children – 'on philosophy', as William Bankes expresses it (p. 36). From the window Mrs. Ramsay looks out on life, irradiating and transforming the human landscape; from the world beyond others gaze back on her, just as her own gaze reaches out to meet and mirror the lighthouse beam. As Mr. Bankes stood admiring Mrs. Ramsay with Lily beside him,

looking along his beam she added to it her different ray. . . . This ray passed level with Mr. Bankes's ray straight to Mrs. Ramsay. . . . But now while she still looked, Mr. Bankes had done. (pp. 75–6, 80)

This alternating attention parallels the flashes of the lighthouse later in the evening; human vision, inspiration, and active attention to others are intermittent but real, like the lighthouse beam itself.

The light of a lighthouse is refracted out of a revolving prism, to emerge as long tapering beams separated by wedges of darkness which widen as they extend farther away from the tower. The individual character of a particular light depends upon the relation between the intervals of light and darkness; the lighthouse in the novel casts three successive beams, the third lasting somewhat longer than the others.[25] Similarly, Mrs. Ramsay sends out successive flashes of sympathy and illumination to mark the way in life to others. But when she is left alone and at rest, she muses that 'one shrunk . . . to being oneself, a wedge-shaped core of darkness, something invisible' (p. 95). In such moments she sinks down into the dark and deeper unity, like Lawrence's realm of carbon beneath individual character, that lies beneath conscious awareness of the self. Mrs. Ramsay thinks that 'beneath it is all dark, it is all spreading, it is unfathomably deep; but now and again we rise to the surface and that is what you see us by'. When she subsides beneath consciousness into this deeper stream she is not limited to any particular place: 'This core of darkness could go anywhere, for no one saw it' (p. 96). The darkness between the beams of light, which alone defines and delimits them, spreads off into the illimitable universe and ultimately merges with it.

In this consciousless unity with a universal darkness, Mrs. Ramsay feels at peace:

> Not as oneself did one find rest ever, in her experience (she accomplished here something dexterous with her needles) but as a wedge of darkness. Losing personality, one lost the fret, the hurry, the stir. (p. 96)

This mood is like that which Keats found in momentary identification with the nightingale, leaving behind 'The weariness, the fever, and the fret' of human suffering.[26] Keats's 'negative capability' and the mystic's *via negativa* are both struggles, in different spheres of activity, to achieve the selfless mental state that Mrs. Ramsay is able to enter habitually and almost without effort. As a woman and a Muse she understands, like Ursula Brangwen, that 'self was a oneness with the infinite'.[27] Like Penelope, she is also figuratively able to translate this understanding instantly and dextrously into the fabric she is knitting together. Further, as several critics have observed, it is this essentially impersonal self that Lily sees in Mrs. Ramsay and expresses in her painting as a 'triangular purple shape' (p. 81), because 'a light here required a shadow there' (p. 82).[28]

Mrs. Ramsay's own most powerful moment of vision in the novel occurs after James has been sent away to bed and she continues to sit in the window, casting her own gaze outward into the answering flash, 'the steady light, the pitiless, the remorseless, which was so much her, yet so little her'. Visible instantly when she wakes in the night, 'bent across their bed, stroking the floor', the light is a reflection of her consciousness, which now flashes over her 'as if it were stroking with its silver fingers some sealed vessel in her brain whose bursting would flood her with delight'. She thinks about the happiness she has known, the light 'silvered the rough waves a little more brightly', and finally the waves curved and swelled and broke upon the beach and the ecstasy burst in her eyes and waves of pure delight raced over the floor of her mind and she felt, It is enough! It is enough! (pp. 99–100)

The emotional climax is generated by a perceptual interaction between the sea and the light, between the dark source of life and the light of consciousness. It is a moment poised precariously between anonymous merging with the infinite and individual action; recalling it at dinner, Mrs. Ramsay has again

the feeling she had had once today, already, of peace, of rest. Of such moments, she thought, the thing is made that endures. . . . Here, she felt, putting the spoon down, was the still space that lies about the heart of things, where one could move or rest. (p. 158)

In this 'still space that lies about the heart of things' eternity intersects with time, and inarticulate life with human consciousness; having access to it, Mrs. Ramsay is able to perform the daily miracle of translating darkness into light, the chaos of nature into humanly perceptible order.

Mrs. Ramsay's physical beauty becomes a recurrent symbol for her extraordinary spiritual power to create order, meaning, and form in human experience. But by the end of the first section it has become clear that even she cannot do everything; she runs wearily up against facts which resist her power and her charm. The stocking represents her efforts to make form and order out of the materials of life; at the end of the evening Mr. Ramsay says, 'You won't finish that stocking tonight', and she concedes the point: ' "No," she said, flattening the stocking out upon her knee, "I shan't finish it" ' (p. 184). Her final words in the novel embody a parallel concession: 'Yes, you were right. It's going to be wet tomorrow. You won't be able to go' (p. 186). These two speeches, transparently simple on the realistic surface of the narrative, suggest the working of deep and mysterious forces beneath. Mrs. Ramsay's power to create and shape the world of concrete reality has been so great up to this point that this final prophecy seems self-fulfilling; here as elsewhere, her language appears to possess inescapable effectual power. This final acquiescence of her intuition and sympathy to Mr. Ramsay's fact seems almost to usher in the succeeding ten years of darkness; it is as if the power of hope has voluntarily submitted itself to the power of contingency.

This symbolic capitulation is paid as the price of a personal triumph; Mrs. Ramsay's individual problem in this scene is to convey her love to her husband without saying that she loves him in so many words. As a

Muse figure whose language is effectual rather than merely expressive, Mrs. Ramsay can say 'I love you' only by creating the feeling anew out of inarticulate materials, then giving it up into the world of fact and reality. Such creations of meaning, like the sympathy she gave to Mr. Ramsay earlier in the day, are draining and difficult experiences for her to undertake. Because her words demand such effort and carry such power, she can feel her own emotions more keenly in silence, which Lily later recalls as part of her character: 'Aren't things spoilt then, Mrs. Ramsay may have asked . . . by saying them?' (p. 256). Instead, she successfully communicates her love here by conceding to Mr. Ramsay's wisdom on another matter. But shortly after this night Mrs. Ramsay dies, before she has a chance to resume her habitual creative control over the contingent world. The question to be resolved at the end of the novel is whether, in her absence, the possibility of any such control can be reaffirmed.

II

The central section of *To the Lighthouse* breaks the unity of time that governs both *Ulysses* and *Mrs. Dalloway*, interposing a long night of ten years' duration between the opening and closing movements of the novel. In terms of Frank Kermode's model for the structure of fictions, the ticking of a clock, the structure of *To the Lighthouse* contains a single large progression from *tick* to *tock*. But the interval between the two movements stretches out for so many years that it calls into serious question the supposition that 'an end will bestow upon the whole duration and meaning'.[29] As the long night opens 'a downpouring of immense darkness began. Nothing, it seemed, could survive the flood' (p. 189). In this interval Mrs. Ramsay dies, like Mrs. Wilcox, away in London (pp. 194, 204); Prue Ramsay, the daughter most like her, succumbs to 'some illness connected with childbirth' (p. 199); and Andrew, the son most like his father, is blown up in the great war that sweeps over Europe (p. 201). As its title suggests, 'Time Passes' renders an interval of what Kermode calls *chronos*, 'passing time' or 'waiting time'. In order for the events it chronicles to make sense in some larger pattern, 'the interval must be purged of simple chronicity', must become 'a significant season, *kairos* poised between beginning and end'.[30] In the end temporal order prevails; the last movement establishes a pattern of consonance with the first that confers 'organization and form' upon the structure of the whole. The first day is retrospectively charged with meaning by the completion of its two central actions – Lily's painting and the trip to the lighthouse – that had been planned but left unfinished.

But just as the 'certain airs, detached from the body of the wind', test and toy with the house and its contents (pp. 190–1), the interval of inhuman time that invades the structure of the novel tests and questions the strength of an ordering vision rooted, like Mrs. Ramsay's, in the power of nature. Mrs. Ramsay's ability to create human meaning out of an inhuman natural world parallels the power of the singer in *The Idea of Order at Key West*, after whose song the narrator and his companion turn 'toward the town' to find that

> The lights of the boats at anchor there,
> As the night descended, tilting in the air,
> Mastered the night and portioned out the sea,
> Fixing emblazoned zones and fiery poles,
> Arranging, deepening, enchanting night.[31]

Similarly, in *To the Lighthouse*, when Mrs. Ramsay looks 'over her shoulder, at the town', she finds that

> The lights were rippling and running as if they were drops of silver water held firm in a wind. And all the poverty, all the suffering had turned to that, Mrs. Ramsay thought. The lights of the town and of the harbour and of the boats seemed like a phantom net floating there to mark something which had sunk. (p. 104)

In both passages the Muse figure has harmonized the man-made world of boats and lights with the natural forces of darkness, wind and sea, creating meaning and order that transcend such hardships as poverty and suffering. But no Muse appears in 'Time Passes'; natural forces become much more disturbing, and the possibility that they can be brought into harmony with man becomes much less certain.

Wordsworth is the most powerful literary advocate of the belief that the creative imagination, sustained by nature, can incorporate and make meaning out of human loss and suffering; in its testing of this proposition, 'Time Passes' can be read as a meditation on the continuing viability of a Wordsworthian vision in the modern world.[32] Woolf posits a Wordsworthian observer who rises in the night to seek companionship and reassurance from nature, but as this figure walks the sand, 'no image . . . comes readily to hand bringing the night to order and making the world reflect the compass of the soul' (p. 193). One cannot always rely upon the intercession of a Muse to translate forces of nature into ideas of order; already the observer's search for answers in the night seems 'almost' useless. But with the coming of summer such an observer can again sustain 'imaginations' of

> cliff, sea, cloud, and sky brought purposely together to assemble outwardly the scattered parts of the vision within. In those mirrors, the minds of men . . . it was impossible to resist the strange intimation which every gull, flower, tree, man and woman, and the white earth itself seemed to declare . . . that good triumphs, happiness prevails, order rules. (pp. 198–9)

In this implicitly Wordsworthian vision of nature, the mind creates order within by mirroring the order it sees in the world without; the external order seems to have been created 'purposely' to make this act of internal ordering possible. Spring even 'seemed to have taken upon her a knowledge of the sorrows of mankind'. But nature's apparent declaration of order exists only by an act of human faith; 'if questioned' she will 'at once' withdraw the affirmation (p. 199).

Thus the mere act of doubting nature's capacity to offer order and affirmation undermines her power to provide them. During the war, those who 'ask of the sea and sky what message they reported or what vision they affirmed', would see

> something out of harmony . . . the silent apparition of an ash-n-coloured ship for instance . . . a purplish stain upon the bland surface of the sea as if something had boiled and bled, invisibly, beneath.

Such 'intrusion' on the landscape reverses the earlier model: instead of finding an order in nature that makes it possible to create a mirroring order in the mind, man seems to be projecting his internal disorder outward upon the face of nature herself. Since one cannot simply overlook these intrusions or 'abolish their significance', it becomes difficult to continue 'to marvel how beauty outside mirrored beauty within' (p. 201).

Gradually the observer comes to suspect that Nature offers no active consolation, no order 'brought purposely together to assemble outwardly the scattered parts of the vision within', but looks on man only with indifference:

> Did Nature supplement what man advanced? Did she complete what he began? With equal complacence she saw his misery, his

meanness, and his torture. That dream, of sharing, completing, of finding in solitude on the beach an answer, was then but a reflection in a mirror . . . to pace the beach was impossible; contemplation was unendurable; the mirror was broken. (pp. 201–2)

At this point in the novel, as in *Ulysses* when Penelope's suitors seem to have seized control of the narrative web, it appears likely that no positive interchange can exist between the mind and nature. The power of a Muse to translate natural order into human order is apparently illusory; life offers no *kairos*, no 'still space' of intersection between eternity and time in which the thing can be made that endures; human order, activity and language are not grounded in any meaningful relationship to the external world.

In *Mrs. Dalloway*, the war experience of Septimus Warren Smith leads him to entertain this vision of reality as truth: 'It might be possible, Septimus thought . . . that the world itself is without meaning'.[33] In raising this possibility – the acceptance of which leads Septimus to insanity and suicide – Woolf anticipates, as Joyce had done, the arguments of contemporary literary theory. In a modern world which has rejected any divine order, the possibility for meaning can be grounded only in a Wordsworthian interchange between man and nature, between mind and external world. If there is no romantic lamp, no active reciprocity between internal and external worlds, then mind and nature become merely an endless hall of mirrors, a series of illusory reflections. The dream of 'sharing, completing, of finding in solitude on the beach an answer, was then but a reflection in a mirror', or, as Jonathan Culler argues, 'lamps are only another version of mirrors and belong to the same system of specularity . . . subject reflected in object and object reflected in subject'.[34] If this vision prevails, to pace the beach will indeed become ultimately impossible, contemplation unendurable, and the mirror of the mind be broken. In Woolf's rendition, such a vision creates an utterly disordered world of 'gigantic chaos streaked with lightning', the waves of the sea 'like leviathans whose brows are pierced by no light of reason', lunging 'in idiot games, until it seemed as if the universe were battling and tumbling, in brute confusion and wanton lust aimlessly by itself'. In this meaningless cosmos 'the stillness and the brightness of the day were as strange as the chaos and tumult of the night', and even the flowers stand 'beholding nothing, eyeless, and so terrible' (pp. 202–3). The terror that Mrs. Ramsay hears occasionally in nature has utterly obliterated nature's compensating messages of consolation.

But into this world there wanders, flickering and intermittent, a ray of memory. The charwoman who remembers is old and ignorant, poor and weary, as she struggles with a task that is 'too much for one woman' (p. 206), the task of restoring order to this world of meaninglessness run riot. Yet the memory of Mrs. Ramsay that she brings to the house hints faintly at the continuing presence of a transforming light among the meaningless plungings of water and wind:

> She could see her now . . . and faint and flickering, like a yellow beam or the circle at the end of a telescope, a lady in a grey cloak, stooping over her flowers, went wandering over the bedroom wall, up the dressing-table, across the wash-stand, as Mrs. McNab hobbled and ambled. (p. 205)

Though Mrs. Ramsay never consciously intended it, Mrs. McNab is one of those for whom 'wound about in their hearts, however long they lived she would be woven'. Empowered by her memories, Mrs. McNab's eyes cast a faint irradiating light over the external world, sending Mrs. Ramsay's image across the empty rooms like the lighthouse beam that Mrs. Ramsay identified with herself. This flickering transformation of the scene depends entirely upon a human presence; after Mrs. McNab leaves, her 'dream of a lady . . . had wavered over the walls like a spot of sunlight and vanished. . . . Only the Lighthouse beam entered the rooms for a moment' (p. 207). But later, when Mrs. McNab and Mrs. Bast come to clean the house, 'once more . . . the telescope fitted itself to Mrs. McNab's eyes, and in a ring of light she saw the old gentleman, lean as a rake, wagging his head' (p. 210). As in *Tintern Abbey*, the picture of the mind here superimposes itself upon the external landscape, half-creating what the mind perceives. By introducing a role for memory into the process, these passages tentatively reaffirm the possibility of meaningful interchange between the mind and outward things.

III

Toward the end of 'Time Passes', as Mrs. McNab and Mrs. Bast work at getting the house ready for the Ramsays to return, Woolf suggests that 'some rusty laborious birth seemed to be taking place' (p. 210). This theme of rebirth and renewal permeates the novel's final section. The intervening vision of nature as a process of eyeless and terrible indifference gradually subsides; in its place the setting in the Hebrides becomes a pastoral green world, the novel an elegiac romance. As in Wordsworth and in the late romances of Shakespeare, suffering and loss are woven up into a larger pattern of affirmation. In the final revelation of time's power to heal as well as to destroy, the ten-year interval comes to resemble the gap of sixteen years at the centre of *The Winter's Tale* and the twelve years that interpose in *The Tempest* between the beginning of the plot and the opening of the action.[35] In all these works, sensitivity to the working of time is crucial to the final resolution; characters must be ready to seize upon the fleeting moment of *kairos*, the intersection of eternity with daily life, in order to create consonance with the past and meaning in the present. Like *The Tempest*, the final section of *To the Lighthouse* is suffused with the atmosphere of recent storm and shipwreck; the problem in both works is to find in the scattered fragments of human suffering the materials of a new order.

For Lily Briscoe and Mr. Ramsay, as for the shipwrecked characters in *The Tempest*, the central step necessary in creating this new order is to acknowledge fully their own identities. In Mr. Ramsay's case, this step involves shedding an assumed histrionic grief and rediscovering his own self-sufficient independence; in Lily's, it involves qualifying an assumed pose of unemotional independence and recognizing her need to grieve. The two characters receive unexpected help from each other in solving these opposite problems; by the end of the novel, they have gradually drawn each other together toward a more stable emotional balance between the two extremes. Lily's development is more self-conscious than Mr. Ramsay's, however, because it is bound up with her struggle to record the experience in a work of art. The special problem she faces, but does not at first recognize, is a need to supplement her initial creative reaction against Mrs. Ramsay with an acknowledgement of the compensating love, indebtedness, and grief she has not yet admitted to feeling for the older woman. In psychological terms, she must come to terms with her full and complex response to a woman who stands in relation to her as a mother to a daughter.

At first, Lily insist to herself that she feels 'nothing that she could express at all', having 'come back after all these years and Mrs. Ramsay dead' (p. 217). She is aware that Mrs. Ramsay's absence has created an atmosphere of pervasive disorder; it is 'as if the link that usually bound things together had been cut', leaving a house 'full of unrelated passions' (pp. 219, 221). But she has neither the skill nor the inclination to begin Mrs. Ramsay's work of merging and creating. Nancy Ramsay, who seems to have had her mother's role thrust unwillingly upon her, packs lunches and ties up charity bundles clumsily 'as if she were forcing herself to do what she despaired of ever being able to do' (p. 218). Sitting alone at breakfast, Lily is feeling only an urgent wish to escape, when suddenly she remembers her abandoned paining:

ten years ago there had been a little sprig or leaf pattern on the table-cloth, which she had looked at in a moment of revelation. There had been a problem about a foreground of a picture. . . . She would paint that picture now. (p. 220)

She cannot create order in the social sphere for herself or for the Ramsays, but she decides to do what she can in the medium with which she is familiar. In the process, she will unexpectedly discover both the feelings and the expression of them that had at first eluded her.

Lily had originally seen this revelation about her painting as a defence against Mrs. Ramsay and the life of female self-sacrifice she represented. Mrs.Ramsay had hoped to make a match between Lily and William Bankes, believing as she did that 'an unmarried woman has missed the best of life' (p. 77) and that 'one could not take [Lily's] painting very seriously' (p. 29). To help ward off this match, Lily objects to herself at the dinner party that Mrs. Ramsay is wrong to see Bankes as lonely and pitiable, because he has his work. The objection reminds her that she, too, has a vocation:

> In a flash she saw her picture, and thought, Yes, I shall put the tree further in the middle; then I shall avoid that awkward space. . . . She took up the salt cellar and put it down again on a flower in pattern in the table-cloth, so as to remind herself to move the tree. (p. 128)

As the dinner progresses, the salt cellar comes to symbolize for Lily her artistic identity, which saves her from the 'degradation' and 'dilution' of marriage (p. 154). This renewed commitment to art enables her to remain partially independent of Mrs. Ramsay's social order, much as the poet Augustus Carmichael seems able to keep himself aloof from Mrs. Ramsay's power. The salt cellar is Lily's own personal version of the lighthouse, a marker to prevent her life as an artist from running on the rocks of marriage.

Standing before a fresh canvas on the lawn, however, Lily begins to realize that the solution she has borne in mind 'all these years' only 'seemed' to be right; the answer now ten years old is no longer adequate (p. 221). Both the state of her feelings and the scene itself have changed. Mrs. Ramsay is dead; 'The step where she used to sit was empty' (p. 224). Originally Lily had felt 'that she would move the tree to the middle, and need never marry anybody . . . now she could stand up to Mrs. Ramsay' (p. 262). But standing up to Mrs. Ramsay is no longer Lily's central problem. She has never married, and her artistic vocation is much more firmly established than it would have been on the morning after the dinner party ten years before. In recalling her creative insight, she never remembers the mnemonic pillar of salt she had placed on the tablecloth; the insight itself remains, but she no longer need cling to a sterile symbol of her artistic identity. Lily can now create art unselfconsciously out of that identity, freed from the aesthetically damaging need to assert it. Woolf believed strongly that such mental freedom from spite, grievances, and hardship is necessary to the production of creative work.[36] Lily's problem now is that her original insight emerged as a defensive response to what seemed threatening in Mrs. Ramsay's influence; ultimately, such negative inspiration must be supplemented with something more positive.

Lily's painting is clearly an attempt to repeat and improve upon the post-impressionist rendition of house and garden, as seen from the lawn, that she was painting on the first day of the novel. A number of readers have contended that her easel is now facing in the opposite direction, that she is painting the harbour, sea, and lighthouse; one critic, Avrom Fleishman, tries to establish that the bay and lighthouse lie over the wall between the hedge and the house, thus becoming available for incorporation into this second painting.[37] But such readings, though schematically attractive, cannot be supported from the text. Woolf repeatedly makes it clear that the sea and the lighthouse are behind Lily as she paints; every time she wants to follow Mr. Ramsay's progress, she must turn away from her easel and walk over to the edge of the lawn: we see her 'turning back, reluctantly again, to her canvas' after looking out at the bay (p. 255); later she is watching the sea, then 'she turned to her picture' (p. 287); on the last page of the novel she is gazing out toward the lighthouse with Mr. Carmichael, and then 'quickly, as if she were recalled by something over there, she turned to her canvas' (p. 309). But the desire of several readers somehow to incorporate Mr. Ramsay and the lighthouse into the painting reflects accurately the importance of Lily's emotional tie to Mr. Ramsay in the progress of the work.

The structure of Lily's painting, no less than artistic structures in the work of male artists, will require both male and female elements. Even on the earlier day's work, she insists that she does not see the scene as 'Paunceforte would have seen it' – the colour 'thinned and faded; the shapes etherialised'. Rather, 'she saw the colour burning on a framework of steel; the light of a butterfly's wing lying upon the arches of a cathedral' (p. 75).[38] Again ten years later she affirms these formal principles:

Beautiful and bright it should be on the surface, feathery and evanescent . . . but beneath the fabric must be clamped together with bolts of iron. (p. 255)

The need for a 'framework of steel' and 'bolts of iron' is a need for the stern code of facts and logic according to which Mr. Ramsay lives and works. Lily's awareness that art needs to incorporate an element of male rationality parallels Mrs. Ramsay's reliance upon it in her weaving together of life:

> she let it uphold her and sustain her, this admirable fabric of the masculine intelligence, which ran up and down, crossed this way and that, like iron girders spanning the swaying fabric, upholding the world. (p. 159)

This masculine intelligence corresponds to the warp of rationality in *Ulysses* into which the Muse weaves the woof of words to create Joyce's narrative web; in *To the Lighthouse*, Mrs. Ramsay's unfinished stocking becomes a similar symbol for the structure of the novel's opening section. Lily's painting completes the web of the novel by shifting Mrs. Ramsay's fabric onto a different loom: 'The Window' concerns the creation of meaningful order in human relations; 'The Lighthouse' concerns the completion of that order in the medium of art.

The problem for the female artist is that she needs assistance from outside herself which a traditional Muse figure, also a woman, cannot provide. In *A Room of One's Own*, Woolf argues that because great men have 'admired, sought out, lived with, confided in, made love to, written of, trusted in' women over the centuries, women must have more to offer than 'comfort, flattery and the pleasures of the body'. What these men received from women

> was something that their own sex was unable to supply; and it would not be rash, perhaps, to define it further . . . as some stimulus, some renewal of creative power which is in the gift only of the opposite sex to bestow.[39]

By implication, a woman striving to create lasting achievements will also need some form of stimulus from the opposite sex, but it will clearly be of a different character from the stimulus that men receive from women. Lily realizes that 'the human apparatus for painting or for feeling . . . always broke down at the critical moment; heroically, one must force it on' (p. 287); Mr. Ramsay, with his determined ability to lead mankind onward even in the face of discouragement and failure, offers precisely the example and inspiration she needs. In her repeated trips to the edge of the lawn, watching the voyage to the lighthouse, she renews her consciousness of his firm determination and logical clarity of vision. But ultimately she must also prevent Mr. Ramsay's positive qualities from completely dominating and controlling her vision, just as in *Ulysses* the artist and the Muse must ward off the attempts of male rationality to take over the web of art. She must 'achieve that razor edge of balance between two opposite forces; Mr. Ramsay and the picture' (p. 287). In Woolf's complex reshaping of the Muse convention, Lily must sustain her initial inspiration by drawing on Mr. Ramsay's strengths, but can only achieve final balance in recognizing her positive inheritance from Mrs. Ramsay as well.

At first Lily finds Mr. Ramsay distracting and threatening; when he comes up demanding the sympathy Mrs. Ramsay used to give him, she has none to offer. Quite by accident, however, she happens to praise his boots, only to discover with surprise that this simple gesture will suffice. She has shown herself sensitive to something he cares about deeply. As he responds by tying her shoe according to his own special method, she feels genuine sympathy for him and wishes to say something, but 'her feeling had come too late ... he no longer needed it' (pp. 230–1). When he departs, she is left with her unused sympathy 'troubling her for expression' (p. 232). But although the feeling continues to disturb her, it gradually takes on the character of a tentative connection between them:

> She felt curiously divided, as if one part of her were drawn out there – it was a still day, hazy; the Lighthouse looked this morning at an immense distance; the other had fixed itself doggedly, solidly, here on the lawn. (p. 234)

This connection is like one Woolf describes in *Mrs. Dalloway* between Lady Bruton and two men, Richard Dalloway and Hugh Whitbread, who in walking down the street from her house still remain 'attached to her by a thin thread (since they had lunched with her) which would stretch and stretch, get thinner and thinner as they walked across London'.[40] Lily's unexpressed sympathy for Mr. Ramsay becomes such a thread; during the remainder of the novel, she is repeatedly 'driven by the discomfort of the sympathy which she held undischarged', to follow the progress of his voyage to the lighthouse (p. 241). For a long time she still feels that her unused sympathy 'weighed her down' (p. 254), but ultimately she will realize that it has become a more positive tie.

This thin thread of Lily's unexpressed sympathy is one of two strands out of which Woolf weaves the scene changes in the third part of the novel; most of the shifts from lawn to boat and back are managed by a shuttling back and forth along the line of this connection. As Lily watches the boat set sail at the end of section III, her gaze shifts the narrative perspective out into the boat and begins section IV (p. 242). The second thread in this narrative fabric is Cam's gaze cast backward from the boat to the island; at the end of section IV, as 'she looked doggedly and sadly at the shore' (p. 253), the scene returns to Lily on the lawn. Lily, still looking out at the beginning of Section V, unconsciously meets her gaze: 'Yes, that is their boat, Lily Briscoe decided, standing on the edge of the lawn' (p. 253). Section VI stands in brackets partly because Woolf shifts the narrative perspective abruptly into the boat without either Cam's or Lily's help (p. 268). At the end of section VII Lily, 'looking out to sea', again shifts the scene out to where Cam sits, at the beginning of Section VIII, 'looking at the shore' (pp. 271–2). Section IX stands in parentheses; although Cam is not at the moment looking back at the island, Lily's line of vision has remained constant: she is 'still standing and looking out over the bay' (p. 279). Cam draws the narrative back to the boat by looking again at the island at the beginning of section X (p. 280), and Lily draws it back to the island by looking out to the boat at the beginning of section XI (p. 284). The last two shifts in scene, which I shall discuss more fully below, are managed by Lily alone (pp. 300, 308). By unconsciously weaving their lines of vision together, Cam and Lily – like Penelope weaving her web and Mrs. Ramsay knitting her stocking – are figuratively engaged in binding up the disordered world of the novel.

Mr. Ramsay also looks back at the island during the course of the voyage. He finds the house and, 'seeing it, he had also seen himself there . . . walking on the terrace, alone' (p. 247). For the first time in the novel he seems ready to escape the prison of his egotism, to look back at himself from an external perspective. Yet immediately he begins a process of self-dramatization:

> he seemed to himself very old and bowed. Sitting in the boat, he bowed, he crouched himself, acting instantly his part – the part of a desolate man, widowed, bereft. (pp. 247–8)

But in his present high spirits, he cannot maintain the pose for long. Glancing up from his internal drama, he thinks that Cam looks frightened and decides to make her smile. He is for once thinking of someone other than himself; he works actively to express interest in her concerns (p. 250). As the voyage takes him out of himself he begins acting more and more like his wife, making a social effort to please his daughter, ultimately praising his son for steering the boat 'like a born sailor' (p. 306). But unlike Mrs. Ramsay, he has resources other than the creation of social order; he does not feel it necessary to badger people into a harmony they may not desire. When Cam resists his efforts to please, he uncomplainingly opens his book.

Mr. Ramsay has arranged this trip to fulfil the terms of an old promise and to assuage his guilt toward the memory of his wife. Ten years before, when Mrs. Ramsay conceded to his position on the next day's weather, she told James that they could not go to the lighthouse tomorrow, 'but soon, she promised him; the next fine day' (p. 173). With death and war interposing years of turmoil, today has belatedly become the first fine day on which the promise can be kept. Ironically, James and Cam no longer have any interest in going; they think of Mr. Ramsay's journey as 'these rites he went through for his own pleasure in memory of dead people, which they hated' (p. 246). They were too young when their mother died for them to think of her now with particular grief. But on the way to the lighthouse, they both have memories of Mrs. Ramsay that parallel Lily's more fully visualized experience on the lawn. Thinking that Cam will 'give way' to Mr. Ramsay's charm and break their silent compact to resist his tyranny, James remembers his mother's outpouring of consoling energy for his father on the first day of the novel:

> They look down he thought, at their knitting or something. Then suddenly they look up. There was a flash of blue, he remembered, and then somebody sitting with him laughed, surrendered, and he was very angry. (p. 251)

But Cam does not give in to her father's sudden affability; unlike Mrs. Ramsay, she feels for the present a stronger loyalty to James. Cam herself, looking back at the island, gradually drifts off into sleep remembering the words and the scene her mother conjured up to put her to sleep at the end of the first day of the novel (pp. 172, 303). In remembering experiences with their mother on the day that this voyage was promised, both children are subconsciously in touch with the temporal consonance between this day and that particular day in the past. Like Mr. Ramsay, each experiences an emotional transformation in the course of the voyage; their resentment gradually falls away, and by the time they arrive all three characters are at peace with each other and with themselves.

IV

Shortly before beginning *To the Lighthouse*, Woolf described the process of writing as 'this dash at the paper of a phrase, and then the typing and retyping – trying it over; the actual writing being now like the sweep of a brush'.[41] In the novel itself she uses similar language to describe the process of painting: Lily 'attained a dancing rhythmical movement as if the pauses were one part of the rhythm and the strokes another, and all were related' (p. 236). Both descriptions suggest the rhythm of the lighthouse beam that symbolizes Mrs. Ramsay; painter and writer are at rest in the pauses between the strokes of brush or pen, just as Mrs. Ramsay rests in the darkness between the strokes of light and sympathy she casts out into the world of human relations. In the rhythm of their work, the artists in life, paint, and words are all participating in different forms of the same essential process. For Lily the work gradually seems to fall in with

> some rhythm which was dictated to her . . . so that while her hand quivered with life, this rhythm was strong enough to bear her along with it on its current. Certainly she was losing consciousness of outer things. (pp. 237–8)

The thread of Lily's sympathy for Mr. Ramsay, which links her to the outer world of fact and reason, is still being woven up into this rhythm; but her conscious awareness is coming to rest on the same deeper current beneath external reality that Mrs. Ramsay draws upon in creating social order. As she becomes aware of this connection, Lily must unexpectedly revise her earlier vision of art as a defence against Mrs. Ramsay; ultimately, the common current beneath artistic and social order makes her artistic vocation not a new departure from Mrs. Ramsay's world, but an inheritance.

Working in rhythm with this deeper current, Lily's mind is gradually unburdened of resentment, distraction, and unacknowledged grief. As a female artist, she has been unconsciously crippled by her justified resentment of male prejudice against her; now she remembers that it was Charles Tansley who said 'women can't paint, can't write' (p. 238). In associating this sentiment with a specific person, she can escape her resentment by recalling a 'moment of friendship and liking' between them – a time when she and Charles played ducks and drakes together while Mrs. Ramsay wrote letters on the beach. Remembering the occasion now permanently alters her opinion of Charles Tansley, retrospectively reshaping the past; 'she dipped into it to re-fashion her memory of him'. But Lily simultaneously realizes that she is indebted to Mrs. Ramsay for her possession of this moment, folded up in memory, that can free her creative mind from the distraction of resentment. It was Mrs. Ramsay who had smoothed over the usual antagonism between Lily and Charles that day, creating the occasion which has now become available to memory; Mrs. Ramsay who made out of ordinary time a moment 'which survived, after all these years complete . . . affecting one almost like a work of art' (p. 240).

Lily's acceptance of this debt immediately cascades into the larger recognition that Mrs. Ramsay's art draws, no less than her own, upon the fleeting moments when eternity intersects with time, those 'little daily miracles, illuminations, matches struck unexpectedly in the dark'. Mrs. Ramsay is concerned with 'making of the moment something permanent (as in another sphere Lily herself tried to make of the moment something permanent)'. While Lily thought she was rejecting Mrs. Ramsay's example, she was in fact unconsciously learning and applying it to her own endeavours. The goal of social and artistic order was the same all along:

> In the midst of chaos there was shape; this eternal passing and flowing (she looked at the clouds going and the leaves shaking) was struck into stability. Life stand still here, Mrs. Ramsay said. "Mrs. Ramsay! Mrs. Ramsay!" she repeated. She owed it all to her. (pp. 240–1)

In experiencing and affirming the power of memory and art to strike moments of illumination into stability, Lily also implicitly overcomes the view advanced in 'Time Passes' that such permanance is impossible.

Acknowledging her debt to Mrs. Ramsay leads Lily to recognize at last her sense of personal loss; in this process, the power of the external world to reflect unacknowledged emotions within comes to her aid. Looking at the scene and thinking of Mrs. Ramsay, she realizes that 'It must have altered the design a good deal when she was sitting on the step with James. There must have been a shadow' (p. 239). Gradually the space where Mrs. Ramsay used to sit comes to suggest a corresponding emptiness in Lily: 'For how could one express in words these emotions of the body: express that emptiness there? (She was looking at the drawing-room steps; they looked extraordinarily empty)' (p. 265). Finally the feeling called up by the empty space before her becomes insistent, obliterating all other thoughts and emotions:

> To want and not to have, sent all up her body a hardness, a hollowness, a strain. And then to want and not to have – to want and want – how that wrung the heart, and wrung it again and again! (p. 266)

All the other elements of the scene have become 'like curves and arabesques flourishing round a centre of complete emptiness' (p. 266). As she looks back at her picture, 'she was surprised to find that she could not see it. Her eyes were full of a hot liquid (she did not think of tears at first)' (p. 267). Her consciousness is the last part of her to acknowledge the experience of grief. When finally the emptiness breaks through her mental defenses, she feels that if she and Mr. Carmichael 'both got up' and 'demanded an explanation',

> beauty would roll itself up; the space would fill, those empty flourishes would form into shape; if they shouted loud enough Mrs. Ramsay would return. "Mrs. Ramsay!" she said aloud, "Mrs. Ramsay!" The tears ran down her face. (p. 268)

In allowing herself to grieve, Lily at last overcomes the mood of rebellion against Mrs. Ramsay in which her original artistic insight was achieved. She is now ready to accept Mrs. Ramsay as an ally, to work in partnership with her memory rather than against it.

Lily's acceptance and expression of grief for Mrs. Ramsay allows her to achieve a mood of cathartic calm: 'the pain of the want, and the bitter anger . . . lessened; and of their anguish left, as antidote, a relief that was balm in itself'. In the quiet after her experience of human suffering, Lily has reached what Wordsworth called the 'blessed mood' in which 'the heavy and the weary weight / Of all this unintelligible world, / Is lightened'.[42] Again, Lily's inner experience is reflected externally, in her mysterious sense that Mrs. Ramsay is somehow present, 'relieved for a moment of the weight that the world had put on her' (p. 269). This presence is not completely new and strange; in the past, Lily has frequently superimposed over the scenes of daily life a consoling image of Mrs. Ramsay being summoned like Persephone, walking quickly through the flowers across the fields of death.[43] But interruptions 'waked her, required and got in the end an effort of attention, so that the vision must be perpetually remade' (p. 270). Today, however, her mind has been freed from distraction and interruption; she has achieved the state of mental calmness necessary to experience creative vision. Lily has reached the 'still space that lies about the heart of things' where, with a Wordsworthian eye 'made quiet by the power / Of harmony, and the deep power of joy', she can 'see into the life of things'.[44] But, she reminds herself, 'one got nothing by soliciting urgently. . . . Let it come, she thought, if it will come' (pp. 287–8). She is unconsciously echoing Mrs. Ramsay, who approached her moment of vision in 'The Window' thinking to herself 'It will end, it will end', and 'It will come, it will come' (p. 97); but she is also echoing Hamlet's words to Horatio before his duel with Laertes:

'If it be now, 'tis not to come; if it be not to come, it will be now; if it be not now, yet it will come – the readiness is all'.[45] Vision dwells on the borders of life and death; like tragic action, it requires that a fully achieved identity give itself up to the rhythm of a power beyond the self, beyond, in Keats's words, 'any irritable reaching after fact and reason'.[46]

The final step in Lily's movement toward her culminating vision is to fuse the two forms of inspiration out of which the experience is being shaped. She is still connected to Mr. Ramsay's male world of fact and perseverance by a thread of interest and sympathy; now she has established her link with Mrs. Ramsay's female access to order and consolation. Lily relates these opposing influences by working out her own vision of how two such disparate individuals as the Ramsays came to be married in the first place. She recalls a time when Mr. Ramsay

> stretched out his hand and raised her from her chair. It seemed somehow as if he had done it before; as if he had once bent in the same way and raised her from a boat. . . . Letting herself be helped by him, Mrs. Ramsay had thought (Lily supposed) the time has come now. Yes, she would say it now. Yes, she would marry him. And she stepped slowly, quietly on shore. . . . Time after time the same thrill had passed between them – obviously it had, Lily thought. . . . She was not inventing; she was only trying to smooth out something she had been given years ago folded up. (p. 295)

Lily has apparently reconstructed this moment accurately; earlier, Mrs. Ramsay has thought of her husband 'again as she had first known him, gaunt but gallant; helping her out of a boat, she remembered' (p. 150). Lily's reconstructed vision of the Ramsays' engagement parallels Molly Bloom's visionary remembrance of her engagement to Bloom. But Lily's ability to visualize the moment of affirmation without having participated in it herself confirms her identity as a visionary artist, capable of creating within her own creative imagination a marriage of male and female, fact and vision, reason and intuition.

This internal union between male and female forms of inspiration will make it possible for Lily to achieve the single vision that Woolf found lacking in Forster's art.[47] Lily understands now that she wants to perceive the simultaneous presence of the real and the symbolic, of this world and the world beyond:

> to be on a level with ordinary experience, to feel simply that's a chair, that's a table, and yet at the same time, It's a miracle, it's an ecstasy. (p. 300)

Earlier, Lily has had no difficulty seeing these two worlds in alternation, as when the Ramsays suddenly became representative,

> the symbols of marriage, husband and wife. Then, after an instant, the symbolical outline which transcended the real figures sank down again, and they became . . . Mr. and Mrs. Ramsay watching the children throwing catches. (pp. 110–11)

In visionary experience, this instant of delay between the two ways of seeing disappears; the everyday and symbolic identities exist together. Such simultaneity characterizes our experience of enduring art; thus the sonnet Mrs. Ramsay reads at the end of Part One contains both male and female elements, is at once 'beautiful and reasonable, clear and complete' (p. 181). On the way to the lighthouse, James and Cam glimpse the nature of this simultaneous vision in moments which parallel Lily's more fully realized experience on the lawn. James, comparing the mythic, misty lighthouse of his childhood and the starkly real tower before him, realizes that both visions of it are true, 'for nothing was simply one thing' (p. 277). Cam, a potential artist like Lily or Woolf herself, imagines during the voyage that they are survivors of a shipwreck, 'telling herself a story but knowing at the same time what was the truth' (p. 304). The single vision is what allows Molly Bloom to be at once Dublin housewife and mythical earth goddess; things are both themselves and their transfigurations.

Lily's vision arises out of her simultaneous attentiveness to surface reality and symbolic meaning. Drawing upon the sources of Mrs. Ramsay's own creative power, Lily gradually recreates her presence, conjures her up into the living world again. She sits down briefly on the lawn, as Margaret Schlegel does near the climax of *Howards End*; 'here sitting on the world', Lily is as closely in touch as it is possible to be with the earth (p. 288).[48] As she sits musing, her attention persistently strays to the window where Mrs. Ramsay used to sit; she realizes that 'the drawing-room step was empty, but it had no effect on her whatever. She did not want Mrs. Ramsay now' (p. 290). Mrs. Ramsay is with her already, has in a sense entered into her: 'Lily looked up, as she had seen Mrs. Ramsay look up; she too heard a wave falling on the beach' (p. 294). A sudden movement at the window suggests that someone has come into the drawing room, settling 'so as to throw an odd-shaped triangular shadow over the step'. This apparent accident duplicates exactly the conditions of the original setting, in which the triangular shadow was cast by Mrs. Ramsay, but Lily merely thinks now that 'It altered the composition of the picture a little. It was interesting. It might be useful.' Yet she has an acute sense that some power is intensely at work: returning to her painting, she thinks to herself that 'one must keep on looking without for a second relaxing the intensity of emotion' (p. 299). Suddenly she sees a movement at the window again.

"Mrs. Ramsay! Mrs. Ramsay!" she cried, feeling the old horror come back – to want and want and not to have. Could she inflict that still? And then, quietly, as if she refrained, that too became part of ordinary experience, was on a level with the chair, with the table. Mrs. Ramsay – it was part of her perfect goodness – sat there quite simply, in the chair, flicked her needles to and fro, knitted her reddish-brown stocking, cast her shadow on the step. There she sat. (p. 300)

The external space of vacancy and absence is filled by the overflowing of Lily's internal grief and desire; the lines between subject and object are blurred, and Mrs. Ramsay's presence becomes part of 'ordinary experience'. Woolf has carefully constructed the novel to make this moment believable, to affirm the possibility that for an instant the world of eternity can intersect the world of time.[49]

In standing as the climax of the work, Lily's vision of Mrs. Ramsay resembles Tennyson's momentary communion with the spirit of Arthur Hallam in section 95 of *In Memoriam*. Like Woolf, Tennyson prepares earlier for the visionary experience, calling for Hallam to 'wear the form by which I know / Thy spirit in time'.[50] But he is troubled by the problem of distinguishing vision from memory, fearing that if he should see Hallam's likeness, he 'might count it vain / As but the canker of the brain', a mere 'wind / Of memory murmuring the past' (92.1–8). Woolf solves this problem by bringing male and female ways of seeing momentarily together in a 'single vision', so that Mrs. Ramsay's appearance in both an ordinary fact and a 'veil through which we see infinity'. Tennyson, untroubled by Woolf's complicating need to reconcile male and female perspectives, simply decides that a reliable visual experience cannot occur, but that a contact of 'Spirit to Spirit, Ghost to Ghost' (93.8) may be possible. Like Woolf, Tennyson recognizes that the visited soul must be at peace (94.5–8); he is rereading Hallam's letters one evening on the lawn,

> And all at once it seem'd at last
> The living soul was flash'd on mine,
> And mine in this was wound, and whirl'd
> About empyreal heights of thought,
> And came on that which is, and caught
> The deep pulsations of the world. (95.35–40)

Woolf once suggested that 'elegy' might be a more appropriate description of *To the Lighthouse* than 'novel'; the work finally becomes a tribute to the memory of her own parents, especially her mother.[51] Its climax affirms the possibility that even in a post-Christian universe, souls 'wound about' each other in their hearts may meet amid the 'deep pulsations' of a world 'which is', transcending transience and death.

Lily responds immediately to her vision by walking to the edge of the lawn, 'as if she had something she must share', thinking, 'Where was that boat now? And Mr. Ramsay? She wanted him.' She wants to share her vision with Mr. Ramsay, but she also needs to receive assurance from him that the world of fact and reason still exists, that her vision has not subsumed or destroyed the everyday world. She can 'hardly leave her easel, so full her mind was of what she was thinking, of what she was seeing' (p. 300). The escape back into reality from the borders of vision is as difficult as the initial movement toward the visionary world; the risk is of remaining in a perpetual state of vision, such as Woolf herself seems to have known in her periods of madness. Lily now needs all of Mr. Ramsay's best qualities to bring her back into everyday life; thus *To the Lighthouse* does not end, as the earlier visionary novels of the modernists end, with the visionary experience itself. The novel's final achievement will be to record the vision in the moment of recovering the contingent world, an achievement embodied in the line that Lily draws at the centre of her painting to define the boundary between this world and the world beyond.

V

Lily's act of gazing out toward Mr. Ramsay immediately after her vision again shifts the scene of the narrative back to the boat. There the reader finds that, like himself, Mr. Ramsay 'had almost done reading. . . . He was reading very quickly, as if he were eager to get to the end. Indeed they were very close to the Lighthouse now' (p. 301). For the reader, as for Mr. Ramsay, the goal that has been in sight since the first line of the novel is now at hand. An entry in Woolf's diary, written as she was beginning Part Three, indicates the conflicting demands she faced in bringing the book to a close:

> The problem is how to bring Lily and Mr. R[amsay] together & make a combination of interest at the end. . . . I had meant to end with R. climbing on to the rock. If so, what becomes [of] Lily & her picture?

Should there be a final page . . . looking at the picture and summing up R.'s character? In that case I lose the intensity of the moment. If this intervenes, between R. and the lighthouse, there's too much chop & change, I think. Could I do it in a parenthesis? So that one had the sense of reading the two things at the same time?[52]

Her desire to conflate the experiences of Lily and Mr. Ramsay in the reader's mind underlies and helps to create the sense that two different worlds have merged in these concluding pages; the effect is a more powerful version of what Forster tried to achieve in *Howards End* by making Margaret Schlegel's culminating vision coincide with the instant when the cutting of the hayfield is completed.

In the complex process of interchange which has occurred between Lily, Mr. Ramsay, and the spirit of his wife, Mr. Ramsay has emerged – as always – renewed and reinvigorated. At the instant of landing, he 'rose and stood in the bow of the boat, very straight and tall, for all the world, James thought, as if he were saying, "There is no God"'. Whereas Henry Wilcox is bowed and broken by the conclusion of *Howards End*, Mr. Ramsay now 'sprang, lightly like a young man, holding his parcel, on to the rock'. The thread of connection between Lily and Mr. Ramsay remains; looking outward, she is aware that 'he must have reached it'. She realizes that 'whatever she had wanted to give him, when he left her that morning, she had given him at last', but for her the experience has been a draining one: 'the effort of looking' at the lighthouse and 'the effort of thinking of him landing there . . . both seemed to be one and the same effort' (pp. 308–9). As he has spun out the thread of her sympathy in travelling toward his distant goal, Mr. Ramsay has at last come to terms with himself. He is for the moment no longer a man 'afraid to own his own feelings, who could not say, This is what I like – this is what I am' (p. 70). At the same time, by reaching his goal he has unconsciously given something important back to Lily: the example and inspiration of his own best qualities, which are as essential as those of Mrs. Ramsay to the struggle of life and the fabric of artistic achievement.

Mr. Ramsay's journey is repeatedly associated with allusions and images which suggest that it is a proleptic version of his own life's voyage toward death. When he set out, Lily had reflected that 'there was no helping Mr. Ramsay on the journey he was going' (p. 230). Near the end of the voyage, Mr. Ramsay remarks to Macalister that 'they would soon be out of it' – life – but that 'their children would see some strange things' (p. 304). In describing his landing Lily echoes the final words of Christ: 'It is finished' (p. 309; John 19:30). As the goal of this voyage, the lighthouse is thus associated symbolically with death. But in the Christian cosmology that Lily's words fleetingly evoke, what is 'finished' as Christ dies is not life itself, but only the suffering associated with life on earth. The words spoken from the cross mark a boundary between two worlds, indicate both the end of life in one world and its beginning in another. The lighthouse is a similar boundary, a line figuratively suggesting the border between human time and eternity; in approaching this border by sea Mr. Ramsay exactly parallels Lily's course toward her visionary experience on the lawn. On this proleptic voyage Mr. Ramsay is accompanied by two of his children, just as two others followed his wife out of this world; in leaping onto the rock 'lightly like a young man' he prefigures his entrance into the next world, ready to turn back and help Mrs. Ramsay out of the boat once again.

From this moment, the simultaneity of the two worlds – of reality and vision, time and eternity – begins to break down. On the novel's final page Mr. Carmichael rises, 'looking like an old pagan god, shaggy, with weeds in his hair and the trident (it was only a French novel) in his hand.' In the visionary world Mr. Carmichael carries a trident, in the everyday one a French novel; the parenthesis that makes the distinction begins to split the two worlds apart. But just before the moment is irremediably lost, Lily turns back to her canvas, 'quickly, as if she were recalled by something over there'.

> She looked at the steps; they were empty; she looked at her canvas; it was blurred. With a sudden intensity, as if she saw it clear for a second, she drew a line there, in the centre. It was done; it was finished. Yes, she thought, laying down her brush in extreme fatigue, I have had my vision. (pp. 309–10)

The identity of this final line is not particularly important; what matters is knowing where to put it. It defines the border between life and death, fact and vision, the real and the symbolic, this world and the world beyond. In this sense it fulfils the same function in the painting that the lighthouse fulfils in the novel: 'a central line down the middle', as Woolf wrote to Roger Fry, 'to hold the design together'. To know where to place this line, writer and painter must each draw upon experience of both worlds, blending and reshaping the contrasting forms of inspiration that the Ramsays provide.[53]

In the painting, Lily's final line brings hedge, house and spectator into a new relationship with one another; in the novel, Woolf's need to reshape the conventions of artistic inspiration ultimately redefines the interrelations among men, women, and the external world. The novel's first scene located Mrs. Ramsay in what must be a French window, open to the terrace and the lawn; she sits between the home and the world of action, sallying out occasionally to visit the sick and the poor, but fundamentally still tied to her responsibility for house and children. Mr. Ramsay affirms the Victorian values of this world, which Woolf can clearly admire but not accept:

> He liked that men should labour and sweat on the windy beach at night; pitting muscle and brain against the waves and the wind; he liked men to work like that, and women to keep house, and sit beside sleeping children indoors, while men were drowned, out there in a storm. (p. 245)

Woolf's male precursors in modernist visionary closure felt no special impetus to realize the form's possibilities for changing this pattern. In *The Rainbow*, for example, Lawrence gives Ursula Brangwen her culminating vision from woman's traditional perspective within the home; the novel's final pages find her looking out through the window on the male world of external achievement. In contrast, Woolf places Lily out on the lawn from the start; though Lily does not travel as far into the world of action as Mr. Ramsay, Cam, representing the next generation, is in the boat with the men themselves. Unlike Forster, who struggles for an entire novel to get Margaret Schlegel into a house, Woolf wants to get her women out of the house and beyond it. Forster sought a haven where the world of Mrs. Wilcox and Mrs. Ramsay could be preserved, but by the mid 1920's that world has been irrevocably destroyed; Woolf must rather try to affirm the possibility and define the form of a new order.

In confronting her art, Lily Briscoe finds the 'passage from conception to work as dreadful as any down a dark passage for a child' (p. 32). The dread of this passage is embodied in the 'Time Passes' section of the novel, which evokes the extraordinary difficulty of the 'passage' from house to lighthouse, from starting point to goal. *To the Lighthouse* itself underwent a sea-change while making this voyage. In Woolf's original conception of the novel, her father's character was to be its central subject:

> This is going to be fairly short: to have father's character done complete in it; & mother's; & St. Ives; & childhood; & all the usual things I try to put in – life, death &c. But the centre is father's character, sitting in a boat, reciting We perished, each alone, while he crushes a dying mackerel.[54]

But as she worked the emphasis shifted; she was unexpectedly diverted into coming to terms with her mother, who stands for most readers of the finished novel at the centre of the work.

Virginia was only thirteen when her mother died, but her sister Vanessa, a few years older, testifies to the uncanny accuracy of the portrait she created in *To the Lighthouse* by the play of imagination over memory:

> you have given a portrait of mother which is more like her to me than anything I could have conceived of as possible. It is almost painful to have her so raised from the dead. . . . It was like meeting her again with oneself grown up and on equal terms and it seems to me the most astonishing feat of creation to have been able to see her in such a way.[55]

The meeting with her mother as if 'raised from the dead' that Vanessa describes here is the same experience that Lily has as she works on her painting, and that Woolf must have had as she worked on the book. By weaving into the climax of the novel this unexpected encounter in the passage from conception to work, Woolf transformed the tradition she inherited in a strikingly original way; Lily's experience on the lawn, which Woolf herself was not altogether sure she had pulled off, is the novel's great experimental achievement.[56] In using Lily's encounter with Mrs. Ramsay to reshape the model of visionary closure from a female perspective, Woolf discovers that self-definition for a woman artist involves a process far more complex than simply rejecting her mother's life and values. She must learn how to accept the daughter's positive inheritance from both parents and how to weave these two strands together into the fabric of her own chosen medium.

6

Tragic Vision in *The Sound and the Fury*

I

Critics have long been troubled to reconcile Faulkner's personal belief that man will 'endure and prevail', as he expressed it in accepting the Nobel Prize, with the darkness of his fictional world, where he often seems to be writing 'as though he stood among and watched the end of man'.[1] Because the novels seem greater and more believable than Faulkner's personal optimism, many readers have been tempted to conclude that his heart saw deeper and embodied in his works a truth darker than his mind was able to accept. His persistent claims that the novels are all failures, and *The Sound and the Fury* his 'most splendid failure', often seem to reflect the man's unwillingness to acknowledge the artist's profound success in envisioning the defeat of man by men.[2] But I believe that the form and closure of *The Sound and the Fury* contradict both Faulkner's view that the book fails in affirming man's potential triumph, and the persistent critical view that it succeeds in affirming man's defeat.[3] Although the novel is about characters who fail or merely endure, it defines out of their suffering – as does all tragedy – the missing values which would make it possible for them to prevail.

I am aware, in turning to *The Sound and the Fury*, that it is not altogether customary to look at Faulkner in the context of English modernism; and, indeed, he probably did not know the work of Forster, Lawrence, or Woolf.[4] But criticism has steadily retreated from early views of Faulkner as an untutored backwoods genius; studies by Richard P. Adams and Michael Millgate firmly establish that he was profoundly versed in the same literary traditions as his English contemporaries. Surveying the available evidence, Millgate argues that Faulkner is more 'actively aware of American and European literary traditions than any other important American novelist of this century', and that *The Sound and the Fury* 'stands in the direct tradition of the modern psychological and experimental novel'.[5] Later in life, Faulkner frequently recommended extensive reading as the best training for young writers, and

143

Richard Adams has persuasively traced the results of such reading in Faulkner's own novels, discerning the influence of Shakespeare, the King James Bible, Keats, Conrad, and others.[6]

In addition to possessing this general literary background, Faulkner almost certainly knew *Ulysses* before he began *The Sound and the Fury*. Joseph Blotner reports that in 1924, Faulkner's friend Phil Stone gave him a copy of *Ulysses* and said 'this fellow is trying something new. This is something you should know about'. Faulkner wrote his name and the year in it.[7] By the end of his life he also owned copies of Joyce's *Poems, Dubliners, Portrait,* and *Stephen Hero*, which suggests that he was seriously interested in Joyce's work.[8] Early in his career, however, he repeatedly denied having read Joyce – probably, as Michael Groden contends, to 'counter the comparisons' that were made between *The Sound and the Fury* and *Ulysses* almost from the first.[9] Faulkner's fluctuating response to Joyce, like Virginia Woolf's, suggests the necessary struggle of a great artist to evade the shadow of a major contemporary. In 1931, Faulkner observed that his *response* to people who said he'd been influenced by Joyce was that he hadn't read Joyce.[10] In the same year, Estelle Faulkner told an interviewer that Faulkner gave her *Ulysses* to read on their honeymoon in 1929; when she did not understand it on a first reading, he insisted she read it again – scarcely the behaviour of a man who had not read it himself.[11] Finally, in 1955, Faulkner admitted that he had read *Ulysses* in the middle twenties, but he still claimed that Joyce could not have influenced him because by then his own 'career as a writer was already fixed'.[12] Nevertheless, Groden sees Joyce as a major influence on *The Sound and the Fury* – rightly, I believe – and offers convincing internal evidence from Faulkner's early works to suggest that his use of internal monologue was indebted to Joyce, particularly to *Penelope*.[13]

I would like to take this argument a step further, and suggest that the entire formal structure of *The Sound and the Fury* is a response to that of *Ulysses*. Each of the first three sections of *The Sound and the Fury* is narrated by one of the three Compson brothers; structural logic suggests that the fourth section should be narrated by their sister Caddy, whose female perspective – like Molly Bloom's in *Ulysses* – might be expected to unveil the final affirmative order and meaning of the whole. But such a conclusion becomes impossible because Caddy has been cast out of her family; by duplicating this loss in the structure of the novel, Faulkner creates a new version of tragic form. Dilsey, rather than Caddy, experiences an affirmative vision in the novel's final section; but Dilsey is the isolated survivor of a waning Christian tradition, and her vision cannot provide adequate closure for a novel set in the modern world. In *Howards End* and *To the Lighthouse*, the representatives of older systems of ordering values – Mrs. Wilcox and Mrs. Ramsay – die unexpectedly, and younger women – Margaret Schlegel and Lily Briscoe – eventually grow to fill, in different ways, the void left in the lives of the characters and at the centre of the novel. In *The Sound and the Fury* this situation is reversed: Dilsey, the elder centre of spiritual values, endures, but her potential spiritual heir has been lost. Caddy alone in the novel might have grown to inherit and embody the contact with natural order that Dilsey shares with Mrs. Wilcox and Margaret, Mrs. Ramsay and Lily, Ursula Brangwen, and Molly Bloom. Like the younger women in the earlier novels, Caddy should eventually have reenvisioned that contact in secular rather than religious terms, reshaping it into a form capable of making order and meaning out of modern experience.

Caddy Compson's reputation, like Molly Bloom's, has suffered at the hands of literary critics; early readers often saw Caddy with the eyes of her mother and brothers, as simply a 'fallen' woman so promiscuous and immoral that no positive values could ultimately attach to her. But as in Molly's case, a more positive evaluation of Caddy has emerged in recent decades. Faulkner himself always referred to Caddy in unqualifiedly positive terms; he calls her 'the beautiful one', 'my heart's darling', and locates her at the novel's thematic centre, asserting that *The Sound and the Fury* is 'the tragedy of two lost women: Caddy and her daughter'.[14] Taking up these suggestions, Catherine Baum argues that Caddy is the novel's heroine, possessing the qualities of unselfish 'love, compassion, pity, and sacrifice in a family which is destroying itself through lack of those qualities'. But in such a family, Baum suggests, Caddy's best qualities ultimately destroy her: she loves Dalton Ames but sends him away thinking he has hurt Quentin; when she finds herself with child, she thinks only of her father and Benjy in marrying Herbert Head; she gives up the daughter she loves to remove her from the life of prostitution to which Caddy, cast out by both husband and family, is finally reduced. Baum concludes that the loss of Caddy's capacity for love is a tragic and 'terrifying waste', and that the final section 'comments on life without Caddy and the love she represents'.[15] Sally Page suggests further that because Mrs. Compson refuses to love or care for her children, Caddy 'assumes the false role of playing "mother" to her brothers'. But when Caddy begins the 'natural process of seeking love outside her family, she is faced with a frustrating problem of identity – the confusion of her real self with the role she has assumed'. Because Quentin, in particular, clings to her as a substitute mother, she is forced 'at a crucial moment to withdraw from the natural life process'; through his jealous interference, Caddy loses the man she loves.[16]

In a book-length study of *The Sound and the Fury*, André Bleikasten moves beyond revaluing Caddy's character to identify her as 'the very soul of the novel'. Faulkner comments that in writing the book, 'I, who never had a sister . . . set out to make myself a beautiful and tragic little girl'.[17] The novel, Bleikasten suggests, was written out of this sense of lack of loss, 'reduplicated in the figure of Caddy'; it 'grows out of and refers back to an empty centre' which 'represents at once the novel's origin and its *telos*'. But Caddy 'was elusive to her creator; so she is to her brothers in the novel, and so she must remain to the reader . . . a dream of beauty wasted and destroyed'. Caddy is not the novel's heroine in any traditional sense, but is the 'ambiguous and evasive object of desire and memory' who 'exists only in the minds and memories of her brothers'. We can 'never discover what she actually is'; she remains, rather, woman as seen in man's imagination, 'the other, a blank screen onto which he projects both his desires and his fears, his love and his hate'. Her brothers

> form the plural *subject* of the narration; the sister . . . turns out to be its primary *object* . . . the absent/present figure ceaselessly *evoked* – or *invoked* – in their monologues.

She is the 'novelist's secret Muse', a symbolic reminder 'of the mythic mediating function of woman through whom, for man, passes all knowledge about the origins, all knowledge about the twin enigmas of life and death'. Bleikasten observes her persistent association with natural images: the swiftness and lightness of wind in her movements, the warmth of fire in her nurturing capacity, the fecundity of the land in her association with trees and mud, the purification of water in her appearances at the branch and in the rain.[18]

This association with nature is an essential attribute of the Muse figure who can mediate between inhuman life process and human order. Like Molly Bloom, Caddy is in part a symbolic earth goddess; to Benjy, until he loses her, she always 'smelled like trees'.[19] To Quentin's anguish at Caddy's sexual activity, Mr. Compton responds, aptly, that 'it's nature is hurting you not Caddy' (p. 143). But while Dublin at least tolerates Molly's natural sexuality, the Compson South ultimately turns Caddy's into something that tortures and destroys her; as a result, her capacity for contact with nature becomes a tragic loss in the novel rather than a comic presence. As the author's Muse in *The Sound and the Fury*, Caddy is thus neither merely *invoked* as a source of inspiration, nor fully *evoked* as a character. If Beatrice and Molly Bloom can be categorized as embodied

Muse figures, Caddy is perhaps best conceived as a disembodied Muse, who can now be seen only through the minds of other characters.

When Faulkner was asked why Caddy did not narrate a section of her own, he replied that 'Caddy was still to me too beautiful and too moving to reduce her to telling what was going on, that it would be more passionate to see her through somebody else's eyes, I thought'.[20] He will not reduce his Muse to explaining or justifying herself; the only way to keep his vision of Caddy intact is for her to remain silent in the novel. Although Joyce attempts to render Molly's voice directly in *Penelope*, it is in any case unusual for a writer to report the words of the Muse herself. She stands in a mediating role between inarticulate nature and human speech; it is not her own words that matter, but the power that animates them, as the women themselves understand. Just as Mrs. Ramsay prefers to convey her love to her husband without speaking of it, Caddy tells Quentin that she loves Dalton Ames by letting the surge of nature itself within her speak:

> she took my hand and held it flat against her throat
> now say his name
> Dalton Ames
> I felt the first surge of blood there it surged in strong
> accelerating beats (p. 203)

Faulkner's narrative strategy makes the vision of Caddy more 'passionate' because we see her through the eyes of tellers who are less admirable, less coherent selves than she is; our perspective is made to correspond with that of the brothers who have lost her, so that we can win through to understanding the role their own failings have played in causing that loss only by sharing their sense of emptiness and their suffering. As in *Ulysses*, the novel's nihilistic surface arises because the author refuses to make the meaning of his story more accessible to his readers than it is to his characters. The family has banished the one figure who might make their lives meaningful and connected; each tale that remains is only a fragment of a larger and broken whole. But Faulkner's ordering of those fragments achieves a coherent, albeit elusive, tragic unity that stands in contrast to the failure of the characters to make sense of their lives.[21]

II

Faulkner invariably gave the same response to questions about the genesis of *The Sound and the Fury*:

It began with the picture of the little girl's muddy drawers, climbing that tree to look in the parlor window with her brothers that didn't have the courage to climb the tree waiting to see what she saw.[22]

The problem Faulkner faced in writing the novel was to describe the meaning of that image, to figure out for himself and for the reader how to view it: 'it took the rest of the four hundred pages to explain why she was brave enough to climb the tree to look in the window'.[23]

The originating image is a mythic one, a symbolic repetition of man's fall. Versh reminds Caddy that 'your paw told you to stay out of that tree', but she rationalizes the objection away: ' "That was a long time ago." Caddy said. "I expect he's forgotten about it. Besides, he said to mind me tonight" ' (p. 46). Caddy climbs the forbidden tree to gain knowledge, to find out what the adults are doing; she thinks they are having a party, and expects the vision through the window to be a pleasant one. What she actually sees from the tree without understanding it is her grandmother's funeral; later, when she finds out what has happened, she will connect death with a vision of emptiness and inaction: ' "they're not doing anything in there." Caddy said. "Just sitting in chairs and looking" ' (p. 55). But while Caddy is looking at the adults who are looking on the nothingness of death, learning to see as an adult sees, her brothers are looking up at the muddy bottom of her drawers. When they find out what has happened, they will subconsciously associate the knowledge of death with this view of Caddy; the image will become a symbol for the connection between sin and death and a prediction of her fall. She is like a darkened mirror in the tree; they gain the knowledge of death only as it is reflected from her. For her brothers, death becomes not simply the consequence of sin, but the consequence of Caddy's sin.

For Benjy, this moment beneath the tree represents both the beginning and end of time. The day of Damuddy's death is the earliest one of which he has any memory; it marks his first separation of an objective world from a subjective self, a division understood through the experience of seeing: 'We watched the muddy bottom of her drawers' (p. 47). But this entry into remembered time also marks the end of his mental development: on his thirty-third birthday in 1928, another boy astutely remarks to Luster that 'he been three years old thirty years' (p. 19). Benjy's mental progress remains permanently arrested at the point he had reached in 1898. His capacities are roughly those of a three year old throughout his life: he understands simple speech but cannot employ it; he 'could manage solid food pretty well for himself' (p. 376), but otherwise he has to be fed. Damuddy's death also elicits his first demonstration of the special power of smell which will later enable him to perceive and react violently to strained emotions in the people around him. While he is going to sleep, 'Caddy held me and I could hear us all, and the darkness, and something I could smell' (p. 90). On this first encounter with the smell he does not yet find it disturbing, but later he will come to connect it with those periods when the even tenor of his uneventful contentment is most grievously disrupted. Damuddy's death is the first occasion on which his position in the midst of a fallen world impinges seriously on the Eden of his innocence; in his pre-rational awareness, the coming of death and all its woe into his world is adventitiously but permanently associated with the memory of Caddy 'all wet and muddy behind' (p. 21). For Jason, two years older and unhampered by congenital idiocy, the same connection becomes not merely adventitious but logical; woman's sin – Caddy's sin – is the cause of all evil in his world.

Quentin is not present to witness this mythic, ordering image at the pear tree that is for Faulkner the crucial moment in the novel – a point most readers seem to miss. When the children follow Caddy down to Versh's house after dinner, Benjy observes that 'Roskus came with the milk buckets. He went on. Quentin wasn't coming with us. He was sitting on the kitchen steps' (p. 33). At Versh's, Caddy decides that they will go back to the main house to look in the parlor window; once they arrive she climbs the tree (pp. 38–40, 43–7). During this time Benjy never mentions that Quentin has rejoined the other children, and we never hear Quentin speak. While Caddy is in the tree, Dilsey arrives and asks where Caddy and Quentin are (p. 54); after removing Caddy from the tree, Dilsey repeats 'Where's Quentin'. Versh is sent off to find him; according to Dilsey, 'Roskus say he seen him going towards the barn' (p. 55). Later, when the children are going to bed, Quentin and Versh come in (p. 90). Quentin presumably started for the barn sometime after the other children left for Versh's house and remained there alone until Versh came later to find him. In the interval, Quentin was seen only by Roskus, whom Benjy had just observed coming (either to or from the barn) with the milk buckets. In Quentin's own narration the only explicit recollection of this night makes no allusion to the scene at the tree: he asks Caddy 'do you remember the day damuddy died when you sat down in the water in your drawers', and a page later refers to the scene at bedtime: 'Caddy do you remember how Dilsey fussed at you because your drawers were muddy' (pp. 188–9). He remembers only those events at which Benjy's narration also confirms that he was present.[24]

Quentin is the most intelligent and imaginative of the Compson sons, the only one who might have been able, like Faulkner himself, to perceive the mythic significance of Caddy's position in the tree. Unlike the younger children, Quentin gradually works out the knowledge that Damuddy has died: he identifies the sound of his mother crying, loses interest in eating dinner, and asks Caddy how they can have a party when Damuddy is sick (pp. 29–31). Alone in the barn he apparently becomes certain of his suspicions; he returns crying but otherwise silent, and once in bed he turns his face to the wall (pp. 90–1). In contrast, Caddy, who has actually seen the funeral, persistently refuses the knowledge of death, assuring Jason that he can sleep with Damuddy when she gets well (p. 89). Quentin's behaviour at the branch earlier in the evening suggests why he alone seems receptive to a correct understanding of the day's events. When Caddy takes off her dress so that it will dry, Quentin interprets her innocent action as sexual provocation in an attempt to deny his own dawning sexual awareness; by punishing Caddy, he tries to make her responsible for his response (pp. 19–21). His stirring of sexual desire and guilt marks a fall from the innocence of childhood and prepares him for the knowledge of death which is to follow. Like his brothers, he will later find his recollection of this day – his first encounter with death – inextricably associated with the memory of Caddy's muddy drawers; unlike his brothers, he consciously understands this image as prophetic of Caddy's fall. But he misses the moment at the pear tree which places the image in the wider archetypal context of universal human failing and loss. As Mr. Compson will tell him later,

> you are still blind to what is in yourself to that part of general truth the
> sequence of natural events and their causes which shadows every mans
> brow even Benjys (p. 220)

Quentin can neither understand nor accept his position in a fallen world, can never see in his sister's fall the image of his own.

Quentin's absence in the scene at the pear tree results from his refusal to participate in the human community represented by his sister, his brothers and the negro children.[25] According to Caddy, his absence is the result of being 'mad because he had to mind me tonight' (p. 55); more generally, Quentin refuses to accept Caddy's role as a leader among the children because it conflicts with his false image of himself. As the eldest son in a family with aristocratic traditions, he thinks he ought to possess chivalric courage and exercise active leadership; when he fails to demonstrate such qualities, he is consistently discouraged and baffled. His culminating failure is the attempt to fight Caddy's lover, Dalton

Ames, who merely catches hold of both his wrists with one hand; Quentin struggles and finally passes out 'like a girl' (pp. 199–201). Quentin is incapable of acting the heroic role in which he has cast himself; like Conrad's Lord Jim, he cannot reconcile his romantic ideals with his defective courage. Unable to lead and unwilling to follow, he is repeatedly forced – ultimately in the extreme expedient of suicide – to withdraw from the community of shared human experience.

Quentin's brothers share his unheroic isolation, but not the imagination, intelligence and heroic standard of conduct which make it quickly unbearable and self-destructive. Jason repeatedly refuses in principle to mind Caddy on the night of Damuddy's death (pp. 28, 32, 39, 46), but he follows her lead all evening; unlike Quentin, he is untroubled by inconsistencies between his plans and his actions. Later in life he is as ineffectual in action as his brother, but he generally has a ready excuse for himself: his failure in disciplining his niece is the result of interference by his mother and Dilsey; his failure in cotton speculation is the fault of the telegraph office or the Jews; his general inability to get ahead is the result of Caddy's promiscuity and her daughter's untimely birth, which cost him his promised job in Herbert Head's bank. Jason's self-justifying rationalizations preserve his sanity by bridging the gap between what he intends and what he achieves, but he lacks the moral courage necessary to trust his future security even in part to anyone but himself. The inevitable result is that in spite of saving, stealing and speculating obsessively in the attempt to get ahead of his neighbours, he continually falls behind them. Like Quentin and Benjy, he is forced by his behaviour into isolation from the human community: in his earliest chronological appearance in the novel, Jason is playing 'by himself further down the branch' (p. 21). His isolation never alters; as an adult he has no friends, only greater and lesser adversaries.

All three brothers miss the significance of the moment beneath the pear tree because they are too self-involved to see themselves as merely part of a larger, universal human pattern of failure, loss and possible redemption. Characters in fiction who grow from initial self-involvement to genuine maturity – Elizabeth Bennet and Emma Woodhouse, for example – must acquire the ability to imagine themselves in someone else's place; by shifting their point of view, they can see themselves as part of a wider human community, and look back at themselves to assess and judge their own actions. None of the Compson brothers ever becomes capable of such imaginative projection; they are incapable of losing themselves long enough to find themselves. Benjy's solipsism differs from that of his brothers only in appearing more involuntary than theirs. He is conscious of little beyond his own needs and the perpetual anguish of his incapacity to satisfy them; he can neither know courage in the face of loss, nor participate actively in a human community by acknowledging the needs of its other members. Jason acknowledges his neighbours merely in fearing their ability to harm him; he must continually battle his self-centredness with rationalizations and self-extenuations. Benjy and Quentin are unable to adopt any such pattern of self-justification – Quentin because he is too intelligent to delude himself, and Benjy because he is not intelligent enough. In embracing courage and chivalric action as romantic ideals of conduct, Quentin alone attempts to redirect his self-love toward external goals, but is finally unable to do so. His love of Caddy is love of the one woman in the world most like himself; when she falls, becoming 'to death devote', he makes the easy transition from love of self to love of death through the mediating image of her fate.[26] Benjy's idiocy, Jason's paranoia and Quentin's suicide are all forms of behaviour which place the fate of the self above all other concerns.

Caddy alone among the Compson children possesses both the strength and the will to shift her point of view, to see the world imaginatively through eyes other than her own. Such imaginative sympathy is the secret of her success with Benjy: she realizes that his hands are cold and warms them (p. 5); she understands at the branch that he is crying because she has threatened to run away, and she reassures him that she will not (pp. 21–2); she discovers his interest in T. P.'s bottle of lightening bugs and negotiates with T. P. and Frony so that he can hold them (pp. 43–4). Because Benjy cannot use words to express his needs, he can be comforted and satisfied only by someone who can persistently shift her perspective to identify it with his. The novel's originating image at the pear tree offers a physical metaphor for this imaginative capacity: Caddy climbs the tree to see the world from a different angle, one above and beyond her normal range of vision. This unthinking willingness to shift her point of view is the source of her courage, the reason why she was 'brave enough' to climb the tree. But the image also promises uncompromisingly that Caddy's finest qualities will themselves become the agents of her fall; her courage is the courage of man's disobedience as well as the courage of his capacity for unselfish love. Her capacity to see and her compassionate desire to satisfy the needs of others will lead her, in adolescence, to the sexual surrender that her family can interpret only as the sin of promiscuity. In a fallen world, even the greatest human virtues contribute to 'the sequence of natural events and their causes which shadows every mans brow'.

Caddy's story is tragic not because she falls – an inevitable event for all

men and women in a fallen world – but because her family stedfastly fails
to forgive her.[27] Mrs. Compson sees Caddy only from an unchanging
perspective like the one her sons find beneath the pear tree, where
Caddy's muddy drawers are clearly visible but their own are out of sight;
they see the speck in Caddy's eye but miss the beam in their own. Mrs.
Compson sees only her own loss of reputation in Caddy's dishonour, not
the failure of maternal love which makes that loss fully merited. Benjy
sees only his personal loss of contentment, Jason only the loss of his
promised job, Quentin only his own failure to act a chivalric role. Mr.
Compson means better; Jason – certainly not a favourably biased witness
– testifies to his father's persistent attempts at charity after Caddy is cast
off by her husband: he reminds his mother that Mr. Compson 'was trying
all the time to persuade you to let her come home when Herbert threw her
out' (p. 274).[28] But Mr. Compson drinks himself to death before he can
insist effectively upon forgiveness. Caddy is cast out by a manipulation of
traditional values in which Jason and his mother set the Word against the
Word, sexual morality against the higher moral law of Christian love.
When Mr. Compson brings Caddy's daughter home, Mrs. Compson
insists that Caddy's name never again be spoken in the house. As Jason
remembers the scene, she invokes divine authority in support of her
moral stand; she knows 'that people cannot flout God's laws with
impunity' (p. 247). But Faulkner turns this statement ironically against
her; in flouting the law of Christian forgiveness, she and Jason banish
from the family not merely Caddy, but also the spirit of unselfish love she
represents.

III

The Sound and the Fury, like a Greek tragedy, begins near the end of its
dramatic action; by Easter Weekend 1928, the tragedy of Caddy and her
daughter is nearly complete. Faulkner presents earlier events in the form
of memories and flashbacks, both within the individual narratives and in
the structure of the book as a whole; Quentin's entire section is a long leap
into the past. From the characters' scattered fragments of a remembered
past, the reader must build up his own version of Caddy's fall and the
Compsons' failure of moral vision. But the narrative present of the novel
itself focuses on the end of the story; it is organized around the moment
when the Compson failure to forgive Caddy becomes humanly
irrevocable.

    Despite its narrative complexities, *The Sound and the Fury* is essentially a movement between two symbolic images which establish, in Frank Kermode's terms, a consonance between past and present, origin and end.[29] In the novel's originating image, Caddy climbs up the pear tree to look in the parlour window; thirty years later, in its culminating image, her daughter climbs out of a bedroom window and down the same tree to escape from the house. The events of the day Damuddy dies are Benjy's earliest memories; Quentin's escape on 7 April 1928 is, correspondingly, the latest event described in his narration:

We went to the window and looked out. It came out of Quentin's window and climbed across into the tree. We watched the tree shaking. The shaking went down the tree, then it came out and we watched it go away across the grass. (pp. 90–1)

Faulkner further emphasizes the connection between the two events by framing Benjy's description of this final incident between two fragments of the scene in which the children go to bed on the day of Damuddy's death. The first incident in the pear tree symbolically initiates the chain of events which comes to an end in the second: Quentin's presence in the Compson household is a direct consequence of Caddy's fall, but her presence has also provided the family's most inescapable continuing link to Caddy herself.

While Quentin is in the household, Caddy and her capacity for love are still distantly associated with the family. She has bribed Jason for the right to visit her daughter 'once or twice a year sometimes' (p. 262), frustrating Mrs. Compson's plan to bring the child up 'never to know that she had a mother' (p. 247). From these infrequent meetings, Quentin seems to have acquired some sense of her mother's love as a potential protection and refuge from the miseries of her life: when Jason abuses her physically and verbally she says 'Dilsey, I want my mother' (p. 230); earlier, apparently when she first began to plan her escape, she wrote to her mother for money (pp. 263–8). Quentin is deeply shocked when Jason tells her that the money order Caddy has sent is only for ten dollars; much as she wants the money, she seems even more anxious to prove to herself that Jason rather than Caddy has betrayed her:

"Will you let me see it?" she says. "I just want to look at it. Whatever it says, I wont ask for but ten dollars. You can have the rest. I just want to see it."

Jason refuses and Quentin 'stood there with her head bent and the pen

shaking in her hand. Just like her mother' (p. 267). Most critics have
emphasized Quentin's differences from Caddy, pointing in particular to
their dramatically opposed attitudes toward Benjy. But Quentin is not
totally incapable of her mother's sympathy and compassion; as Michael
Millgate has observed, it is she who gives Luster the quarter he so
anxiously desires.[30] Because Luster's small loss on Saturday 7 April
parallels Benjy's larger one, the gift suggests Quentin's more general
potential to give back what the family has lost – both directly in her power
to draw Caddy back to Jefferson, and indirectly in her own unnurtured
capacity to see and satisfy the needs of others.

Until Easter 1928, it is still possible – however remotely – that Caddy
might be forgiven and asked to return home. Because Jason's financial
interest is involved in maintaining her banishment, he works to keep his
mother's moral outrage alive, but without his efforts Mrs. Compson
might by now have found it more comfortable to slip by degrees away
from principle:

> She looked at the check a while. "I'm glad to know she's so . . . she
> has so much . . .
> "I could bring myself to accept them," she says, "For my childrens'
> sake. I have no pride . . . .
> "It's not myself," she says, "I'd gladly take her back, sins and all,
> because she is my flesh and blood. It's for Quentin's sake." (pp. 272–4)

But Jason deftly manoeuvres her into once more renouncing flesh and
blood (and money). At the same time, because Caddy's concern for
Quentin is genuine, it seems at least possible that she would be willing to
endure the personal abuse at the hands of her mother and Jason which
would be an unstated condition of permission to return home and care for
her daughter.

Caddy's continuing concern for Quentin appears in her final letter to
Jason: 'Is she sick? Let me know at once or I'll come there and see for
myself. You promised you would let me know when she needed things'
(p. 236). Jason remembers that earlier she wanted him to

> "promise that she'll – that she – you can do that. Things for her. Be
> kind to her. Little things that I cant, they wont let. . . . But you wont.
> You never had a drop of warm blood in you."

Caddy tried to offer a thousand dollars to get Quentin back, but she gave
up when Jason suggested that Caddy could only bring Quentin up to

become another fallen woman: 'Oh, I'm crazy,' she said, 'I'm insane. I can't take her' (pp. 259–60). Caddy has accepted her family's judgement that she herself is not fit to bring up a daughter. But she sent Quentin home when her father was still alive and Jason was less influential, thinking perhaps also of Dilsey's presence in the household; she cannot have envisioned the environment of selfishness and deceit that has grown up under Mrs. Compson and Jason. When Quentin climbs down the pear tree for the last time, repeating her mother's public fall, Caddy's hope to have saved her daughter by renouncing her is completely lost. After Easter 1928, Caddy, as Faulkner observes in the Compson Appendix, '*hasn't anything anymore worth being saved for nothing worth being lost that she can lose*' (p. 420). Caddy's tragedy is now complete; she has no possible further tie to her family, no hope of redeeming herself or anyone else by sacrfice or love.

None of this significance is apparent to Benjy and Luster as they watch Quentin climb down the tree. Apparently they have made a routine of watching her nightly sorties:

> *Luster . . . went to the window and looked out. He came back and took my arm. Here she come, he said. Be quiet, now. We went to the window and looked out.* (p. 90)

Earlier, Luster told the man with the red tie that 'they comes every night she can climb down the tree. I don't keep no track of them' (p. 61). Luster has no suspicion that tonight will be in any way unusual. But this night's difference from the immediate past and its connection with a more distant origin are what call up the novel's organization around Easter Weekend 1928, just as Molly Bloom's decision to commit adultery on 16 June 1904 is what ultimately determines the date of *Ulysses*. Beverly Gross argues that 'Miss Quentin's escape with Jason's cache' does not seem 'much of a conclusion to the manifold experience this novel deals with'.[31] But the loss of Jason's cache is a red herring for both Jason and the reader, one which obscures the more serious final loss of any bond between Caddy and her family; the novel has at last reached a moment of tragic consonance with its origin.

This narrative consonance acquires special power from Faulkner's innovative use of Benjy as a narrator. Benjy is the only character who actually witnesses both events at the pear tree, yet he is completely incapable of perceiving any temporal organization.[32] As a result, Faulkner can create a formal consonance which organizes the structure of the novel without imposing any direct influence on the actions of his characters. Through Benjy's eyes, the reader sees the pattern that connects the events of 1928 to those of 1898, making sense in the process of many events between; but since none of the characters sees and understands this pattern, all act as if they were free moral agents unfettered by their existence within the boundaries of art. Like real people, they can prevail over empty time by constructing their own meanings and consonances; endure time by mediating suffering and loss with received patterns of order such as religious faith; or fail in struggling with time by seeing life as essentially meaningless, mere sound and fury signifying nothing. But at no point do their choices seem forced or limited purely by the aesthetic exigencies of their position within a work of art. Faulkner thus achieves an unusually elegant solution to the formal problem E. M. Forster identified in novelistic endings: the damage generally done to the characters by the writer's need to wind up the plot.[33] *The Sound and the Fury* achieves satisfying aesthetic closure without conspicuously compromising the freedom of its characters; it releases them in the reader's mind from the deterministic boundaries of its own artistic order.[34]

Faulkner's unusual success in freeing the characters from being dominated by the plot enables him to take the equally unusual risk of revealing the culminating formal consonance at the end of the first section, rather than at the end of the novel. In a traditional narrative, such a strategy would work to undermine the plausibility of the characters by subordinating them to a clearly predetermined action. Even here, since Benjy's section provides a complete formal microscosm of the novel, the succeeding sections are all in a sense structural appendices – explications of what happens in the first – as Faulkner himself insisted:

> I told the idiot's experience of that day, and that was incomprehensible, even I could not have told what was going on then, so I had to write another chapter . . . then [another] . . . then another . . .[35]

But as long as the reader remains uncertain about the central action, this prolonged deferral of closure becomes itself a further source of narrative power. Since we have already seen but not understood the central structural consonance, the sense of an ending is, in Kermode's terms, vividly immanent throughout.

IV

The first three sections of *The Sound and the Fury* are like the synoptic gospels, in the literal sense of *synoptic* as 'a seeing together'.[36] Different as the three narrators are, they all see the tragedy of Caddy and her daughter from similar perspectives. But the fourth section, like the fourth gospel, offers a new and visionary 'seeing' of the story. Because Dilsey's affirmative religious experience occupies a central position in this section, many readers have argued that the final narrative provides an unqualifiedly positive ending in Christian terms. But this final narrative perspective cannot be identified entirely with Dilsey's, as Walter Slatoff first suggested: 'the emphasis on Dilsey and her trip to church is at the beginning of the final section and is only one of several emphases in that section'.[37] In a detailed structural analysis, John V. Hagopian identifies four parts in the last section: a Prologue (dawn to 9.30 a.m.), Dilsey's trip to church (9.30 a.m. to 1.30 p.m.), Jason's trip to Mottson (also 9.30 a.m. to 1.30 p.m.), and Benjy and Luster's trip to the monument (1.30 to about 3 p.m.). Hagopian argues that the later scenes completely overturn the tentative resolution provided by Dilsey's experience, and that the novel's final terms of closure are nihilistic.[38] But while his analysis effectively refutes religious interpretations of the final section, it need not follow that the novel achieves no final ordering vision at all. By continuing the narrative beyond the moment when Dilsey's experience could have provided visionary closure, Faulkner deliberately and vividly evokes the tragic loss of Caddy in the structure of the novel itself.

It is easy to overvalue the role of Dilsey's Christian vision in the novel's structure, because it indeed comes the closest of any experience in the final section to comprehending Faulkner's own vision of the Compson story. Shortly before leaving for church, Dilsey hears Luster's suspicion that Quentin has left the house:

> Dilsey looked at him. "How you know she aint here?"
> "Me and Benjy seed her clamb out de window last night. Didn't us, Benjy?"
> "You did?" Dilsey said, looking at him.
> "We sees her doin hit ev'y night," Luster said, "Clamb right down dat pear tree."

After Benjy and Luster go out, Dilsey 'stood quietly for awhile at the table' (pp. 357–8). Faulkner holds out the possibility, but withholds the certainty, that she may be able to see back through this recent image to an earlier scene at which she herself was present:

> "Who in what tree." Dilsey said. She came and looked up into the tree. "Caddy." Dilsey said. The branches began to shake again.
> "You, Satan." Dilsey said. "Come down from there." (p. 54)

Dilsey's identification of Caddy with Satan suggests her persistent awareness of the reigious resonances in human experience. Even if she never consciously grasps the consonance between the widely separated scenes at the pear tree, she believes in a mythic repetition, patterning and ordering of experience which is directly antecedent to the formal ordering strategies of art.

Dilsey's visionary experience is inspired by Reverend Shegog's incantatory sermon, which is composed less of words chosen to convey meanings than of mythic verbal patterns arranged rhythmically to stimulate the brain and conjure up visual images:

> "When de long, cold – Oh, I tells you, breddren, when de long, cold – I sees de light en I sees de word, po sinner! Dey passed away in Egypt, de swinging chariots; de generations passed away. Wus a rich man: whar he now, O breddren? Wus a po man: whar he now, O sistuhn?" (pp. 368–9)

The preacher's words evoke the entire pattern of Christian history: the long cold of the uncreated abyss becomes the light and the word of creation, which begins in turn the march of human generations. But human history is one of universal passing and loss; all men fall and die, a process which reaches its nadir in the crucifixion:

> "I sees hit, breddren! I sees hit! Sees de blastin, blindin sight! I sees Calvary, wid de sacred trees, sees de thief en de murderer en de least of dese."

But out of this dark tale of sound and fury there appears light:

> "I sees de darkness en de death everlastin upon de generations. Den, lo! Breddren! Yes, breddren! Whut I see? Whut I see, O sinner? I sees de resurrection en de light; sees de meek Jesus sayin Dey kilt Me dat ye shall live again; I died dat dem whut sees en believes shall never die." (p. 370)

Faith in this sudden replacement of darkness by light cannot be justified or explained in words; it can only be experienced as a moment of vision, a sudden shift of perspective which places the seer – like Saul on the Damascus road or Wordsworth on Snowdon – in a new world.

Dilsey's vision is in many ways similar to the concluding visionary experiences of Margaret in *Howards End*, Ursula in *The Rainbow*, Molly in *Ulysses* and Lily in *To the Lighthouse*. Like theirs, Dilsey's experience is not communicable or fully reducible to words:

> "I've seed de first en de last," Dilsey said. "Never you mind me."
> "First en last what?" Frony said.
> "Never you mind," Dilsey said. "I seed de beginnin, en now I sees de endin." (p. 371)

The novel has all along developed an implied antithesis between sound and sight: sound, from the simplicity of Benjy's moaning to the complexity of Mr. Compson's discussions with Quentin, seems capable only of expressing the utterer's subjective awareness; sight, in contrast, takes a character out of himself in a moment of vision and understanding. Such experience can be shared through actions but not described in words. Just as Caddy affirms her capacity to see beyond herself by caring for Benjy, Dilsey shows her selfless understanding in her unrewarded devotion to the Compsons. Donald Kartiganer argues that Dilsey's understanding is available to neither the other characters nor to the reader; 'what Dilsey really knows, as Frony's comment makes clear, is for Dilsey alone'.[39] But Dilsey's understanding is simply not available through language. Frony has had the same opportunity to be taken out of herself in the church service, and both the Compsons and the reader have before them the daily expression of Dilsey's understanding in her exemplary and unselfish actions.

Dilsey's phrase 'the first and the last' is a rhetorical counterpart to the novel's title. According to Christian history, the world begins in the first sound of the word – 'Let there be light' – and ends in the last fury of final apocalypse. Dilsey's moment of seeing origin and end together thus takes her temporarily into the world outside of time which Benjy inhabits permanently. Benjy, for whom time is simultaneous rather than sequential, is always lost in an instantaneous present which contains birth and death, origin and end, all confused together in an unintelligible sound and fury which signifies nothing to him because he cannot escape from it back into time. His world is always just being born and just being destroyed. Unlike his brother Quentin, whose memories of the past often blot out and obliterate his awareness of the present, Benjy can relive long scenes from the past and return to the present without having missed anything; his memories take place completely outside of ordinary time. His constant cry, over which he has no conscious control, resembles the glossalalia that sometimes accompanies religious vision; in his case it echoes the traumatic agony he suffers from being trapped in his own eternal moment. But for most people time is plotted out in a more orderly and humanly manageable succession, except in rare moments of overarching vision. This spatialized successiveness gives man the power to remember the past and to predict the future, the freedom to forget and the capacity to imagine. Such power and freedom enable moments of vision to bestow meaning on experience, to create out of the flux of time orders and concords that become for man 'the pillars to help him endure and prevail'.[40] *The Sound and the Fury* is a protracted attempt to achieve some such visionary consonance and meaning, to discover its own beginning and end. For Dilsey, the tale of loss and suffering she has witnessed – the sound and fury of the Compson tragedy – acquires meaning in its correspondence with the larger pattern of Christian history. But for Faulkner, Christian significance alone is not enough.

Unlike the culminating visions in other modernist novels, Dilsey's experience is unmediated by the Romantic secularization of vision. Her vision belongs to a purely Christian tradition; she 'sees en believes' in an ancient religious system of order that seems admirable but finally inadequate to deal with the complexity of modern life. Faulkner implicitly acknowledges such doubts about Christianity in the setting and structure of the final section. Dilsey's vision occurs in 'Nigger Hollow' (p. 377), a location which inverts the traditional place of vision on the mountaintop; mental sight is cut off here from any correspondingly far-reaching physical vision. Faulkner's description of the setting further suggests religion's two-dimensional perspective on the modern world; it is

a scene like a painted backdrop. Notched into a cut of red clay crowned with oaks the road appeared to stop short off, like a cut ribbon. Beside it a weathered church lifted its crazy steeple like a painted church, and the whole scene was a flat and without perspective as a painted cardboard set upon the ultimate edge of the flat earth. (p. 364)

Sunk amidst the Compson tragedy, Dilsey's experience has little real effect on the lives of the other characters. Because Caddy has been lost, Dilsey's values are not supported by any authority within the family; as a result, her efforts to hold the family together are largely ineffectual. In returning to the sound and the fury of Jason's day after recounting the visionary moment in Dilsey's, Faulkner's artistic vision embraces a wider perspective than Dilsey's religious one. But in Kermode's terms, Dilsey's apocalypse is 'disconfirmed without being discredited'; an ending will still come 'as expected, but not in the manner expected'.[41]

After Dilsey's vision passes and her daily routine resumes, the novel offers a second version of the same hours of the day by following Jason's pursuit of his niece. Jason's trip is a parodic repetition of Dilsey's walk to church and back, but it climaxes in an unexpected visionary experience exactly parallel to hers, one which takes him momentarily out of himself for the first, and perhaps only, time in his life. As he drives to Mottson, rage and the headache induced by the smell of gasoline gradually break down his hardbitten rational consciousness; his ordinarily suppressed imagination inflates his self-centredness to Satanic proportions:

> he passed churches. . . . "And damn You, too," he said, "See if You can stop me," thinking of himself, his file of soldiers with the manacled sheriff in the rear, dragging Omnipotence down from His throne, if necessary; of the embattled legions of both hell and heaven through which he tore his way and put his hands at last on his fleeing niece. (p. 382)[42]

As he loses the ability to think rationally and sinks deeper into solipsism, Jason's sense of smell quickens to resemble that of his nearly subhuman brother Benjy: 'the fact that he must depend on that red tie' to recognize the man 'seemed to be the sum of the impending disaster; he could almost smell it' (p. 384). Like his brother Quentin, Jason wants to defeat the apparent meaninglessness of time with an end that centres on himself:

> He could see the opposed forces of his destiny and his will drawing swiftly together now, toward a junction that would be irrevocable. . . . That [his niece and the man in the red tie] should not be there . . . would be opposed to all nature and contrary to the whole rhythm of events. (pp. 384–5)

But when Jason storms into the show trailer at Mottson, he encounters, in the furious little old man, a crisis totally different from the one he is seeking.

The desperate sound and fury of this meaningless encounter opens Jason's eyes: 'for the first time Jason saw clear and unshadowed the disaster toward which he rushed' (p. 386). In the face of immediate and totally unexpected danger, his perspective suddenly shifts to embrace a vision of the world beyond himself:

> Jason glared wildly about, holding the other. Outside it was now bright and sunny, swift and bright and empty, and he thought of the

people soon to be going quietly home to Sunday dinner, decorously
festive, and of himself trying to hold the fatal, furious little old man
whom he dared not release long enough to turn his back and run.
(p. 387)

For the first time Jason sees himself from the outside as only part of a
larger human pattern; he at last sees 'clear and unshadowed' the
inevitability of his own death, and envisions the process of life itself which
will continue undisturbed after he is gone.

The moment of vision gives Jason the strength and courage to escape,
but when he hesitates outside the trailer he is attacked again by the old
man, now wielding a hatchet. He falls, thinking 'so this is how it'll end,
and he believed that he was about to die' (p. 387). But again he finds
unexpected will and strength: 'a furious desire not to die seized him and
he struggled', amid the sound and the fury of 'the old man wailing and
cursing in his cracked voice' (p. 388). The wider vision of his own relative
unimportance in the world gives Jason, ironically, the will and strength to
survive; like his mother he finds 'in the face of incontroverible disaster
. . . a sort of fortitude' (p. 373) to overcome the peril of an utterly
meaningless personal end. Destructive as it has been in the novel, self-
centredness nevertheless gives man the power to endure, to bide time
until he can discover how to prevail.

Yet unlike Dilsey and Caddy, Jason is only capable of seeing beyond
himself when he stands in the shadow of imminent death. The moment is
likely to remain unique in Jason's life; after he is rescued and revived, an
electric sign admonishes him to keep his mind's eye fixed on his
experience in Mottson. He tells his rescuer that he was 'looking for two
people', echoing the theme of loss which has been central to the novel.
But he can say now, without any further proof than his own change of
perspective, that 'I know they're not here.' Though he still does not
understand as fully as Dilsey what has really been lost and why, he
realizes, as she does, that the loss is now irrecoverable: 'It dont matter,' he
says; 'it dont make any difference' (pp. 389–90). Jason returns to his car
and sits quietly – something he has never done before in the novel – 'with
his invisible life ravelled out about him like a wornout sock' (p. 391). Just
as Macbeth sets himself against natural order by murdering Duncan,
killing the innocent sleep 'that knits up the ravell'd sleave of care', Jason
has killed time and struggled against nature until his life is in tatters. As in
Ulysses, a power beyond rational calculation has unwoven a web of
selfishness, mockery and manipulation; but Jason's sudden shift in
perspective enables him to acquiese in what has happened. In the

Compson appendix, Faulkner grants him the small commercial success that has thus far eluded him and a measure of personal happiness in his relations with Lorraine – both only made plausible by his having once briefly shared Dilsey's overarching vision of time. But Jason has neither the desire to communicate his experience nor the capacity to translate vision into caring and compassion for others; it will remain entirely personal and unshared. His experience is even less universal, less adequate than Dilsey's to stand as a conclusion to the novel. Like hers, his vision of an end is disconfirmed; the novel returns with Jason to Jefferson, where, like his, its life must once again 'resume' (p. 392).

V

The concluding scene of *The Sound and the Fury* is a third and final attempt to replace the loss of Caddy in the structure of the narrative. Dilsey understands that Benjy's anguished wailing symbolically gives voice to the irrevocable loss that she and the Compsons have suffered this Easter weekend: 'Dis long time, O Jesus', she says, rocking him and stroking his head, 'Dis long time' (p. 396). Though she is only an ageing and inadequate surrogate for Caddy, she 'does de bes I kin' to comfort Benjy and restore order to his world. She decides to let Luster drive Benjy to the cemetary at once instead of waiting for T. P. to arrive, even though she knows that Luster has his own share of 'Compson devilment' (p.344). Rather than risk disturbing Mrs. Compson to get Benjy's cap, Dilsey lends him the felt hat she had worn to church earlier: 'We's down to worse'n dis, ef folks jes knowed', she says (p. 396). Dilsey's substitution of her hat for Benjy's own parallels her noble but inadequate attempt to replace Caddy's love in shielding him from the world; Dilsey understands that the need for such replacement has now become permanent.

Luster and Benjy start off for the graveyard, the symbolic end of all journeys, Benjy once more at peace in watching the pattern of passing images which he has seen many times before. As they approach the square, they face the monument of the Confederate Soldier, who 'gazed with empty eyes beneath his marble hand into wind and weather', while Benjy 'sat, holding the flower in his fist, his gaze empty and untroubled' (p. 399). The statue's eyes are permanently fixed, like Benjy's, in an unchanging perspective on the world beyond human time. But because Benjy cannot see the statue's eyes as mirroring his own, the novel's originating image is also suggested here a final time; from Benjy's perspective the reader looks up at the statue, whose eyes are fixed – like

Caddy's in the pear tree – on an unknown sight beyond Benjy's range of vision. The scene also recalls the moment at the branch when Quentin asks Caddy if she loves Dalton Ames: her eyes 'looked like the eyes in the statues blank unseeing and serene' (p. 202). Like Caddy in the tree, the Confederate soldier is simultaneously a symbol of human courage, failing and mortality; as in the scene of Quentin's escape, the reader can perceive here a larger human significance in patterns which offer Benjy merely the familiar consolation of visual repetition.

When Luster tries to show off by driving to the left instead of the right around the monument, Benjy's peace is totally destroyed. For an instant he sits in 'utter hiatus', but then bellows in 'more than astonishment . . . it was horror; shock; agony eyeless, tongueless; just sound'. Jason, who has returned from Mottson, comes 'jumping across the square', saws Queenie violently around 'while Ben's hoarse agony roared about them', and 'swung her about to the right of the monument'. He strikes both Luster and Benjy, jumps down, and orders Luster to 'get to hell on home with him' (p. 400). As Luster sets off,

> Ben's voice roared and roared. Queenie moved again, her feet began to clop-clop steadily again, and at once Ben hushed. . . . The broken flower drooped over Ben's fist and his eyes were empty and blue and serene again as cornice and facade flowed smoothly once more from left to right; post and tree, window and doorway, and signboard, each in its ordered place. (p. 401)

Paradoxically, Jason's savage action in this scene is almost the only one he has performed successfully in the course of the novel. He is probably motivated by the desire to preserve his respectability and get Benjy out of sight and hearing as quickly as he can, but it is also true that his self-interest here accidently coincides with the opportunity to ease Benjy's pain. Without working any significant change in his personality, Jason's experience earlier in the day seems, nevertheless, to have placed him in a less adversarial and more synchronized relationship and the world around him.

Benjy's experience in this final scene retrospectively parallels the reader's experience in *The Sound and the Fury*. Benjy, the simplest imaginable reader, is capable of following only 'humanly uninteresting successiveness', the 'emptiness of tock-tick'.[43] He sees the world as a series of discrete fragments – 'cornice and facade . . . post and tree, window and doorway, and signboard' – which he cannot combine into larger units of significance such as complete houses or the street as a whole. But Luster is a more sophisticated reader than Benjy; he wants to reshape the tradition he inherits and reach the end of the familiar journey by an unexpected route. By going around the statue on the left he destroys the successive world Benjy expects to see, just as Faulkner alters narrative tradition by taking the reader around his story in an unfamiliar direction in the first two sections of the novel. Jason's sudden appearance to turn the cart back around into the traditional path parallels his role in the structure of the novel, where his narrative abruptly begins Faulkner's return from experimental to traditional form. Like Benjy, most readers are content to accept Jason's violent recreation of a familiar world; we are secretly grateful for the restoration of a fictional universe in which the traditional conventions appear 'each in its ordered place'.[44] But as the narrative gets progressively clearer and more conventional, its original subject – Caddy – gets harder to see. For the reader who is capable of altering his perspective, traditional paths offer the least adequate ways of seeing experience. The first two sections of the novel have invited us to shift our point of view as Caddy does and empathetically identify our seeing with unfamiliar visions of the world. Paradoxically, it is Benjy – the character most incapable himself of such projection – whose perspective offers the most unclouded vision of the past, because he is unable to reshape his experience into the distorting orders of interpretation and memory.

The concluding scene provides a final and revealing look at the inner working of Benjy's mind. For Benjy, the familiar paths of daily experience call up scenes from the past; the first flashback in his narrative, for example, is stimulated by Luster's repetition of an action that Caddy had performed long before. They are crawling through a broken place in the fence:

> "Wait a minute." Luster said. "You snagged on that nail again. Cant you never crawl through here without snagging on that nail."
> *Caddy uncaught me and we crawled through.* (p. 3)

In fact, because Benjy cannot make logical connections, such repetitions of external circumstances are the only way he can retrieve remembered images and scenes. In *The Mind of a Mnemonist*, the Russian psychologist A. R. Luria describes his subject's almost identical method for consciously memorizing sequences of unrelated information:

> he would "distribute" [images for each word or object] along some road-way or street he visualised in his mind. Sometimes this was a street in his

home town, which would also include the yard attached to the house he had lived in as a child and which he recalled vividly . . . he would take a mental walk along that street . . . "distributing" his images at houses, gates, and store windows. . . . [To] name the word that preceded or followed one I'd select from the series . . . he would simply begin his walk, either from the beginning or from the end of the street, find the image of the object I had named, and "take a look at" whatever happened to be situated on either side of it. . . .

. . . He had no need for logical organization, for the associations his images produced reconstituted themselves whenever he revived the original situation in which something had been registered in his memory.[45]

The only difference between this system of recall and Benjy's is that Benjy cannot either memorize or remember images consciously; he does not 'distribute' images along a mentally visualized street, but finds them lying in wait for him along the paths of real experience itself. The importance of spatial order for Benjy is that it is the key to memory. The usual route to the cemetary is a mnemonic device which leads, like all of Benjy's ordinary experience, to recollections of Caddy and the greater contentment of childhood. But there is no chance of meeting Caddy in memory on an unexpected route.

Further, since Benjy cannot comprehend temporal order, he has no capacity to imagine that something he can no longer see might still exist. Absence is annihilation; to change his point of view is to destroy his world. His resulting demand that the world proceed according to unvarying patterns is only an extreme case of the rigidity of perspective that Quentin demonstrates in his adherence to a traditional code of honour and Jason in his allegience to a traditional code of prejudice. All three kinds of behaviour reveal a fear to face the future unaided by the past. But in the novel's final scene Benjy is unwillingly forced, as Jason is in Mottson, to change his point of view; he is carried out of the familiar past and into a completely alien present. His change of perspective parallels the earlier experiences of Dilsey and Jason; all three characters find themselves in new worlds after taking unexpected turns on the path to the end. For each character the vision is framed in terms appropriate to his or her own plane of understanding: Dilsey's vision is of Christian apocalypse, Jason's of the personal fate with which his world begins and ends, and Benjy's of the mere perceptual change which itself has the power to destroy his world. Each successive vision represents a further falling off of breadth, power and significance, but the cumulative portrayal of deteriorating vision becomes finally a pattern in itself, one which creates out of the repeated failure of vision a new version of tragic form.

The *Sound and the Fury* contains frequent references to the world of Shakespearean tragedy, from its title to its final phrase, which echoes Malcolm's promise to restore social order at the end of *Macbeth*:

> this, and what needful else
> That calls upon us, by the grace of Grace
> We will perform in measure, time and place.[46]

From Benjy's perspective there can be no awareness of time, but otherwise Malcolm and Benjy envision the restoration of order in similar terms. While the Scottish ancestry of the Compsons makes *Macbeth* a particularly appropriate source of tragic allusion in the novel, *Hamlet, Lear,* and *Antony and Cleopatra* also all end with a final restoration of order which suffers in comparison to the older, original order that has been destroyed. In the long and disruptive transitions from Duncan to Malcolm, Lear to Edgar, Hamlet's father to Fortinbras, Antony to Octavius, there is a pervasive falling off, a sense of loss and diminishment analogous to that which suffuses the ending of Faulkner's novel. Like Lear, the Compsons banish the daughter who represents the ordering social bond of love; like Cordelia, Caddy is the absent hope at the heart of the story whose final destruction makes the loss of love irrevocable. Macbeth, like the Compsons, personifies greatness of human potential corrupted from within; in his loss of moral vision, as in theirs, life is finally seen as merely sound and fury that signify nothing.[47] But because the conventions of dramatic tragedy are clearly understood, few readers have ever seen *Macbeth* as a nihilistic play. Macbeth's view of life in Act V is accepted not as the vision of the play or of the author, but as the final despair, dramatically rendered, of a tragically fallen and defeated man.

In contrast, the history of the novel offers predominantly comic traditions and conventions for the shaping of narrative. Earlier attempts to embody tragic vision in fiction – of which Hardy provides perhaps the most salient examples – are complicated by the tendency of omniscient narration to seem unfairly deterministic; the characters often seem to be destroyed, not by fate or internal weakness, but by an author who has loaded the dice against them. Faulkner's Shakespearean allusions and formal experiments are parallel aspects of his need to create a new tragic narrative tradition in order to tell the tale of Caddy and her family. But the Shakespearean echoes are so mixed and muted that they never threaten to take over the novel as a whole; Faulkner hints at parallels and then withdraws them in favour of his own larger design. The Shakespearean play most similar in design to *The Sound and the Fury* is not a tragedy at all: *The Winter's Tale,* also the story of an unjustly banished mother and daughter, ends with a reconciliation in which vision becomes consonant with reality; this reconciliation is made possible because the moral values of the faithful servant Paulina still possess the power to prevail over the heart and mind of Leontes. The failure of Dilsey's moral vision to possess equivalent power in her world compels the reshaping of this story as tragedy in *The Sound and the Fury.*

Benjy's final experience of order thus emerges from a new and unexpectedly altered narrative context. For Margaret Schlegel, Ursula Brangwen, Molly Bloom, and Lily Briscoe, final vision and affirmation of order are virtually one process; but because Caddy has been lost, *The Sound and the Fury*'s final vision must be repeatedly qualified, the discovery of final order persistently postponed. The tragic vision that finally emerges from this persistent denial of affirmative closure is Faulkner's strikingly original contribution to the evolution of visionary form.[48] As the focus in the final section shifts from Dilsey to Jason to Benjy, the successive narrowing of perspective duplicates for the reader both the Compson failure of moral vision and the novel's own increasingly unsuccessful attempts to look into the wind and weather of the past and see Caddy.

The monument in the concluding scene functions, finally, as a traditional symbol for the enduring world of art. In the envoy to *Epithalamion,* Spenser charges the poem to 'Be unto her a goodly ornament / And for short time an endless moniment'; the end of Shakespeare's sonnet 107 promises that 'thou in this shall find thy monument / When tyrants' crests and tombs of brass are spent'.[49] The image of Caddy, like that of the Confederate soldier, has been cast into a work of art which endures because it mirrors human experience from the ordering perspective of aesthetic form. Faulkner's artistic success in creating *The Sound and the Fury* stands in particular contrast to Quentin's failure to create any meaningful order out of his experience. Like Quentin, Faulkner was the eldest of four children and the heir of ante-bellum aristocracy, but unlike Quentin he was able to disassociate himself fully enough from the chivalric tradition to recognize his own identity as an artist. The sense of spiritual kinship between Caddy and Quentin which pervades the novel is allied to the kinship of Caddy's imaginative sympathy with the empathetic visionary power of art; the artist Quentin fails to become would possess the capacity, like Caddy and like Faulkner, to see the world from unexpected points of view.

Keats, whom Faulkner greatly admired, described this power of projection as the core of poetic identity in his definition of Negative Capability and in other letters: 'if a Sparrow come before my Window I take part in its existince and pick about the Gravel'; 'the Poet . . . is continually . . . filling some other Body – the Sun, the Moon, the Sea and Men and Women'.[50] Like Faulkner, Quentin is a potential artist rather than a potential leader, but in his misconception of himself he misses the crucial image at the pear tree which enabled Faulkner to create tragic order out of Caddy's story. The image suggests the consonance between individual and universal failing which defines the collective social bond and makes acceptance of life possible; it links mythic tradition to new aesthetic ways of seeing order in human experience. Faulkner has shown us, as he shows Benjy in the final scene, how an unexpected route leads back to the familiar; how a tradition can be reshaped to provide new perspectives on 'the old verities and truths of the heart'.[51] For Faulkner, this faith in the visionary power of art to show us ourselves seems to be the firmest reason for hoping that man will be able to prevail; by envisioning the promised end, or an image of that horror, we may find the strength and the will to avoid it.

Notes

1: VISIONARY CLOSURE AND THE EMBODIED MUSE

1. *Aspects of the Novel* (New York: Harcourt, rpt. 1955) p. 95.
2. Works such as Defoe's *Robinson Crusoe* (1718) and *Moll Flanders* (1722) predate the establishment of formal structure and closure as requisities of prose fiction; they are picaresque novels, winding down only when old age leaves the characters with fewer and fewer incidents to report. Laurence Sterne's *Tristram Shandy* (1767) offers a more complex early exception to the common forms of novelistic closure. It was designed, as Ian Watt observes, to provide a form in which Sterne can 'continue writing one or two volumes a years for as long as he wishes' (Introduction to *Tristram Shandy* [Boston: Houghton Mifflin, 1965] p. xxxiii; cf. Tristram's own comment, p. 29). It is in this sense deliberately prepared to be incomplete; when Tristram observes that it has taken him 364 days of writing to chronicle the first day of his life, he realizes that 'I shall never overtake myself' (pp. 213–14). Nevertheless, most readers find the concluding lines of the ninth and final book an aptly self-reflexive comment on *Tristram Shandy* as a whole:

   > L--d! said my mother, what is all this story about? –
   > A COCK and a BULL, said *Yorick* – And one of the best of its kind, I ever heard. (p. 496)

   Fortuitously or deliberately, this offers a unique form of closure.
3. In *The Turn of the Novel* (New York: Oxford University Press, 1966), Alan Friedman structures his history of novelistic endings around a distinction (which I shall challenge later) between closed and open form. His argument that 'experience' in *Bleak House* is left open in the omniscient narrative, and closed in Esther's, would appear unexceptionable (p. 25). Yet the narrative that is repeatedly closed (Esther's) is left, on the novel's final page, rhetorically open:

   > they can do very well without much beauty in me – even supposing –

   while the narrative that is finally open (the omniscient narrator's) is left rhetorically closed:

   > passion and pride, even to the stranger's eye, have died away from the place in Lincolnshire, and yielded it to dull repose.

   (*Bleak House*, ed. George Ford and Sylvère Monod [New York: Norton, 1977] pp. 770, 767). This paradox may hint that a narrative open in one respect tends to be closed in another; or, more broadly, that any narrative with aesthetic value – even one that is only half an aesthetic whole, as here – moves toward some form of closure.

171

4. Dickens, note on the conclusion, in Angus Calder, ed., *Great Expectations* (New York: Penguin, 1965) p. 495.
5. *Moby Dick* (New York: Rinehart, 1957) p. 565.
6. *Anna Karenina*, trans. Louise and Alymer Maude, ed. George Gibian (New York: Norton, 1970) pp. 722, 739, 740.
7. Hardy's footnote to the marriage asserts that the original ending without it is more 'consistent' and 'true'; *Return of the Native*, ed. James Gindin (New York: Norton, 1969) p. 307.
8. 'The Art of Fiction', 1884, rpt. in *Theory of Fiction: Henry James*, ed. James E. Miller (Lincoln: University of Nebraska Press, 1972) p. 32.
9. Preface to *Roderick Hudson*, in *The Art of the Novel*, ed. R. P. Blackmur (New York: Scribner's, 1934) pp. 6, 5, 14.
10. Preface to *The Ambassadors*, in *The Art of the Novel*, p. 309.
11. *The Ambassadors*, ed. S. P. Rosenbaum (New York: Norton, 1964) pp. 344–5).
12. *The Art of the Novel*, p. 322.
13. *Aspects of the Novel*, p. 95.
14. *Poetics 6*, trans. Preston H. Epps (Chapel Hill: University of North Carolina Press, 1942) p. 13.
15. 'Mr. Bennett and Mrs. Brown' in *The Captain's Death Bed* (New York: Harcourt, 1950) pp. 102, 94, 104.
16. *Aspects of the Novel*, pp. 159–62.
17. *The Letters of D. H. Lawrence*, II, ed. George J. Zytaruk and James T. Boulton (New York: Cambridge University Press, 1981) pp. 182–4.
18. *Character and the Novel* (Ithaca: Cornell University Press, 1965) p. 23. But in recent structuralist thinking, plot has regained its Aristotelian priority: Roland Barthes, for example, defines character 'according to participation in a sphere of actions' in 'Introduction to the Structural Analysis of Narratives' in *Image – Music – Text*, trans. Stephen Heath (New York: Hill & Wang, 1977) p. 107.
19. In *Forms of Life: Character and Moral Imagination in the Novel* (New Haven: Yale University Press, 1983), Martin Price argues that increasingly, as the novel evolves, 'plot is internalized, so that external event seems more a vehicle than the action proper' (p. xii).
20. *The Disappearance of God* (Cambridge, MA: Harvard University Press, 1963, rpt. 1975) p. 12.
21. *Strains of Discord* (Ithaca: Cornell University Press, 1958); 'Narrative Time and the Open-Ended Novel', *Criticism*, 8 (Autumn 1966).
22. Friedman, pp. 180, 32, 187.
23. Friedman, pp. 204, 32.
24. *The Rhetoric of Fiction* (University of Chicago Press, 1961, rev. edn. 1983) p. 298. Booth also argues that 'whatever verisimilitude a work may have always operates within a larger artifice', p. 59.
25. *Closure in the Novel* (Princeton University Press, 1981).
26. *Fable's End* (University of Chicago Press, 1974) pp. 4, 178.
27. *Structuralist Poetics* (Ithaca: Cornell University Press, 1975) pp. 209, 230.
28. *Narrative and its Discontents: Problems of Closure in the Traditional Novel* (Princeton University Press, 1981) p. ix.
29. Smith, *Poetic Closure* (University of Chicago Press, 1968) pp. viii, 1–6,

10–12, 33–6. See also Robert Scholes and Robert Kellogg, *The Nature of Narrative* (New York: Oxford University Press, 1966) p. 212.

30. Smith, pp. 95, 110, 213.

31. Kermode, *The Sense of an Ending* (New York: Oxford University Press, 1967) pp. 17–18, 44–7.

32. 'Mr. Bennett and Mrs. Brown', p. 112.

33. *The Divine Comedy*, trans. John D. Sinclair (New York: Oxford University Press, 1939, rpt. 1976), *Paradiso*, XXXIII.145, 43, 61–3; subsequent references appear in the text.

34. *Paradise Lost*, ed. Scott Elledge (New York: Norton, 1975) XI.377–8 and 763; XII.469 and 573.

35. See M. H. Abrams, *Natural Supernaturalism* (New York: Norton, 1971) and Kermode for extended discussions how the Romantics secularize religious vision and apocalypse. Abrams shows that God is almost entirely inactive in *The Prelude*; in the poetry of Wordsworth and his heirs, as in Romantic philosophy, the traditional cosmological trinity of God, Man, and Nature becomes a duality of Man and Nature, subject and object, with the attributes of divinity shared between the two remaining elements (pp. 89 ff.). Abrams also defines and discusses the 'Moment' in Romantic and modern literature, pp. 385–90, 418–27.

36. Kermode, p. 53.

37. The most interesting and influential readings of *The Prelude* tend to minimize or ignore the structural significance of the Snowdon episode in the poem as a whole. Geoffrey Hartman locates the power of the passage merely in the greatness of Wordsworth's failure to achieve an 'apocalyptic' vision, comparable to that of Book VI, which abandons and transcends Nature to rely on human imagination alone. For Hartman, the poem's climax occurs at Simplon Pass; by contrast, Snowdon is Wordsworth's 'most astonishing avoidance of apocalypse' (*Wordsworth's Poetry* [New Haven: Yale University Press, 1971] pp. 45–61). Jonathan Wordsworth challenges Hartman's view; one cannot 'categorize "The Climbing of Snowdon" as an avoidance (of apocalypse, or anything else)' he argues; 'the poetry is triumphantly positive'. But in his own reading of the passage as a nearly autonomous lyric, neither the poetic language nor its evocative power seems able to 'distinguish the passage from others that seem inherently slighter' ('The Climbing of Snowdon', in *Bicentenary Wordsworth Studies* [Ithaca: Cornell University Press, 1970] pp. 473–4, 462). M. H. Abrams places the episode in its larger context as climax to the poem: 'The last book of *The Prelude*, in symmetry with its first book, also opens with a literal walk which translates itself into a metaphor for the climactic stage both of the journey of life and of the imaginative journey which is the poem itself' (*Natural Supernaturalism*, p. 286). But because his primary concern is to locate Wordsworth within the broad historical contours of Romanticism, Abrams does not explore in detail the episode's climactic function in the structure of *The Prelude*.

38. For the past thirty years, critics have been revising earlier views that modernism reacts against or rejects Romanticism. Those who discuss modernism as it emerges from and interacts with Romantic traditions include Robert Langbaum in *The Poetry of Experience* (New York:

Norton, 1957); Kermode in *Romantic Image* (New York: Macmillan, 1957) and in *The Sense of an Ending*; Abrams in *Natural Supernaturalism*; Morris Beja in *Epiphany in the Modern Novel* (Seattle: University of Washington Press, 1971); and Charles Schug in *The Romantic Genesis of the Modern Novel* (University of Pittsburgh Press, 1979). In an essay on 'The Epiphanic Mode in Wordsworth and Modern Literature' in *New Literary History*, 14:2 (winter 1983), Langbaum distinguishes the structure and operation of modern epiphany from those of traditional vision; he also observes that Wordsworth influenced the modern emphasis on character in his belief that feeling 'gives importance to the action and situation, and not the action and situation to the feeling' (p. 346).

39.   *The Prelude: 1799, 1805, 1850*, ed. Jonathan Wordsworth, M. H. Abrams, Stephen Gill (New York: Norton, 1979) XIII.2. Subsequent references to *The Prelude* appear in the text; they are, except where noted, to Book XIII and to the 1805 version. The modernists of course could not have known this version, first published in 1926; I have employed it here because Wordsworth's meaning, while not essentially changed in the 1850 text, is generally clearer in the 1805. References in subsequent chapters, where Wordsworth is considered explicitly as an influence, will be to the 1850 text.

40.   Readers who prefer metaphysical or modern poetic tautness often criticize the mediative passages of *The Prelude* as laboured and unnecessarily discursive. But in Wordsworth's attempt to create a philosophical poetics, the meditative passages seem in part an answer to the Platonic charge that poets possess no true knowledge because they cannot give a rational explanation of their art (*Apology*, 22a–c).

41.   On the dating of the episode, see R. D. Havens, *The Mind of a Poet* II (Baltimore: Johns Hopkins Press, 1941) pp. 607–8.

42.   The meditation that follows Wordsworth's description of the Snowdon vision is not merely a 'gloss', as Jonathan Wordsworth argues (p. 466), because it reveals that poet's crucial self-conscious understanding of the poetic process in which he is engaged. On the other hand, the meditation does not reveal, as Hartman suggests, that 'full understanding comes immediately after the event' (p. 62). Wordsworth clearly achieves full understanding of the vision's significance only in the process of writing *The Prelude*.

43.   Augustine's literary reshaping of his experience is discussed by Abrams, p. 85; by Northrop Frye in *Anatomy of Criticism* (Princeton University Press, 1957) p. 307; and by Scholes and Kellogg, p. 169.

44.   Mark Reed argues, though without relation to the Snowdon passage, that '*The Prelude* is a poem that both describes the growth of Imagination and demonstrates the Imagination as a living and present mode of vision' in 'The Speaker of The Prelude', *Bicentenary Wordsworth Studies*, p. 280.

45.   From *The Recluse*, in *Wordsworth: Selected Poems and Prefaces*, ed. Jack Stillinger (Boston: Houghton Mifflin, 1965) ll. 754, 778–80, 793–4; pp. 45–7.

46.   Graves, *The White Goddess* (rpt. New York: Octagon, 1972) pp. 9–12, 24, 386, 390–1.

47.   *Illiad*, trans. Andrew Lang, Walter Leaf, Ernest Myers (London:

Macmillan, 1883) I.1; *Odyssey*, trans. S. H. Butcher and A. Lang (New York: Macmillan, 1895) I.1.

48. *Paradise Lost* I.1–6. Milton's Muse, however, derives its power of inspiration not from sexual otherness – it is not really feminine at all – but from association with the creative aspect of divinity:

> thou from the first
> Wast present, and with mighty wings outspread
> Dove-like sat'st brooding on the vast abyss
> And mad'st it pregnant (I.19–22)

Later, in calling this muse Urania, he invokes 'The meaning, not the name ... for thou / Nor of the muses nine, nor on the top / Of old Olympus dwell'st' (VII.5–7).

49. 'Apostrophe' in *The Pursuit of Signs* (Ithaca: Cornell University Press, 1981) pp. 143, 142, 149.

50. Graves, p. 24.

51. Graves, p. 444.

52. *The Symposium*, trans. Walter Hamilton (New York: Penguin, 1951) 202a–212c.

53. *Confessions*, trans. R. S. Pine-Coffin (New York: Penguin, 1961) VI.5; subsequent references appear in the text.

54. *Two Cheers for Democracy* (New York: Harcourt, 1951) p. 117.

55. Sinclair, *Inferno*, p. 44, *Purgatorio*, p. 411, *Paradiso*, p. 29.

56. In Stillinger, ll. 15–24, 44–8; pp. 111–12.

57. From notes on the poems dictated to Isabella Fenwick in 1843, quoted in Stillinger, p. 517.

58. From *The Recluse*, ll. 805–7, 810–11.

59. *Shelley's Poetry and Prose*, ed. Donald H. Reiman and Sharon B. Powers (New York: Norton, 1977) I.50–9, 303–5; I.152–86, 272–5; II.iv.116; IV.164–5.

60. *Selected Poems and Letters*, ed. Douglas Bush (Boston: Houghton Mifflin, 1959) I.61 ff.; I.245; I.256–62.

61. *She Dwelt Among the Untrodden Ways*, ll. 5 and 7; *Three Years She Grew in Sun and Shower*, ll. 1–6, 29–30; *A Slumber Did My Spirit Seal*, ll. 7–8; in Stillinger, pp. 113–15.

62. No literal answer is possible, since she is singing in Erse; see note in Stillinger, p. 567.

63. *The Solitary Reaper*, in Stillinger, p. 367–8.

64. *The Idea of Order at Key West*, in *The Palm at the End of the Mind* (New York: Vintage, 1972) pp. 97–9. Many Stevens critics discuss Wordsworth's general influence on Stevens, and several note the particular similarity of this poem to *The Solitary Reaper*; see, for example, A. Walton Litz, *Introspective Voyager: The Poetic Development of Wallace Stevens* (New York: Oxford University Press, 1972) p. 195, and Harold Bloom, *Wallace Stevens: the Poems of Our Climate* (Ithaca: Cornell University Press, 1977) p. 103. Stevens himself discusses Wordsworth in 'The Noble Rider and the Sound of Words', *The Necessary Angel* (New York: Vintage, 1951) pp. 13, 21, 31.

65.   I have deliberately avoided discussing Proust, who represents an important parallel case, but who lies outside the scope of the present study; I touch briefly on *Finnegans Wake*, which also contains a visionary ending, at the end of my chapter on *Ulysses*.

66.   Auerbach, *Mimesis* (1946), trans. Willard R. Trask (Princeton University Press, 1953) p. 555.

67.   Auerbach, pp. 548–53.

68.   Many other early twentieth-century writers fall altogether outside the tradition that has come to be associated with the term 'modernism'; David Lodge suggests that throughout the century two quite different kinds of fiction have coexisted, which he identifies as 'modern' and 'contemporary' in his *Language of Fiction* (New York: Columbia University Press, 1966) pp. 243–5, and as 'metaphorical' and 'metonymical' in *The Modes of Modern Writing* (Ithaca: Cornell University Press, 1977). Incidentally, Lodge's *Changing Places* (1975) is probably the only novel ever written that concludes with a dialogue about problems of fictional closure.

69.   *One Hundred Years of Solitude* (1967), trans. Gregory Rabossa (New York: Avon, 1971) p. 383.

2: IDEAS OF ORDER IN *HOWARDS END*

1.   See the array of early reviews reprinted in Philip Gardner, ed., *E. M. Forster: the Critical Heritage* (Boston: Routledge & Kegan Paul, 1973) pp. 127–57.

2.   Trilling, *E. M. Forster* (London: Hogarth, 1944) pp. 44, 116. For similar assessments, see James McConkey, *The Novels of E. M. Forster* (Ithaca: Cornell University Press, 1957) p. 8; Frederick Crews, *E. M. Forster: the Perils of Humanism* (Princeton University Press, 1962) p. 112; Alan Wilde, *Art and Order: a Study of E. M. Forster* (New York University Press, 1964) p. 117; Robert Langbaum, 'A New Look at E. M. Forster', *Southern Review* (Winter 1968) p. 43; Wilfred Stone, 'Forster on Love and Money' in Oliver Stallybrass, ed., *Aspects of E. M. Forster* (New York: Harcourt, 1969) p. 117; Peter Widdowson, *E. M. Forster's Howards End* (London: Sussex University Press, 1977) pp. 98, 101; Barbara Rosecrance, *Forster's Narrative Vision* (Ithaca: Cornell University Press, 1982) p. 147. For an unusual defence of the ending as a triumph of androgyny, see Bonnie Finkelstein, *Forster's Women: Eternal Differences* (New York: Columbia University Press, 1975) p. 92. But her defence remains unconvincing; Forster clearly values traditionally feminine qualities more highly than masculine ones, and wishes Margaret Schlegel to dominate the end of the novel. The traditional reading is not necessarily 'antifeminist', as Finkelstein argues; it merely holds that the feminine victory seems too easy, that the novel fails to establish its plausibility.

3.   Letter to Jonathan Spence, quoted from Spence, 'E. M. Forster at Eighty', *The New Republic* (9 May, 1959) p. 21, by J. B. Beer, *The Achievement of E. M. Forster* (London: Chatto & Windus, 1962) p. 177.

4.   Woolf, *Collected Essays*, I (New York: Harcourt, 1966) p. 345.

5.   Trilling, p. 102. This passage also appears on the back cover of the Vintage

edition of the novel. Numerous subsequent critics emphasize this theme; see, for example, Laurence Brander, *E. M. Forster* (London: Rupert Hart-Davis, 1968) p. 127; Langbaum, p. 42; John Colmer, *E. M. Forster: the Personal Voice* (Boston: Routledge & Kegan Paul, 1975) pp. 85–6; Rosecrance, p. 121; and note the subtitle of Widdowson's book-length study of the novel: *Fiction as History*.

6. Woolf, p. 345.

7. Abrams, *The Mirror and the Lamp* (New York: Oxford University Press, 1953) pp. 26–8.

8. Bradley, 'Poetry for Poetry's Sake' in *Oxford Lectures on Poetry* (London: Macmillan, 1909) pp. 4–5.

9. *Two Cheers for Democracy* (New York: Harcourt, 1951) pp. 79–82, 43, and 118. In *The Cave and the Mountain* (Stanford University Press, 1966), Wilfred Stone also notes the relation of Forster's aesthetic theory to Bradley's (pp. 102–4), and locates the aesthetic theory of Forster's Bloomsbury friend Roger Fry in the same tradition (p. 66). But Stone does not read *Howards End* against this aesthetic model; he makes the usual argument in the Trilling line that the 'question of the book' is 'who shall inherit England' (p. 242).

10. 'Art for Art's Sake', in *Two Cheers for Democracy*, p. 89. Compare, again, this passage with one of Bradley's:

> The offensive consequences often drawn from the formula 'Art for Art' . . . attach not to the doctrine that Art is an end in itself, but to the doctrine that Art is the whole or supreme end of human life. . . . This latter doctrine, which seems to me absurd, is in any case quite different from the former. . . . Poetry has its place in a many-sided life. (p. 5)

11. *Two Cheers for Democracy*, p. 276.

12. *Two Cheers for Democracy*, p. 116.

13. *Two Cheers for Democracy*, pp. 59, 95, 92.

14. *Two Cheers for Democracy*, pp. 89–90, 94.

15. *Two Cheers for Democracy*, pp. 114–15.

16 *Howards End* (New York: Vintage, 1921) p. 1. Subsequent references appear in the text.

17. Brander, p. 150.

18. *Two Cheers for Democracy*, p. 67.

19. 'Dover Beach' in *Poetry and Criticism of Matthew Arnold*, ed. A . Dwight Culler (Boston: Houghton Mifflin, 1961) pp. 161–2.

20. For a useful discussion of the author's subjective consciousness in modern fiction, see Daniel R. Schwarz, ' "I Was the World in Which I Walked": The Transformation of the British Novel', *University of Toronto Quarterly* (Spring 1982) pp. 279–97. Forster surely must have read Wordsworth at Cambridge if not earlier, though specific external evidence is scanty. In July 1907 he visited Grasmere and seemed to regard Wordsworth with respect; see *Selected Letters of E. M. Forster* I, ed. Mary Lago and P. N. Furbank (Cambridge, MA: Belknap, 1983). Later in life he knew Wordsworth well. See *Two Cheers for Democracy*, p. 178, and his *Commonplace Book*, ed. Philip Gardner (Stanford University Press, 1985)

pp. 119, 188, 243; he gave a radio talk on Wordsworth in 1944 (B. J. Kirkpatrick, *A Bibliography of E. M. Forster* [Oxford: Clarendon, 1985] p. 241).

21.   In *The Palm at the End of the Mind* (New York: Vintage, 1972) pp. 97–9.

22.   A few readers have attempted to make the narrative voice more centrally important than Forster's primary focus on the characters seems to warrant; see Francis Gillen, '*Howards End* and the Neglected Narrator', *Novel*, 3 (1970), and Kinley E. Roby, 'Irony and the Narrative Voice in *Howards End*', *The Journal of Narrative Technique* (May 1972).

23.   Widdowson, p. 12.

24.   Kermode, *The Sense of an Ending* (New York: Oxford University Press, 1966) p. 23.

25.   David Lodge notes the relation of these three terms in *The Modes of Modern Writing* (Ithaca: Cornell University Press, 1977) p. 46. The sources for the terms are *Aspects of the Novel*, ch. 8; Gilbert, *James Joyce's Ulysses* (New York: Random House, 1930; rev. edn 1952; rpt. 1955), Part I, ch. 2; and Frank, 'Spatial Form in Modern Literature', *Sewanee Review* (1945).

26.   Stone sees *Howards End* as Forster's 'first major experiment with the technique of "rhythm,"' arguing that as such it is an 'important novel, and perhaps a great one' (*Cave and the Mountain*, p. 267).

27.   For a sensitive discussion of this 'deeper stream' in *Howards End*, see McConkey, who links Margaret's moment of resignation to the pattern of water imagery running through the novel (pp. 121–4, 132).

28.   For objections that Forster is telling rather than showing Mrs. Wilcox's character, see McConkey (pp. 78, 80), Wilde (p. 118), Widdowson (p. 77), and Rosecrance (p. 135). Robert Langbaum almost alone among critics feels that Forster portrays Mrs. Wilcox 'authentically through negative qualities – passivity and stillness' (p. 42).

29.   The names of Forster's characters are almost all symbolically allusive, creating part of the novel's power to invoke worlds beyond that of the story itself. 'Ruth' conjures up the world of Old Testament tradition and suggests connection with a mythic spiritual past. 'Helen' suggests classical beauty and, by implication, the classical absolutes Helen idealizes. 'Margaret' and 'Henry' appear frequently in the geneology of the English royal family, suggesting their place at the centre of Forster's English society. 'Charles' is the heir symbolically dispossessed; 'Paul' goes off to spread the gospel of capitalism to the African gentiles. 'Howard' is an ancient name in English nobility, in fact the family name of the highest nobles in the land, the Dukes of Norfolk. 'Wilcox' suggests a pun on 'will' and 'cox', or 'coxswain', an appropriate designation for men who 'have their hands on all the ropes' (p. 28) and who steer the ship of England. Critics have frequently noted the obvious implications of 'Bast'.

30.   Unsigned notice, *Standard* (28 Oct. 1910), rpt. in Gardner, pp. 128–9.

31.   Many critics have discussed the process by which Margaret comes to resemble Mrs. Wilcox; see McConkey (p. 119), Crews (p. 108), Wilde (p. 118), Stone, *Cave and the Mountain* (p. 259), Colmer (p. 89), Widdowson (p. 81).

32.   This phrase, a recurrent motif in the book, is from Matthew Arnold's 'To a

Friend'. In the poem the phrase refers to Sophocles, whom 'Business could not make dull, nor Passion wild: / Who saw life steadily, and saw it whole' (Culler, p. 7). This opposition between business which sees life steadily and passion which sees it whole is the central one of *Howards End*, lying behind the antinomies of business and art, prose and passion, the monk and the beast (p. 187), and behind the opposing characters of Henry and Helen. Stone observes that Arnold's phrase is 'heard intact four times in the novel, at intervals of roughly one hundred pages' (*Cave and the Mountain*, p. 271).

33. *Aspects of the Novel* (New York: Harcourt, 1927) p. 95.
34. *The Prelude*, ed. Jonathan Wordsworth, M. H. Abrams, Stephen Gill (New York: Norton, 1979) 1850, XIV.199–201.
35. Kermode, p. 18.
36. Beer, p. 48. Beer feels, however, that visionary moments in *Howards End* 'do not carry the same burden of significance' as in the earlier novels (p. 101). Colmer has also discussed the visionary moment in Forster, arguing that like the Romantics 'he believes that the imagination has the power to seize on the symbolic moments of truth (Wordsworth's "spots of time"; Pater's "present moment" which "alone really is"): such moments, treasured in the memory, become "the master light of all our seeing" ' (p. 12).
37. The rejected stone has also frequently been identified with Jesus himself; see the New Oxford Annotated Bible, Herbert G. May and Bruce M. Metzger, eds (New York, 1973) p. 1324 note. See Kermode, p. 47, for a discussion of Christ's power to rewrite history.
38. *The Prelude*, 1805, XIII.69.
39. The circuitous journey in Wordsworth and other Romantics is discussed extensively by M. H. Abrams in *Natural Supernaturalism* (New York: Norton, 1971).
40. *Two Cheers for Democracy*, pp. 92, 71.
41. Introduction to *The Celestial Omnibus* (New York: Vintage, 1976) p. vii.
42. Mansfield's Journal (May 1917) rpt. in Gardner, p. 162.
43. *Aspects of the Novel*, p. 78.
44. Wilde voices a general consensus among critics in suggesting that 'Henry makes contact by submission, not connection' and that 'the last chapter represents not Margaret's search for meaning, but Forster's' (pp. 120–1). Many readers also find Margaret's marriage to Henry as psychologically unbelievable as Helen does.
45. *The Rainbow* (1915; rpt. New York: Viking, 1961) p. 495. Beer also observes this connection between the two rainbows, and suggests that 'the closing scenes of the two novels, with harsh new houses engulfing the countryside in each, have a strange similarity' (p. 196).
46. *A Passage to India* (New York: Harcourt, 1924; rpt. 1952) p. 2.
47. McConkey suggests that *Howards End* is an 'epic' in which the characters are voyagers upon the sea, like Ulysses, who finally reach home 'in spite of all hazards' (p. 123).
48. In his unsuccessful attempt to bring Jacky to life, Forster gives her qualities which Joyce will later ascribe to Molly: 'She was fond of flowers, generous with money, and not revengeful' (p. 318).

3: *THE RAINBOW* AND THE FLOOD OF CONSCIOUSNESS

1. See *The Letters of D. H. Lawrence*, ed. James T. Boulton and George J. Zytaruk (New York: Cambridge University Press, 1979 and 1981), I p. 278; II, pp. 266, 275.
2. *The Letters of D. H. Lawrence*, ed. Aldous Huxley (New York: Viking, 1932) p. 558.
3. See Charles L. Ross, *The Composition of The Rainbow and Women in Love* (Charlottesville: University of Virginia Press, 1979) p. 5.
4. Boulton, *Letters*, II, p. 67.
5. Boulton, *Letters*, II, p. 142.
6. See Ross, pp. 27–31.
7. Leavis, *D. H. Lawrence* (New York: Knopf, 1956) pp. 170–2.
8. Friedman, *The Turn of the Novel* (New York: Oxford University Press, 1966) p. 204. Virtually every influential Lawrence critic since Leavis has registered dissatisfaction with the ending. See Graham Hough, *The Dark Sun* (London: Duckworth, 1956) pp. 71–2; Marvin Mudrick, 'The Originality of *The Rainbow*' in *A D. H. Lawrence Miscellany*, ed. Harry T. Moore (Carbondale, IL: Southern Illinois University Press, 1959) pp. 76–7; Roger Sale, 'The Narrative Technique of *The Rainbow*', *Modern Fiction Studies* (Spring 1959) p. 59; S. L. Goldberg, 'The Rainbow: Fiddle-bow and Sand', *Essays in Criticism* (Oct. 1961) pp. 425, 427, 431–2; Julian Moynahan, *The Deed of Life* (Princeton University Press, 1963) p. 72; George Ford, *Double Measure* (New York: Holt, Rinehart & Winston, 1965) pp. 161–2; H. M. Daleski, *The Forked Flame* (London: Faber & Faber, 1965) p. 125; Colin Clarke, *River of Dissolution* (New York: Barnes & Noble, 1969) pp. 42, 67; Scott Sanders, *D. H. Lawrence* (New York: Viking, 1973) p. 92. One of the few previous critics to find the ending successful is Edward Engleberg, in 'Escape from the Circles of Experience: D. H. Lawrence's *The Rainbow* as a Modern *Bildungsroman*', *PMLA* (Mar. 1963).
9. Friedman, p. 139.
10. The two most useful discussions of Lawrence's debt to Romanticism are Herbert Lindenberger's 'Lawrence and the Romantic Tradition' in *A D. H. Lawrence Miscellany*, and the chapters on Lawrence in Robert Langbaum's *The Mysteries of Identity* (New York: Oxford University Press, 1977). Colin Clarke's *River of Dissolution: D. H. Lawrence and English Romanticism* is a lengthier but less helpful study. The best discussion of *The Rainbow's* relation to the Bible is in George Ford's *Double Measure*.
11. Eliot, *Criterion* (July 1931), rpt. in *D. H. Lawrence: the Critical Heritage*, ed. R. P. Draper (New York: Barnes & Noble, 1970) p. 361.
12. For a detailed discussion of Christian tradition in the Romantic age, see M. H. Abrams, *Natural Supernaturalism* (New York: Norton, 1971).
13. Eliot, p. 363.
14. *Women in Love* (1920; rpt. New York: Viking, 1960) p. 51.
15. *The Rainbow* (1915; rpt. New York: Viking, 1961) pp. 1, 494. Subsequent references appear in the text.
16. *The Prelude*, ed. Jonathan Wordsworth, M. H. Abrams, and Stephen Gill (New York: Norton, 1979) 1850, XIV.81–6.

17. *Tintern Abbey* in Wordsworth, *Selected Poems and Prefaces*, ed. Jack Stillinger (Boston: Houghton Mifflin, 1965) ll. 67–75; pp. 108–11. I have conflated, for purposes of comparison, Wordsworth's complex distinction between boyhood and youth.

18. *Tintern Abbey*, ll. 106–7.

19. *Tintern Abbey*, ll. 96–102.

20. Boulton, *Letters*, II, pp. 182–4.

21. Friedman, p. 174.

22. Langbaum, p. 251.

23. Lindenberger, p. 331. He also quotes a remark Lawrence made to Forster on *A Passage to India*: 'Life is more interesting in its undercurrents than in its obvious' (p. 329; in Huxley, *Letters*, pp. 605–6).

24. *Phoenix*, II (New York: Penguin, 1978) p. 478.

25. Langbaum, p. 255.

26. *The Rainbow* also resembles *The Prelude* in its oscillation between dramatic scenes and narrative responses. Just as critics often dislike Wordsworth's meditative passages, many object to Lawrence's practice of 'telling' rather than 'showing' much of *The Rainbow*. See, for example, Goldberg, pp. 419, 426, 429; Daleski, p. 78; Ford, p. 150. Leavis defends Lawrence's long stretches of narrative as necessary discussion of themes raised in the dramatic scenes (p. 164); Mark Kinkead-Weekes sees 'a continual "systole and diastole" of poetry and analytic prose, exploration and understanding' in the novel ('The Marble and the Statue' in *Imagined Worlds*', ed. Maynard Mack and Ian Gregor [London, Methuen, 1968] p. 384.

27. Lawrence, *Psychoanalysis and the Unconscious* (1921, rpt. New York: Viking, 1960) pp. 5–6.

28. *Psychoanalysis and the Unconscious*, pp. 9, 13. Recent research by psychologists suggests that Lawrence was surprisingly accurate in his view of the range of mental activity performed by the unconscious; many researchers now see the unconscious as playing a much larger role in mental life than Freud envisioned. Perceptions and even decisions may be processed largely in the non-conscious mind and only submitted to the consciousness when non-habitual actions are demanded (*The New York Times*, 7 Feb, 1984, Sec. C, p. 1).

29. Boulton, *Letters*, II, p. 165.

30. Boulton, *Letters*, II, p. 173. He also writes that at first he 'could not get my soul into' the novel 'because of the struggle and resistance between Frieda and me. Now you will find her and me in the novel, I think and the work is of both of us', p. 164.

31. Boulton, *Letters*, II, p. 182.

32. *Howards End* (1910; rpt. New York: Vintage, 1921) p. 90.

33. *Howards End*, pp. 33 ff.; Ford also observes this resemblance, p. 128.

34. *Apocalypse and the Writings on Revelation* (1931), ed. Mara Kalnins (New York: Cambridge University Press, 1980) pp. 54–5.

35. In *The Palm at the End of the Mind* (New York: Vintage, 1972) pp. 97–9.

36. *Prelude*, 1850, XII.210–15.

37. For an extended discussion of the circuitous journey in Romantic poetry and philosophy, see Abrams, *Natural Supernaturalism*. Abrams places Lawrence's commentary on Revelation, *Apocalypse*, in the tradition of this motif (pp. 323–4).

38. Compare Anna's fear of the dark sensuality in herself and Will: 'in all the happiness a black shadow, shy, wild, a beast of prey, roamed and vanished from sight' (p. 177).
39. *Prelude*, 1850, I.454–60.
40. Goldberg sees Ursula's progress as a *'via negativa'*, in which she rejects a series of inadequate forms of love, leaving her 'clarified in herself, in a state of vital receptivity' (p. 421). Similarly, Geoffrey Hartman sees in Wordsworth a progress which he calls *'naturaliter negativa'*, related 'to what mystics have called the negative way', but 'achieved without violent or ascetic discipline', in which 'nature itself led him beyond nature' (*Wordsworth's Poetry* [New Haven: Yale University Press, 1971] p. 33).
41. Daleski, p. 125.
42. Frank Kermode also contends that this final chapter is explicitly apocalyptic. He suggests that 'Lawrence's discussion of the horse in *Apocalypse* establishes a direct connexion with Revelation' and points out that Lawrence saw himself as living in a time of crisis, of apocalyptic potential; in a September 1915 letter to Lady Ottoline Morell, he claimed a need for 'new heaven and new earth' ('Lawrence and the Apocalyptic Types' in *Continuities* [London: Routledge & Kegan Paul, 1968] pp. 131, 125, 127).
43. Cf. *Howards End*, p. 339.
44. *Prelude*, 1850, XIV.450–6. Lawrence's rainbow may derive from the rainbow of Wordsworth's *Intimations Ode* (1. 10) and *My Heart Leaps Up*, where it inspires the poet to wish his 'days to be / Bound each to each in natural piety'. The rainbow also looks back to Forster's 'rainbow bridge' (*Howards End*, p. 186), and forward to Forster's 'overarching sky' (*A Passage to India* [1924; rpt. New York: Harcourt, 1952] p. 8).
45. Boulton, *Letters*, II, pp. 132, 134.

4: UNWEAVING THE WIND: *PENELOPE* AND *CLARITAS* IN *ULYSSES*

1.   *Letters of James Joyce* I, ed. Stuart Gilbert (London: Faber & Faber, 1957) p. 170.
2.   French, *The Book as World* (Cambridge, MA: Harvard University Press, 1976) p. 259.
3.   *Ulysses* (New York: Random House, 1961) p. 377. Subsequent references appear in the text.
4.   A. Walton Litz identifies these two poles in *Ulysses* criticism as elements in an extended conversation 'between the spiritual descendents of Pound and Eliot': Pound sees *Ulysses* as a realistic novel of character; Eliot sees it as a symbolic novel of mythic correspondences. In our own time, Hugh Kenner is the most prominent of Pound's inheritors, Richard Ellmann of Eliot's. ('Pound and Eliot on *Ulysses*: The Critical Tradition', *James Joyce Quarterly* [Autumn 1972] p. 16). Since Litz's essay appeared in 1972, these two perspectives have tended to move into unpredictable alignments with the broader dialectic between traditional criticism and contemporary theory. Alliances are most often formed in current debates between

interests in realism, character and humanistic value at one extreme; between such concepts as myth, symbol, language and structuralism at the other. In *Ulysses* criticism, by contrast, critics in the Pound tradition seem inclined to move – as Kenner does in his 1978 *Joyce' Voices* (Berkeley: University of California Press) – from interest in the book&ae;s realism toward analysis of *Ulysses* as a nearly autonomous linguistic process; whereas in the Eliot line, books such as Ellmann's 1972 *Ulysses on the Liffey* (New York: Oxford University Press) firmly join a concern with Joyce's use of myth and allegorical schema to an emphasis on his affirmation of humanistic meaning. These unusual alignments suggest that Joyce has created a work with the power to mix, subvert and finally transcend our contemporary debates. Attempts to read *Ulysses* as a realistic novel of character run aground on the stylistic shoals of the later chapters, and critics whose interests lie initially with the characters are forced to account somehow for the pervasive stylistic complexity which ultimately seems to conceal the characters and 'subvert' the novel. Such problems do not arise for the mythic perspective, which can attempt to connect human meaning to symbolic occurrences without reference to the stylistic context in which the symbols appear. But as a consequence of its very difficulties, the realistic perspective has given rise to some of the most probing and illuminating accounts of the novel: Arnold Goldman's *The Joyce Paradox* (London: Routledge & Kegan Paul, 1966); David Hayman's *Ulysses: the Mechanics of Meaning* (1970, rev. edn. Madison: University of Wisconsin Press, 1982); Marilyn French's *The Book as World* (1976); C. H. Peake's *James Joyce: the Citizen and the Artist* (Stanford University Press, 1977); James Maddox's *James Joyce's Ulyssess and the Assault Upon Character* (New Brunswick, NJ: Rutgers University Press, 1978); Hugh Kenner's *Joyce's Voices* (1978) and *Ulysses* (London: Allen & Unwin, 1980).

5. 'The Genre of *Ulysses*' in *The Theory of the Novel*, ed. John Halperin (New York: Oxford University Press, 1974) p. 119.
6. Goldberg, *The Classical Temper* (New York: Barnes & Noble, 1961) p. 2.
7. *Anatomy of Criticism* (Princeton University Press, 1957) p. 308.
8. Rader, 'Exodus and Return: Joyce's *Ulysses* and the Fiction of the Actual', *Univ. of Toronto Quarterly* (Winter 1978–79) p. 154.
9. Goldberg, p. 56.
10. *The Mirror and the Lamp* (New York: Oxford University Press, 1953) p. 23.
11. *A Portrait of the Artist as a Young Man* (1916; rpt. New York: Viking, 1964) p. 213.
12. The other three orientations for artistic theories that Abrams identifies focus on external reality (mimetic theory), on the effect on an audience (pragmatic theory), and on the artist's internal creative process (expressive theory). Joyce acknowledges the importance of all three at the end of *Portrait*, when Stephen goes out to 'encounter for the millionth time the reality of experience [mimesis] and to forge in the smithy of my soul [expression] the uncreated conscience of my race [pragmatic purpose]' (pp. 252–3). But all three of these orientations seem subordinate for Stephen and for Joyce to the primary, objective theory discussed at length in the preceding pages.

13. *Portrait*, pp. 214–15. At a purely grammatical level, however, as Kenner observes, all three of Joyce's major works begin in the third person and end in the first (Kenner, *Ulysses*, p. 41).
14. *Portrait*, pp. 215, 213.
15. *Odyssey*, trans. S. H. Butcher and A. Lang (New York: Collier, 1909) 2:92 ff.; the passage recurrs almost verbatim at 19:137 ff. and 24:128 ff. According to Fritz Senn, Joyce used this translation (*Joyce's Dislocutions* [Baltimore: Johns Hopkins University Press, 1984] p. 128).
16. *Encyclopaedia Britannica*, 11th edn (New York, 1911) XXVIII pp. 440–5.
17. *Odyssey*, 2:292f.
18. *Ulysses in Progress* (Princeton University Press, 1977) p. 197.
19. 'Ulysses', rpt. in *Joyce: a Collection of Critical Essays*, ed. William Chace (Englewood Cliffs, NJ: Prentice-Hall, 1974) p. 62.
20. Such readings have been proposed several times; they are most explicitly combined by Kenner, whose study of the book's shifting styles leads finally to despair of finding any final meaning beneath its stylistic and linguistic surface (*Joyce's Voices*, p. 91). In his more recent *Ulysses*, Kenner seems at first to retreat from this view, suggesting that the characters do finally rise above the narrative innovations (pp. 41, 63); later he moves toward the symbolist position, seeing a 'metamorphosis' of Stephen and Bloom 'into types and portents' (p. 101); but finally he contends that Molly's affirmation of life is merely an 'expositor's cliche' (p. 146) and returns to his earlier view that there is nothing beneath the linguistic surface of the novel (p. 156). By identifying Penelope's web as an ordering image which underlies this surface, I want to challenge the tendency of *Ulysses* criticism to move toward versions of Kenner's conclusion.
21. See, for example, William York Tindall, *A Reader's Guide to James Joyce* (New York: Farrar, Straus & Giroux, 1959) and Richard Kain, *Fabulous Voyager* (New York: Viking, 1947, rpt. 1959).
22. Kermode, *The Sense of an Ending* (New York: Oxford University Press, 1966) p. 18.
23. Goldman, p. 110.
24. Maddox, p. 208.
25. Maddox, p. 231. Numerous other critics discuss weaving as a connection between Molly and Penelope, but none so far as I know has made the further connection between weaving imagery and the narrative structure of the book. Kenner remarks in discussing *Ithaca* that 'like Homer's Penelope at her tapestry, *Ulysses* unweaves at night what it wove by day', but he does not develop the point further (Kenner, *Ulysses*, p. 141; see also p. 148). For other suggestive but incomplete discussions of weaving in *Ulysses* see R. M. Adams, *James Joyce: Common Sense and Beyond* (New York: Random House, 1966) p. 168; Fritz Senn, 'Weaving, Unweaving' in *A Starchamber Quiry: a James Joyce Centennial Volume*, ed. E. L. Epstein (New York: Methuen, 1982); and Bonnie Kime Scott, 'Penelope's Web' in *Joyce and Feminism* (Bloomington: University of Indiana Press, 1984) pp. 156 ff.
26. *Joyce's Voices*, p. 98.
27. Eliot, '*Ulysses*, Order and Myth', *Dial* (1924), rpt. in *James Joyce: Two Decades of Criticism*, ed. Seon Givens (New York: Vanguard, 1948) p. 201.

28. The use of the wind as a metaphor for meaningless speech or fruitless human endeavour is Biblical in origin: 'Do ye imagine to reprove words, and the speeches of one that is desperate, which are as wind?' (Job 6:16, KJV); 'what profit hath he that hath labored for the wind?' (Eccles. 5:16). See also Prov. 1:29 and 11:27, Eccles, 11:4, Hos. 8:7, Job 8:2 and 15:2; and compare KJV 'vexation of spirit' with the more literal RSV 'striving after wind' in Eccles. 1:14, 1:17, 2:11, 2:17, 2:26, 4:4, 4:6, 4:16 and 6:9.

29. *Allusions in Ulysses* (Chapel Hill: University of North Carolina Press, 1968) pp. 27–8. Thornton misses, however, the chance to associate the weaving imagery with Penelope.

30. Eliot, p. 202.

31. David Hayman explains the narrative structure of *Ulysses* by positing (with no authority from Joyce) 'a nameless creative persona 'or "arranger"'' who 'can be identified neither with the author nor with his narrators'. This figure controls such matters as the interrelationships between the chapters and the intrusion of symbolic details that undermine the realism of the book (pp. 84–6, 122–5). Perhaps because this explanation accounts for a level of order and control beneath the novel's fragmented surface (as does the image of Penelope's web), many critics have adopted Hayman's 'Arranger', notably Kenner, who uses the concept to simplify his earlier model of a complex narrative machinery involving two narrators (see *Joyce's Voices*, pp. 64–78 and *Ulysses*, pp. 67, 98, 153). But neither Hayman nor Kenner offer, for me, fully convincing evidence to establish the Arranger as an internal presence in the text with a role distinct from that of its author.

32. *Letters*, I, p. 172. Joyce's desire to set *Penelope* apart in the formal structure of the novel is also related to its role in Stephen's progression of literary forms. Since the dramatic form is realized only at the end of *Ulysses*, it takes the shape of an epilogue to the whole; part of its function, in the tradition of comedy, is to beg the audience's indulgence and to insist upon the connections between art and life.

33. *James Joyce* (New York: Oxford University Press, 1959) p. 25.

34. Kermode, p. 46.

35. This view was first developed in detail by Stanley Sultan in *The Argument of Ulysses* (Ohio State University Press, 1964) pp. 431–3, and has since been adopted with some variation by Hayman, Ellmann, French, Peake, Kenner, Maddox, and a variety of other critics. The only serious challenge to the consensus lies, I think, in Molly's relationship with Gardner, about which very little specific information is given in the novel. But as Sultan and French (p. 254) argue, Molly's recollections of Gardner are purely romantic, in contrast to her explicitly sexual memories of Mulvey, Bloom, and Boylan; thus while the relationship with Gardner clearly had sexual overtones, it probably did not involve sexual intercourse.

36. In the introduction to his useful *Chronicle of Leopold and Molly Bloom* (Berkeley: University of California Press, 1971), John Henry Raleigh observes that his sequential ordering of the characters' memories and experiences gives Molly a role at least equal to Bloom's; the reader learns as much in *Penelope* about the characters as in the rest of the book combined (p. 8). This observation helps to confirm that Molly's experience can simply appear more concisely in the text because her voice emerges

unimpeded by the vast web of words generated out of Bloom's daytime contact with Dublin life. Raleigh also notices that Molly thinks more about the future than her husband; this prophetic element in her character parallels and reinforces the prophetic role of *Penelope* in the symbolic structure of the novel.

37. Kenner rather ingeniously argues that Molly has misinterpreted Bloom's somnolent muttering, and that Bloom never actually meant to request breakfast in bed at all (*Joyce's Voices*, p. 87 and *Ulysses*, p. 146); but if Kenner is right, Molly's mental construction of such a request suggests that she is even more positively receptive to it, more anxious to discover some change in her husband, than readers had previously realized.

38. Peake identifies essentially the same theme I find in Molly's first sentence: 'Molly's surprise at Bloom's request for breakfast in bed gives rise to guessing about the causes of his behavior . . . [she shows] that she is more concerned than she is prepared to admit, even to herself' (pp. 304–5).

39. See Peake, Sultan, French and Maddox.

40. Yeats, *A Vision* (1937; rpt. New York: Collier, 1966) pp. 67 ff. The diagrams on pp. 71 and 72 are helpful in envisioning these models. See also J. Hillis Miller, *Fiction and Repetition* (Cambridge, MA: Harvard University Press, 1982), for a discussion of repetition with differences as 'Nietzchean', pp. 6 ff.

41. Apparently, DNA – the basic biological component of all life – reduplicates itself by separating at the center of its double helix and unweaving itself outward in an expanding spiral; see *Encyclopaedia Britannica*, 15th edn (Chicago, 1974) 7, diagram p. 986. Joyce and Yeats could not have known this except by prophetic intuition, but it would probably have delighted them.

42. Ernest and Johanna Lehner, *Folklore and Symbolism of Flowers, Plants and Trees* (New York: Tudor, 1960). In *Joyce and Dante* (Princeton University Press, 1981) Mary Reynolds links this imagery to the heavenly rose at the end of Dante's *Paradiso* (see pp. 79, 116, 191).

43. *Natural Supernaturalism* (New York: Norton, 1971) p. 286. On Joyce's general response to Wordsworth, Abrams observes that

in a précis of English literary history which he composed in the spring of 1905, Joyce gave "the highest palms" to Wordsworth, together with Shakespeare and Shelley; and a few months later he wrote to Stanislaus Joyce, "I think Wordsworth of all English men of letters best deserves your word 'genius'" (p. 421).

The quoted passages appear in *Letters*, II, ed. Richard Ellmann (London: Faber & Faber, 1966) pp. 90–1.

44. Maddox, p. 171.

45. Some who make this argument rely on the claim that Molly is impossibly self-contradictory as a character, but such objections can generally be met by rethinking preconceptions about how a character in her situation ought to behave. French, for example, argues that

as an actual character and not just a symbol . . . [Molly presents] a psychological contradiction. A person who is as easy with her own sexuality as Molly is, and as hungry for sexual relations as she describes herself to be, would not wait chastely for 10 years, five months, and eighteen days. She would complain to her husband or find a lover . . . it seems unlikely that it would take Molly all these years in sex-starved Dublin to find a lover. (p. 257).

But French herself finds convincing evidence in the text for Molly's desire to maintain an image of respectability (p. 255), and such a desire would be difficult to reconcile with the search for a lover. Further, despite her strong sexuality, Molly seems to ground her self-respect partially in a tacit adherence to values and double standards of Victorian morality which are certainly still pervasive in the Dublin of 1904.

46.   Much later in life, Joyce apparently said that he 'had sought to end with the least forceful word I could possibly find. I had found the word "yes", which is barely pronounced, which denotes acquiescence, self-abandon, relaxation, the end of all resistance" (Ellmann, *James Joyce*, p. 725.) But shortly after finishing *Ulysses* in 1922 he is reported to have said that 'the book must end with yes. It must end with the most positive word in the human language' (Ellmann, p. 536). This apparent self-contradiction – similar to many of Molly's – emerges from two reported conversations widely separated in time, and cannot represent a serious problem for interpretation of the ending. The heightened rhythm of the final half-page insistently proclaims that Molly views the experience positively.

47.   In *The Palm at the End of the Mind* (New York: Vintage, 1972) pp. 97–9.

48.   *Portrait*, p. 215.

49.   Keats, *Selected Poems and Letters*, ed. Douglas Bush (Boston: Houghton Mifflin, 1959) pp. 207–8.

50.   *Finnegans Wake* (1939; rpt. New York: Viking, 1974).

5: *TO THE LIGHTHOUSE*: RESHAPING THE SINGLE VISION

1.   *Two Cheers for Democracy* (New York: Harcourt, 1951) p. 119. See also Woolf, 'How Should One Read a Book?' in *The Second Common Reader* (New York: Harcourt, 1932, rpt. 1960) p. 235.

2.   See Quentin Bell, *Virginia Woolf* (New York: Harcourt, 1972) II, p. 54.

3.   *The Common Reader* (New York: Harcourt, 1925, rpt. 1953) p. 155. The essay was first published in 1919.

4.   *The Letters of Virginia Woolf*, ed. Nigel Nicolson (New York: Harcourt, 1976) II, p. 231. See also p. 234.

5.   *The Diary of Virginia Woolf*, ed. Anne Olivier Bell (New York: Harcourt, 1978) II, p. 69.

6.   *Diary*, II, pp. 188–9.

7.   *Diary*, II, p. 199.

8.   *Diary*, II, p. 200.

9.   *Letters*, II, p. 476.

10.   Review in *Times Literary Supplement* (2 Dec. 1920), rpt. in *D. H. Lawrence: The Critical Heritage*, ed. R. P. Draper (New York: Barnes & Noble, 1970) p. 141.

11.   See *Letters*, II, p. 82, and *The Bloomsbury Group*, ed. S. P. Rosenbaum
       (University of Toronto Press, 1975) p. 363.
12.   *Letters*, II, p. 198.
13.   *Letters*, II, p. 475.
14.   See, for example, *Diary*, III (1980) p. 24: 'Well, Morgan admires [*Mrs.
       Dalloway*]. This is a weight off my mind' and *Letters* III (1977) p. 189: 'I
       always feel that nobody, except perhaps Morgan Forster, lays hold of the
       thing I have done'. See also Quentin Bell, II, pp. 28, 132–3, and
       Rosenbaum, pp. 166, 204.
15.   *Collected Essays* I (London: Hogarth Press, 1966) pp. 345–7.
16.   The ending of *To the Lighthouse* has provoked both strong criticism and
       praise. For negative views, see Robert M. Adams, *Strains of Discord*
       (Ithaca: Cornell University Press, 1958) pp. 194–5; James Hafley, *The
       Glass Roof* (1954; rpt. New York: Russell and Russell, 1963) p. 78; and
       Ruth Temple, 'Never say "I": *To the Lighthouse* as Vision and Confession'
       in Claire Sprague, ed., *Virginia Woolf: a Collection of Critical Essays*
       (Englewood Cliffs, NJ: Prentice-Hall, 1971) pp. 98–100. More positive
       views emerge from a large number of sensitive and perceptive studies, not
       all of which, however, discuss the ending explicitly: Eric Auerbach's 'The
       Brown Stocking' in *Mimesis*, trans. Willard Trask (Princeton University
       Press, 1953); Sharon Kaehele and Howard German's '*To the Lighthouse*:
       Symbol and Vision', *Bucknell Review*, 10 (May 1962), rpt. in Morris Beja,
       ed., *Virginia Woolf: To the Lighthouse, a Casebook* (London: Macmillan,
       1970); James Naremore's *The World Without a Self* (New Haven: Yale
       University Press, 1973); Phyllis Rose's *Woman of Letters* (New York:
       Oxford University Press, 1978); and Maria Dibattista's *Virginia Woolf's
       Major Novels* (New Haven: Yale University Press, 1980).
17.   Phyllis Rose argues that Woolf's struggle with tradition is complicated
       because she sees the tradition as 'masculine, whereas her talent was
       feminine'; the central questions of *To the Lighthouse* are whether one can
       be both a women and an artist, and how Woolf can 'see herself as her
       mother's heir while still rejecting the model of womanhood she presents'
       (pp. 94, 154, 158, 169).
18.   *To the Lighthouse* (New York: Harcourt, 1927; rpt. 1955) p. 43; the elipses
       in this passage are Woolf's own. Subsequent references appear in the text.
       (Maria Dibattista suggests that Woolf is 'less interested in the mother as
       precursor than in the mother as Muse', p. 65).
19.   *The Prelude*, ed. Jonathan Wordsworth, M. H. Abrams, Stephen Gill
       (New York: Norton, 1979) 1850, I.270–4. Woolf regarded Wordsworth
       with considerable respect. In 1911 she wrote to Saxon Sydney-Turner that
       'I am reading The Prelude. Dont you think it one of the greatest works ever
       written? Some of it, anyhow, is sublime; it may get worse' (*Letters*, I,
       p. 460). Later in life, she offers *Lear*, *Phedre*, and *The Prelude* as examples
       of great poems (*The Second Common Reader*, p. 242).
20.   For a different treatment of the link between Mrs. Ramsay and Penelope,
       see Geoffrey Hartman, 'Virginia's Web', *Chicago Review* (1961), rpt. in
       Thomas Vogler, ed., *Twentieth Century Interpretations of To the Lighthouse*
       (Englewood Cliffs, NJ: Prentice-Hall, 1970).
21.   *Howards End* (1910; rpt. New York: Random House, 1921) p. 332.
22.   *Letters*, III, p. 385.

23. Nancy Topping Bazin also identifies Mr. Ramsay with the tower and Mrs. Ramsay with the light, in *Virginia Woolf and the Androgynous Vision* (New Brunswick, NJ: Rutgers University Press, 1973) p. 46.

24. See M. H. Abrams, *The Mirror and the Lamp* (New York: Oxford University Press, 1953) and *Natural Supernatualism* (New York: Norton, 1971).

25. This description of lighthouse mechanics is a vast simplification of that provided in the *Encyclopaedia Britannica*, 11th edn (1911) XVI, pp. 633–44.

26. *Ode to a Nightingale*, in Keats, *Selected Poems and Letters*, ed. Douglas Bush (Boston: Houghton Mifflin, 1959) l. 23; pp. 203–5.

27. *The Rainbow* (1915, rpt. New York. Viking, 1961) p. 441.

28. See, for example, John Hawley Roberts, ' "Vision and Design" in Virginia Woolf', *PMLA*, 61 (1946), rpt. in Jacqueline E. M. Latham, ed., *Critics on Virginia Woolf* (Coral Gables, FL: University of Miami Press, 1970), p. 66. Naremore also discusses Mrs. Ramsay's closeness to a 'vast dark realm which everyone has in common' and which 'can only be defined negatively', p. 139.

29. Kermode, *The Sense of an Ending* (New York: Oxford University Press, 1967) pp. 44–6.

30. Kermode, pp. 46–7.

31. In *The Palm at the End of the Mind* (New York: Vintage, 1972) pp. 97–9.

32. Allen McLaurin notices a problem of Wordsworthian harmony between Nature and man in 'Time Passes', but does not discuss it in detail (*Virginia Woolf: the Echoes Enslaved* [Cambridge University Press, 1973] p. 197).

33. *Mrs. Dalloway* (New York: Harcourt, 1925; rpt. 1953) p. 133.

34. *The Pursuit of Signs* (Ithaca: Cornell University Press, 1981) pp. 162, 164.

35. For a more extended discussion of the relation between *To the Lighthouse* and *The Winter's Tale*, see Dibattista, pp. 76–94.

36. See *A Room of One's Own* (New York: Harcourt, 1929; rpt. 1957) esp. pp. 58–9, 96, 103.

37. Fleishman, *Virginia Woolf* (Baltimore: Johns Hopkins University Press, 1975) pp. 131–4. If the bay and lighthouse were out behind the house when Lily faces it from the lawn, Mrs. Ramsay would not have been able to see the lighthouse beam from the steps; the house would have intercepted it. For the argument that Lily's easel is now facing away from the house, see Ralph Freedman, *The Lyrical Novel* (Princeton University Press, 1963) p. 237; and Herbert Marder, *Feminism and Art* (University of Chicago Press, 1968) p. 149.

38. The best discussion of Woolf's aesthetic theory and its relation to Lily's painting remains John Hawley Roberts's ' "Vision and Design" in Virginia Woolf' (1946). He links both Woolf's and Lily's formalist aesthetics with those of Roger Fry, who believed that lasting feelings about a work of art are wholly 'dependent on the purely formal relations it expresses'. For Fry, even in a novel with ulterior purposes, aesthetic effect arises only from structures that 'are self-contained, self-sufficing, and not to be valued by their reference to what lies outside' (pp. 61, 65–7). As I have argued in discussing *Howards End*, Forster also shared this formalist aesthetic creed.

39. *A Room of One's Own*, p. 90.

40. *Mrs. Dalloway*, p. 170.
41. *Diary* III, p. 12.
42. *Tintern Abbey*, in *Wordsworth: Selected Poems and Prefaces*, ed. Jack Stillinger (Boston: Houghton Mifflin, 1965) ll. 39–41; pp. 108–11.
43. For an extended discussion of the Persephone myth in the novel, see Joseph Blotner, 'Mythic Patterns in *To the Lighthouse*', *PMLA*, 71 (1956), rpt. in Beja, ed. *Virginia Woolf: To the Lighthouse*.
44. *Tintern Abbey*, ll. 47–9.
45. *Hamlet*, V.ii.220–2, from *The Riverside Shakespeare*, ed. G. Blakemore Evans (Boston: Houghton Mifflin, 1974). Hartman also observes this echo (p. 81).
46. *Letters of John Keats*, ed. Robert Gittings (New York: Oxford University Press, 1975) p. 43.
47. Many critics discuss Woolf's attempt to unite fact and vision, realism and myth. See Freedman, pp. 200–1, Bazin, pp. 22, 25; Marder, pp. 40–1, 45–6. Alice Van Buren Kelley organizes her entire book on Woolf – subtitled *Fact and Vision* – around these two elements (*The Novels of Virginia Woolf* [Chicago University Press, 1973]).
48. See *Howards End*, pp. 333–4.
49. For many readers this preparation is insufficient, and perhaps could not be made sufficient. An extraordinary number of critics fail altogether to mention this culminating vision, or reveal rationalistic bias that makes them unwilling to accept Mrs. Ramsay's presence in the scene. See, for example, Josephine O'Brien Schaefer, *The Three-Fold Nature of Reality in the Novels of Virginia Woolf* (London: Mouton, 1965) p. 134; Morris Beja, 'Matches Struck in the Dark: Virginia Woolf's Moments of Vision', *Critical Quarterly*, IV (Summer 1964), rpt. in Beja, ed., *Virginia Woolf: To the Lighthouse*, p. 227; Sharon Proudfit, 'Lily's Painting: A Key to Personal Relations in *To the Lighthouse*', *Criticism* (Winter 1971) p. 37; Fleishman, pp. 104, 126; Daniel Allbright, *Personality and Impersonality* (University of Chicago Press, 1978) p. 152; James Hafley, 'Virginia Woolf's Narrators and the Art of "Life Itself"', in Ralph Freedman, ed., *Virginia Woolf* (Berkeley: University of California Press, 1980), p. 34. Naremore is one of the few previous critics who finds the moment convincing and moving (p. 149).
50. *Tennyson's Poetry*, ed. Robert W. Hill (New York: Norton, 1971) 91.5–6. Subsequent references appear in the text.
51. *Diary*, III, p. 34.
52. *Diary*, III, p. 106.
53. Several critics discuss Lily's drawing upon these two kinds of inspiration. Kaehele and German argue that Lily's vision results from 'her adopting an attitude which combines the perspectives of both Mr and Mrs Ramsay and makes reality simultaneously factual and miraculous' (p. 205). See also A. D. Moody, 'The Meaning of a Technique', rpt. in Thomas Vogler, ed., *Twentieth Century Interpretations of To the Lighthouse*, pp. 55–6; Kelley, p. 143; Jane Novak, *The Razor Edge of Balance* (Coral Gables, FL: University of Miami Press, 1975) p. 60.
54. *Diary*, III, pp. 18–19.
55. *Letters*, III, appendix, p. 572.
56. See *Diary*, III, p. 132.

6: TRAGIC VISION IN *THE SOUND AND THE FURY*

1. *Essays, Speeches and Public Letters by William Faulkner*, ed. James B. Meriwether (New York: Random House, 1965) pp. 119–20.
2. *Faulkner in the University*, ed. Frederick L. Gwynn and Joseph Blotner (Charlottesville: University of Virginia Press, 1959) p. 77. Gary Lee Stonum argues, for example, that the Nobel Prize Speech reveals a Faulkner unable to grasp the 'daring and complexity of his own best work' (*Faulkner's Career* [Ithaca: Cornell University Press, 1979] p. 64).
3. Critical response to *The Sound and the Fury* ranges from Cleanth Brooks's assertion that it 'has to do with the discovery that life has no meaning' to Lyall H. Powers's insistence that its final statement is 'boldly and affirmatively hopeful' (Brooks, *William Faulkner: The Yoknapatawpha Country* [New Haven: Yale University Press, 1963] p. 347; Powers, (*Faulkner's Yoknapatawpha Comedy* [Ann Arbor: University of Michigan Press, 1980] p. 49). Few literary works of such widely acknowledged stature have provoked such divergent views. Many persuasive and influential readings have emphasized the irresolution, meaninglessness, or nihilism of the ending; see, for example, Walter Slatoff, *Quest for Failure* (Ithaca: Cornell University Press, 1960) pp. 136–7, 149, 157; John V. Hagopian, 'Nihilism in Faulkner's *The Sound and the Fury*', *Modern Fiction Studies*, 13 (Spring 1967) p. 53; Beverly Gross, 'Form and Fulfillment in *The Sound and the Fury*', *Modern Language Quarterly*, 29 (Dec. 1968) pp. 444–9; Donald M. Kartiganer, '*The Sound and the Fury* and Faulkner's Quest for Form', *ELH*, 37 (Dec. 1970) pp. 619, 636. For more positive views, see Hyatt H. Waggoner, *William Faulkner* (University of Kentucky Press, 1959) pp. 59–60; Michael Millgate, *The Achievement of William Faulkner* (1966; rpt. Lincoln: University of Nebraska Press, 1978) p. 101; Lawrence Thompson, *William Faulkner* (New York: Holt, Rinehart and Winston, 1967) p. 47.
4. Faulkner mentions Lawrence's 'tortured sex' in a 1925 review, but this obviously need not imply a first-hand knowledge of his novels (*William Faulkner: Early Prose and Poetry*, ed. Carvel Collins [Boston: Little Brown, 1962] p. 115).
5. Millgate, pp. 289–91. In interviews from 1931 to 1962, Faulkner was often questioned about favourite books and possible literary influences. He speaks positively of the following works and authors, among others: the Bible (particularly the Old Testament), Shakespeare, the Elizabethan poets generally, *Don Quixote*, *Tom Jones*, *Clarissa*, Keats, Shelley, Dickens, Melville (especially *Moby Dick*), Dostoevski (especially *The Brothers Karamazov*), Tolstoy (especially *Anna Karenina*), Balzac, Flaubert (especially *Madame Bovary*), Proust, Mann's *Buddenbrooks*, Conard, See *Lion in the Garden*, ed. James B. Meriwether and Michael Millgate (1968, rpt. Lincoln: University of Nebraska Press, 1980) pp. 11, 17–18, 21, 49, 60, 72, 110–12, 128, 217, 234, 251, 284. Millgate asserts that Faulkner also knew Hawthorne, Swinburne, Wilde, Eliot, Hardy, and James (p. 291). At the time of his death, Faulkner owned multiple editions of Shakespeare, Keats, Dickens, Conrad, Cervantes, and Balzac; Joseph Blotner observes that he could quote Shakespeare and Keats by heart (*Faulkner's Library* [Charlottesville: University Press of Virginia, 1964] pp. 8, 12).

6. *Lion in the Garden*, pp. 55, 276, 280; Adams, 'The Apprenticeship of William Faulkner', rpt. in Linda Wagner, ed. *William Faulkner: Four Decades of Criticism* (Michigan State University Press, 1973) pp. 9–25.

7. Blotner, *Faulkner* (New York: Random House, 1974) p. 352.

8. Blotner, *Faulkner's Library*, p. 77.

9. Groden, 'Criticism in New Composition: *Ulysses* and *The Sound and the Fury*', *Twentieth-Century Literature* 21 (Oct. 1975) p. 265. Groden observes that Joyce would have been difficult for Faulkner to avoid, since Stone and Sherwood Anderson, perhaps his most influential friends in the 1920s, were both Joyce enthusiasts (p. 266).

10. Blotner, *Faulkner*, p. 716. In 1932, true to form, Faulkner told an interviewer who asked about Joyce's influence that he had never read him. But unfortunately, Faulkner's copy of *Ulysses* was out on his desk; he had to pretend to have only recently acquired it (*Lion in the Garden*, p. 30).

11. *Lion in the Garden*, p. 26.

12. *Lion in the Garden*, pp. 197, 112. Later in the year he was still more positive, identifying Joyce and Mann as the two great European writers of his time; he said 'you should approach Joyce's *Ulysses* as the illiterate Baptist preacher approaches the Old Testament: with faith' (*Lion in the Garden*, p. 250).

13. Groden finds echoes of *Penelope* in *Soldier's Pay* (New York: Boni & Liveright, 1926) pp. 277–8; *Mosquitoes* (New York: Boni & Liveright, 1927) pp. 47, 128; and *The Sound and the Fury*, pp. 154, 126–7 (pp. 265–8). He observes that 'Molly's final "yes" attracted Faulkner considerably', finding six instances of it in Faulkner's early poems and fictions (p. 277).

14. *Faulkner in the University*, p. 6; *Lion in the Garden*, p. 222.

15. Baum, 'The Beautiful One: Caddy Compson as Heroine', *Modern Fiction Studies*, 13 (Spring 1967) pp. 33–43. Powers also argues that Caddy is the only Compson capable of unselfish love, seeing her problem as a 'superabundance of love' and her sin as an excess of 'the chiefest virtue' (pp. 24–5).

16. *Faulkner's Women* (Deland, FL: Everett, 1972) pp. 47–65.

17. 'Introduction to *The Sound and the Fury*', ed. James B. Meriwether, *Southern Review* 8 (Autumn 1972) p. 710.

18. André Bleikasten, *The Most Splendid Failure* (Bloomington: Indiana University Press, 1976) pp. 51–74.

19. *The Sound and the Fury* (1929; rpt. New York: Vintage, 1954) pp. 5, 8, 22, 50–1, 54, 58, 88. Subsequent references appear in the text.

20. *Faulkner in the University*, p. 1.

21. Kartiganer argues that the form of the novel is a series of 'fragments struggling to discover their own unity'; he concludes, as I do, that the novel is 'a modern version of tragic form' (pp. 613, 639). But Kartiganer feels that neither Caddy nor the fourth section offers an 'adequate basis for unity in the work' and that the novel is ultimately 'a book of nearly total despair' (p. 619).

22. *Faulkner in the University*, p. 1; for similar statements, see p. 31, and *Lion in the Garden*, pp. 222, 245.

23. *Faulkner in the University*, p. 31.

24.   In the draft introduction for a 1933 edition of *The Sound and the Fury* that
       was never published, Faulkner refers to 'Quentin and Jason and Benjy and
       the negros' looking up at the muddy seat of Caddy's drawers
       ('Introduction to *The Sound and the Fury*', *Southern Review* 8 [Autumn
       1972] p. 710). Faulkner may simply have forgotten by 1933 what he had
       written in 1928; I have not found an explicit reference to Quentin's
       presence beneath the tree in any of Faulkner's other spoken or written
       comments on the novel. Quentin's presence can only be read into the scene
       by assuming that after being left on the kitchen steps, he rejoined the other
       children at some point without Benjy's awareness; that he was utterly
       silent all the time he was with them; and that he departed sometime before
       Dilsey's arrival, again unnoticed by Benjy.
25.   Baum observes that Caddy's disobedience is 'better than Quentin's
       excessive obedience which keeps him from participation in life', all but
       explicitly noting Quentin's absence at the pear tree (p. 37).
26.   Compare Adam after Eve's fall in *Paradise Lost*, IX.952–9.
27.   Olga Vickery argues that Caddy challenges 'the family's capacity for
       understanding and forgiveness' and it fails her (*The Novels of William
       Faulkner* [Baton Rouge: Louisiana State University Press, 1964] p. 48.).
28.   In his cynicism and dipsomania, Mr. Compson clearly bears much
       responsibility for family's deterioration, but Caddy and Quentin
       consistently view him positively. Brooks sees him as a caring but defeated
       man who shows real affection and concern for his children, p. 335.
29.   See Kermode, *The Sense of an Ending* (New York: Oxford University
       Press, 1967) pp. 17–18, 44–7.
30.   Millgate, p. 103.
31.   Gross, p. 444.
32.   Arthur Kinney exaggerates Benjy's abilities in arguing that he is able 'to
       recognize' Quentin's escape as completing the analogy between Caddy and
       Quentin (*Faulker's Narrative Poetics* [Amherst: University of Massa-
       chusettes Press, 1978], p. 142).
33.   *Aspects of the Novel* (New York: Harcourt, 1927; rpt. 1955) p. 95.
34.   Faulkner's interest in the freedom of his characters may help to explain his
       inconsistency in describing Quentin's escape; in the Compson Appendix,
       written 17 years after the novel, he has Caddy's daughter leave the house
       by climbing down a rainpipe rather than the pear tree (cf. pp. 90 and
       424–6). Faulkner may have wished, in following his characters beyond the
       limits of the novel itself, to break the aesthetic pattern so that their later
       actions would not seem predetermined by it; the shift from pear tree to
       rainpipe introduces a useful uncertainty into the telling of the central
       events. He repeats this version in a 1956 comment that explicitly links
       Quentin's escape to the image of Caddy in the pear tree:

       I realized the symbolism of the soiled pants, and that image was replaced
       by one of the fatherless and motherless girl climbing down the rainpipe to
       escape from the only home she had, where she had never been offered love
       or affection or understanding. (*Lion in the Garden*, p. 245)

       Here the rainpipe seems to offer a way to describe the novel's structure without, again, quite creating a deterministic clarity about the central events in the pattern.

35. *Lion in the Garden*, pp. 146–7.
36. The New Oxford Annotated Bible, Herbert G. May and Bruce M. Metzger, eds. (New York: Oxford University Press, 1973) p. 1168.
37. Slatoff, pp. 156–7. Faulkner frequently insisted that Christian allegory was 'just one of several tools' he employed in creating the novel (*Faulkner in the University*, p. 17).
38. Hagopian, pp. 46–53.
39. Kartiganer, p. 638. Kartiganer supports my point, however, that Dilsey's orthodox vision is finally inadequate to order the complexity of experience in the novel (p. 637).
40. Nobel Prize Speech, *Essays, Speeches and Public Letters*, p. 120.
41. Kermode, pp. 8, 53.
42. Hagopian explicitly compares Jason in this scene to Satan in *Paradise Lost*, VI:135 (p. 50).
43. Kermode, p. 46.
44. John Matthews suggests rather ingeniously that 'the reader's demand for a conventional novel is mimicked by Benjy's concluding demand for the regular left-to-right flow of signboards past his eyes, like print on the page' (*The Play of Faulkner's Language* [Ithaca: Cornell University Press, 1982], p. 113).
45. Luria, *The Mind of a Mnemonist*, trans. Lynn Solotaroff (New York: Basic, 1968) pp. 31–2, 63. Luria's subject resembles Benjy in other ways; cf. pp. 34, 58, 76–7, 83, 96, 152, 157, 159.
46. *Macbeth* V.viii.71–3, *The Riverside Shakespeare*, ed. G. Blakemore Evans (Boston: Houghton Mifflin, 1974).
47. Thompson suggests that 'the Compsons, like Macbeth, try to excuse themselves from predicaments of their own making by projecting their own inner chaos outward upon the ordered universe' (p. 51).
48. Kinney argues that Faulkner's contribution to the narrative poetics of epiphany, following Joyce, is 'to move the sense of epiphany from the climax of the plot (Stephen discussing art; Stephen confronting Leopold Bloom) to the conclusion of the book, and to transfer the sense of wholeness from the protagonist to the reader' (p. 33). But my reading of Molly Bloom's final vision in *Ulysses* suggests that Joyce has already made both of these contributions.
49. *Edmund Spenser's Poetry*, ed. Hugh MacLean (New York: Norton, 1968) ll. 433–4, p. 445; *The Riverside Shakespeare*, p. 1768.
50. *Letters of John Keats*, ed. Robert Gittings (Oxford University Press, 1979) pp. 38, 157. Richard Adams (p. 13) finds another passage from the first of these letters echoed in *Go Down, Moses*, which suggests that Faulkner had read it at least by 1942.
51. Nobel Prize Speech, *Essays, Speeches and Public Letters*, p. 120.

Selected Bibliography

General Works

Abrams, M. H., *The Mirror and the Lamp: Romantic Theory and the Critical Tradition* (New York: Oxford University Press, 1953).
——, *Natural Supernaturalism: Tradition and Revolution in Romantic Literature* (New York: Norton, 1971).
Adams, Robert M., *Strains of Discord: Studies in Literary Openness* (Ithaca: Cornell University Press, 1958).
Aristotle, *Poetics*, trans. Preston H. Epps (Chapel Hill: University of North Carolina Press, 1942; rpt. 1970).
Auerbach, Erich, *Mimesis: the Representation of Reality in Western Literature*, trans. Willard Trask (Princeton University Press, 1953).
Augustine, *Confessions*, trans. R. S. Pine-Coffin (New York: Penguin, 1961).
Barthes, Roland, 'Introduction to the Structural Analysis of Narrative' in *Image-Music-Text*, trans. Stephen Heath (New York: Hill & Wang, 1977) pp. 79–124.
Beja, Morris, *Epiphany in the Modern Novel* (Seattle: University of Washington Press, 1971).
Booth, Wayne, *The Rhetoric of Fiction* (University of Chicago Press, 1961; rev. edn 1983).
Culler, Jonathan, *The Pursuit of Signs: Semiotics, Literature, Deconstruction* (Ithaca: Cornell University Press, 1981).
——, *Structuralist Poetics: Structuralism, Linguistics and the Study of Literature* (Ithaca: Cornell University Press, 1975).
Dante, *The Divine Comedy*, trans. John Sinclair (New York: Oxford University Press, 1939; rpt. 1961).
Forster, E. M., *Aspects of the Novel* (New York: Harcourt Brace Jovanovich, 1927; rpt. 1955).
——, *Two Cheers for Democracy* (New York: Harcourt, Brace & World, 1951).
Friedman, Alan, *The Turn of the Novel* (New York: Oxford University Press, 1966).
Frye, Northrop, *Anatomy of Criticism: Four Essays* (Princeton University Press, 1957).
Graves, Robert, *The White Goddess: a Historical Grammar of Poetic Myth* (1948; rpt. New York: Octagon Books, 1972).
Gross, Beverly, 'Narrative Time and the Open-Ended Novel', *Criticism*, 8 (Autumn 1966).
Hartman, Geoffrey, *Wordsworth's Poetry, 1787–1814* (New Haven: Yale University Press, 1971).
Harvey, W. J., *Character and the Novel* (Ithaca: Cornell University Press, 1965).
James, Henry, 'The Art of Fiction' (1884) in *Theory of Fiction: Henry James*, ed. James E. Miller (Lincoln: University of Nebraska Press, 1972).
——, *The Art of the Novel: Critical Prefaces*, ed. R. P. Blackmur (New York: Charles Scribner's Sons, 1934).
Keats, John, *Selected Poems and Letters*, ed. Douglas Bush (Boston: Houghton Mifflin, 1959).

Kermode, Frank, *The Sense of an Ending: Studies in the Theory of Fiction* (New York: Oxford University Press, 1966).

Langbaum, Robert, 'The Epiphanic Mode in Wordsworth and Modern Literature', *New Literary History*, 14:2 (Winter 1983).

——, *The Poetry of Experience: The Dramatic Monologue in Modern Literary Tradition* (New York: Norton, 1957).

Lodge, David, *Language of Fiction: Essays in Criticism and Verbal Analysis of the English Novel* (New York: Columbia University Press, 1966).

——, *The Modes of Modern Writing: Metaphor, Metonymy, and the Typology of Modern Literature* (Ithaca: Cornell University Press, 1977).

Miller, D. A., *Narrative and its Discontents: Problems of Closure in the Traditional Novel* (Princeton University Press, 1981).

Miller, J. Hillis, *The Disappearance of God: Five Nineteenth-Century Writers* (Cambridge, MA: Harvard University Press, 1963).

——, 'The Problematic of Ending in Narrative', *Nineteenth Century Fiction* (June 1978).

Milton, John, *Paradise Lost*, ed. Scott Elledge (New York: Norton, 1975).

Plato, *The Symposium*, trans. Walter Hamilton (New York: Penguin, 1951).

Price, Martin, *Forms of Life: Character and Moral Imagination in the Novel* (New Haven: Yale University Press, 1983).

Richter, David H., *Fable's End: Completeness and Closure in Rhetorical Fiction* (University of Chicago Press, 1974).

Scholes, Robert and Robert Kellogg, *The Nature of Narrative* (New York: Oxford University Press, 1966).

Smith, Barbara Herrnstein, *Poetic Closure: a Study of How Poems End* (University of Chicago Press, 1968).

Schug, Charles, *The Romantic Genesis of the Modern Novel* (University of Pittsburgh Press, 1979).

Schwarz, Daniel R., ' "I Was the World in Which I Walked": the Transformation of the British Novel', *University of Toronto Quarterly* (Spring 1982) 279–97.

Shelley's Poetry and Prose, ed. Donald H. Reiman and Sharon B. Powers (New York: Norton, 1977).

Stevens, Wallace, *The Palm at the End of the Mind* (New York: Vintage, 1972).

Torgovnick, Marianna, *Closure in the Novel* (Princeton University Press, 1981).

Woolf, Virginia, 'Mr. Bennett and Mrs. Brown' (1924) in *The Captain's Death Bed* (New York: Harcourt, Brace & Co, 1950).

Wordsworth, Jonathan, 'The Climbing of Snowdon' in Jonathan Wordsworth, ed., *Bicentenary Wordsworth Studies in Memory of John Alban Finch* (Ithaca: Cornell University Press, 1970).

Wordsworth, William, *The Prelude*, ed. Jonathan Wordsworth, M. H. Abrams, Stephen Gill (New York: Norton, 1979).

——, *Selected Poems and Prefaces*, ed. Jack Stillinger (Boston: Houghton Mifflin, 1965).

E. M. Forster

Beer, J. B., *The Achievement of E. M. Forster* (London: Chatto & Windus, 1962).

Bradley, A. C., 'Poetry for Poetry's Sake' in *Oxford Lectures on Poetry* (London: Macmillan, 1909).

Brander, Laurence, *E. M. Forster: a Critical Study* (London: Rupert Hart-Davis, 1968).

Colmer, John, *E. M. Forster: the Personal Voice* (Boston: Routledge & Kegan Paul, 1975).

Crews, Frederick C., *E. M. Forster: the Perils of Humanism* (Princeton University Press, 1966).

Finkelstein, Bonnie Blumenthal, *Forster's Women: Eternal Differences* (New York: Columbia University Press, 1975).

Forster, E. M., *Howards End* (London, 1910; rpt. New York: Vintage, 1921).

——, *A Passage to India* (London, 1924; rpt. New York: Harcourt, Brace & World, 1952).

Furbank, P. N., *E. M. Forster: a Life* (London: Secker & Warburg, 1977).

Gardner, Phillip, ed., *E. M. Forster: the Critical Heritage.* (Boston: Routledge & Kegan Paul, 1973).

Gillen, Francis, '*Howards End* and the Neglected Narrator', *Novel*, 3 (1970) 139–52.

Langbaum, Robert, 'A New Look at E. M. Forster', *Southern Review* (Winter 1968) 33–49.

McConkey, James, *The Novels of E. M. Forster* (Ithaca: Cornell University Press, 1957).

Roby, Kinley E. 'Irony and the Narrative Voice in *Howards End*', *The Journal of Narrative Technique*, II (May 1972) 116–24.

Rosecrance, Barbara, *Forster's Narrative Vision* (Ithaca: Cornell University Press, 1982).

Stone, Wilfred, *The Cave and the Mountain: a Study of E. M. Forster* (Stanford University Press, 1966).

——, 'Forster on Love and Money' in Oliver Stallybras, ed., *Aspects of E. M. Forster* (New York: Harcourt, Brace & World, 1969).

Trilling, Lionel, *E. M. Forster: a Study* (London: The Hogarth Press, 1944)

Widdowson, Peter, *E. M. Forster's Howards End: Fiction as History* (London: Sussex University Press, 1977).

Wilde, Alan, *Art and Order: a Study of E. M. Forster* (New York University Press, 1964).

Woolf, Virginia, 'The Novels of E. M. Forster' in *Collected Essays*, vol. I (London: The Hogarth Press, 1966).

D. H. Lawrence

Clarke, Colin, *River of Dissolution: D. H. Lawrence and English Romanticism* (New York: Barnes & Noble, 1969).

Daleski, H. M., *The Forked Flame: a Study of D. H. Lawrence* (London: Faber & Faber, 1965).

Eliot, T. S., review of *Son of Woman* by John Middleton Murray, *Criterion* (July 1931), rpt. in *D. H. Lawrence: the Critical Heritage*, ed. R. P. Draper (New York: Barnes & Noble, 1970).

Engelberg, Edward, 'Escape from the Circles of Experience: D. H. Lawrence's *The Rainbow* as a Modern *Bildungsroman*', *PMLA* (Mar. 1963).

Ford, George, *Double Measure: a Study of the Novels and Stories of D. H. Lawrence* (New York: Holt, Rinehart & Winston, 1965).

Goldberg, S. L., '*The Rainbow*: Fiddle-bow and Sand', *Essays in Criticism*, 11 (Oct. 1961).

Hough, Graham, *The Dark Sun: a Study of D. H. Lawrence* (London: Duckworth, 1956).

Kermode, Frank, 'Lawrence and the Apocalyptic Types', *Critical Quarterly*, 10 (Spring/Summer 1968), rpt. in *Continuities* (London: Routledge & Kegan Paul, 1968).

Kinkead-Weekes, Mark, 'The Marble and the Statue: the Exploratory Imagination of D. H. Lawrence' in *Imagined Worlds: Essays on Some English Novels and Novelists in Honor of John Butt*, ed. Maynard Mack and Ian Gregor (London: Methuen, 1968).

Langbaum, Robert, *The Mysteries of Identity: a Theme in Modern Literature* (New York: Oxford University Press, 1977).

Lawrence, D. H., *Apocalypse and the Writings on Revelation* (1932), ed. Mara Kalnins (New York: Cambridge University Press, 1980).

——, *Letters*, ed. Aldous Huxley (New York: Viking Press, 1932).

——, *Letters*, vol. I, ed. James T. Boulton, vol. II, ed. George J. Zytaruk and James T. Boulton (New York: Cambridge University Press; vol. I, 1979; vol. II, 1981).

——, *Psychoanalysis and the Unconscious* (1921; rpt. New York: Viking Press, 1960).

——, *The Rainbow* (London, 1915; rpt. New York: Viking, 1961).

——, *Women in Love* (London, 1920; rpt. New York: Viking, 1960).

Leavis, F. R., *D. H. Lawrence: Novelist* (New York: Alfred A. Knopf, 1956).

Lindenberger, Herbert, 'Lawrence and the Romantic Tradition' in *A D. H. Lawrence Miscellany*, ed. Harry T. Moore (Carbondale, IL: Southern Illinois University Press, 1959).

Moore, Harry T., *The Priest of Love: a Life of D. H. Lawrence*. (New York: Farrar, Straus & Giroux, 1974).

Moynahan, Julian, *The Deed of Life: the Novels and Tales of D. H. Lawrence* (Princeton University Press, 1963).

Mudrick, Marvin, 'The Originality of *The Rainbow*' in *A D. H. Lawrence Miscellany*, ed. Harry T. Moore (Carbondale, IL: Southern Illinois University Press, 1959).

Ross, Charles L., *The Composition of The Rainbow and Women in Love: a History* (Charlottesville: University of Virginia Press, 1979).

Sale, Roger H., 'The Narrative Technique of *The Rainbow*', *Modern Fiction Studies*, V (Spring 1959).

Sanders, Scott, *D. H. Lawrence: the World of the Five Major Novels* (New York: Viking Press, 1973).

James Joyce

Adams, Robert M. *Surface and Symbol: the Consistency of James Joyce's Ulysses* (New York: Oxford University Press, 1962).

Eliot, T. S., '*Ulysses*, Order and Myth', *The Dial* (Nov. 1923); rpt. in *James Joyce: Two Decades of Criticism*, ed. Seón Givens (New York: Vanguard Press, 1948).

Ellmann, Richard, *James Joyce* (New York: Oxford University Press, 1959).

——, *Ulysses on the Liffey* (New York: Oxford University Press, 1972).

French, Marilyn, *The Books as World: James Joyce's Ulysses* (Cambridge, MA: Harvard University Press, 1976).

Gifford, Don and Robert J. Seidman, *Notes for Joyce: an Annotation of James Joyce's Ulysses* (New York: Dutton, 1974).

Gilbert, Stuart, *James Joyce's Ulysses* (New York: Random House, 1930; rev. edn 1952; rpt. 1955).

Goldberg, S. L., *The Classical Temper: a Study of James Joyce's Ulysses* (New York: Barnes & Noble, 1961).

Goldman, Arnold, *The Joyce Paradox: Form and Freedom in His Fiction* (London: Routledge & Kegan Paul, 1966).

Groden, Michael, *Ulysses in Progress* (Princeton University Press, 1977).

Hayman, David, *Ulysses: the Mechanics of Meaning* (1970; rev. edn Madison: University of Wisconsin Press, 1982).

Homer, *The Odyssey*, trans. S. H. Butcher and A. Lang (New York: Collier, 1909).

Joyce, James, *Finnegans Wake* (New York: Viking Press, 1939; rpt. 1958).

——, *Letters*, vol. I, ed. Stuart Gilbert (London: Faber & Faber, 1957).

——, *Letters*, vols. II and III, ed. Richard Ellmann (London: Faber & Faber, 1966).

——, *A Portrait of the Artist as a Young Man* (New York: Viking, 1916; rpt. 1964).

——, *Ulysses* (Paris, 1922; rpt. New York: Random House, 1961).

Kain, Richard, *Fabulous Voyager: a Study of James Joyce's Ulysses*. (New York: Viking, 1947; rpt. 1959).

Kenner, Hugh, *Joyce's Voices* (Berkeley: University of California Press, 1978).

——, *Ulysses* (London: Allen & Unwin, 1980)

Lawrence, Karen, *The Odyssey of Style in Ulysses* (Princeton University Press, 1981).

Litz, A. Walton, 'The Genre of *Ulysses*' in *The Theory of the Novel: New Essays*, ed. John Halperin (New York: Oxford University Press, 1974).

——, 'Pound and Eliot on Joyce: The Critical Tradition', *James Joyce Quarterly*, 10:1 (Autumn 1972).

Maddox, James H. Jr., *James Joyce's Ulysses and the Assault Upon Character* (New Brunswick, NJ: Rutgers University Press, 1978).

Peake, Charles H., *James Joyce: the Citizen and the Artist*. (Stanford University Press, 1977).

Pound, Ezra, 'James Joyce and Pecuchet', trans. Fred Bornhauser (*Shenandoah*, III:3 (Autumn 1952).

Rader, Ralph W., 'Exodus and Return: Joyce's *Ulysses* and the Fiction of the Actual', *University of Toronto Quarterly* (Winter 1978/79).

Raleigh, John Henry, *The Chronicle of Leopold and Molly Bloom: Ulysses as Narrative* (Berkeley: University of California Press, 1971).

Reynolds, Mary T., *Joyce and Dante: The Shaping Imagination* (Princeton University Press, 1981).

Schiffer, Paul S., ' "Homing, Upstream": Fictional Closure and the End of *Ulysses*', *James Joyce Quarterly*, 16:3 (Spring 1979).

Sultan, Stanley, *The Argument of Ulysses* (Ohio State University Press, 1964).

Thornton, Weldon, *Allusions in Ulysses: a line-by-line Reference to Joyce's Complex Symbolism* (1968; rpt. New York: Simon and Schuster, 1973).

Tindall, William York, *A Reader's Guide to James Joyce* (New York: Farrar, Straus & Giroux, 1959).

Wilson, Edmund, 'James Joyce', *Axel's Castle* (New York, 1931), rpt. in *Joyce: A Collection of Critical Essays*, ed. William M. Chace (Englewood Cliffs, NJ: Prentice-Hall, 1974).

Yeats, W. B., *A Vision*. (1937, rpt. New York: Collier, 1966).

Virginia Woolf

Bazin, Nancy Topping, *Virginia Woolf and the Androgynous Vision* (New Brunswick, NJ: Rutgers University Press, 1973).

Bell, Quentin, *Virginia Woolf: A Biography*. (New York: Harcourt Brace Jovanovich, 1972).

Blotner, Joseph, 'Mythic Patterns in *To the Lighthouse*', *PMLA*, 71 (1956); rpt. in Morris Beja, ed., *Virginia Woolf: To the Lighthouse: a Casebook* (London: Macmillan, 1970).

Dibattista, Maria, *Virginia Woolf's Major Novels: the Fables of Anon.* (New Haven: Yale University Press, 1980).

Fleishman, Avrom, *Virginia Woolf: a Critical Reading* (Baltimore: Johns Hopkins University Press, 1975).

Freedman, Ralph, *The Lyrical Novel: Studies in Hermann Hesse, Andre Gide, and Virginia Woolf* (Princeton University Press, 1963).

Hafley, James, *The Glass Roof: Virginia Woolf as Novelist* (1954); rpt. New York: Russell & Russell, 1963).

——, 'Virginia Woolf's Narrators and the Art of "Life Itself"' in Ralph Freedman, ed., *Virginia Woolf: Revaluation and Continuity* (Berkeley: University of California Press, 1980).

Hartman, Geoffrey, 'Virginia's Web', *Chicago Review* (1961); rpt. in Thomas Vogler, ed., *Twentieth Century Interpretations of To the Lighthouse* (Englewood Cliffs, NJ: Prentice-Hall, 1970).

Kaehele, Sharon and Howard German, '*To the Lighthouse*: Symbol and Vision', *Bucknell Review*, 10 (May 1962), rpt. in Morris Beja, ed., *Virginia Woolf: To the Lighthouse: a Casebook* (London: Macmillan, 1970).

Kelley, Alice Van Buren, *The Novels of Virginia Woolf: Fact and Vision* (University of Chicago Press, 1973).

McLaurin, Allen, *Virginia Woolf: the Echoes Enslaved* (Cambridge University Press, 1973).

Marder, Herbert, *Feminism and Art: a Study of Virginia Woolf* (University of Chicago Press, 1968).

Naremore, James, *The World Without a Self: Virginia Woolf and the Novel* (New Haven: Yale University Press, 1973).

Novak, Jane, *The Razor Edge of Balance: a Study of Virginia Woolf* (Coral Gables, FL: University of Miami Press, 1975).

Roberts, John Hawley, '"Vision and Design" in Virginia Woolf', *PMLA*, 61 (1946); rpt. in Jacqueline E. M. Latham, ed., *Critics on Virginia Woolf* (Coral Gables, FL: University of Miami Press, 1970).

Rose, Phyllis, *Woman of Letters: a Life of Virginia Woolf* (New York: Oxford University Press, 1978).

Rosenbaum, S. P., ed., *The Bloomsbury Group: a Collection of Memoirs, Commentary and Criticism* (University of Toronto Press, 1975).
Temple, Ruth S., 'Never Say "I": *To the Lighthouse* as Vision and Confession' in Claire Sprague, ed., *Virginia Woolf: a Collection of Critical Essays* (Englewood Cliffs, NJ: Prentice-Hall, 1971).
Woolf, Virginia, *Collected Essays* (London: Hogarth Press, 1966).
——, *Diary*, ed. Anne Olivier Bell. (New York: Harcourt Brace Jovanovich, vol. II, 1978; vol. III, 1980).
——, *Letters*, ed. Nigel Nicolson. (New York: Harcourt Brace Jovanovich, vol. I, 1975; vol. II, 1976; vol. III, 1977).
——, *Mrs. Dalloway* (New York: Harcourt Brace Jovanovich, 1925; rpt. 1953).
——, *A Room of One's Own* (New York: Harcourt Brace Jovanovich, 1929; rpt. 1957).
——, *To the Lighthouse* (New York: Harcourt Brace & World, 1927; rpt. 1955).

William Faulkner

Adams, Richard P., 'The Apprenticeship of William Faulkner', rpt. in Linda Wagner, ed., *William Faulkner: Four Decades of Criticism* (Michigan State University Press, 1973).
Baum, Catherine B., 'The Beautiful One: Caddy Compson as Heroine', *Modern Fiction Studies*, 13 (Spring 1967).
Bleikasten, André, *The Most Splendid Failure: Faulkner's The Sound and the Fury* (Bloomington: Indiana University Press, 1976).
Blotner, Joseph, *Faulkner: a Biography* (New York: Random House, 1974).
Brooks, Cleanth, *William Faulkner: the Yoknapatawpha Country*. (New Haven: Yale University Press, 1963).
Faulkner, William, *Essays, Speeches and Public Letters*, ed. James B. Meriwether (New York: Random House, 1965).
——, *Faulkner in the University*, ed. Frederick L. Gwynn and Joseph L. Blotner (Charlottesville: University of Virginia Press, 1959).
——, 'Introduction to *The Sound and the Fury*', ed. James B. Meriwether *Southern Review*, 8 (Autumn 1972).
——, *Lion in the Garden: Interviews with William Faulkner*, ed. James B. Meriwether and Michael Millgate (New York: Random House, 1968).
——, *The Sound and the Fury* (New York, 1929; rpt. New York: Random House, 1954).
Groden Michael, 'Criticism in New Composition: *Ulysses* and *The Sound and the Fury*', *Twentieth-Century Literature*, 21 (Oct. 1975) 265–77.
Gross, Beverly, 'Form and Fulfillment in *The Sound and the Fury*', *Modern Language Quarterly*, 29 (Dec. 1968).
Hagopian, John V., 'Nihilism in Faulkner's *The Sound and the Fury*', *Modern Fiction Studies*, 13 (Spring 1967).
Kartiganer, Donald M., '*The Sound and the Fury* and Faulkner's Quest for Form', *ELH*, 37 (Dec. 1970).
Kinney, Arthur F., *Faulkner's Narrative Poetics: Style as Vision* (Amherst: University of Massachusetts Press, 1978).

Matthews, John T., *The Play of Faulkner's Language* (Ithaca: Cornell University Press, 1982).

Millgate, Michael., *The Achievement of William Faulkner* (London, 1966; rpt. Lincoln: University of Nebraska Press, 1978).

Page, Sally R., *Faulkner's Women: Characterization and Meaning* (Deland, FL: Everett / Edwards, 1972).

Powers, Lyall H., *Faulkner's Yoknapatawpha Comedy* (Ann Arbor: University of Michigan Press, 1980).

Slatoff, Walter J., *Quest for Failure: a Study of William Faulkner* (Ithaca: Cornell University Press, 1960).

Stonum, Gary Lee, *Faulkner's Career: an Internal Literary History* (Ithaca: Cornell University Press, 1979).

Thompson, Lawrence, *William Faulkner: an Introduction and Interpretation*, 2nd edn. (New York: Holt, Rinehart & Winston, 1967).

Vickery, Olga, *The Novels of William Faulkner: a Critical Interpretation* (Baton Rouge: Louisiana State University Press, 1964).

Waggoner, Hyatt H., *William Faulkner: From Jefferson to the World* (University of Kentucky Press, 1959).

Williams, David, *Faulkner's Woman: The Myth and the Muse* (Montreal: McGill-Queens University Press, 1977).

Index